Spear and Scepter

AFRICA

0   500   1,000
|____|____|____| miles

ERNEST W. LEFEVER

Spear and Scepter

Army, Police, and Politics
in Tropical Africa

THE BROOKINGS INSTITUTION
Washington, D.C.

THE BROOKINGS INSTITUTION is an independent organization devoted to nonpartisan research, education, and publication in economics, government, foreign policy, and the social sciences generally. Its principal purposes are to aid in the development of sound public policies and to promote public understanding of issues of national importance.

The Institution was founded on December 8, 1927, to merge the activities of the Institute for Government Research, founded in 1916, the Institute of Economics, founded in 1922, and the Robert Brookings Graduate School of Economics and Government, founded in 1924.

The general administration of the Institution is the responsibility of a Board of Trustees charged with maintaining the independence of the staff and fostering the most favorable conditions for creative research and education. The immediate direction of the policies, program, and staff of the Institution is vested in the President, assisted by an advisory committee of the officers and staff.

In publishing a study, the Institution presents it as a competent treatment of a subject worthy of public consideration. The interpretations and conclusions in such publications are those of the author or authors and do not necessarily reflect the views of the other staff members, officers, or trustees of the Brookings Institution.

Foreword

IN THE PAST FIFTEEN YEARS more than twenty former European colonies in tropical Africa have become independent states. This unprecedented shift of sovereignty has confronted the new leaders with the problem of building on political institutions that are largely alien to their indigenous cultures. The present study deals with this basic African problem and the relation to it of the United States, whose policy is designed to encourage African leaders in their determination to create modern states. The study is based on the premise that some degree of stability within and among countries is a necessary but not sufficient condition for political development.

In examining the prerequisites for constructive political adaptation and change in the Third World, most American scholars have focused on economic factors. More recently, they have given attention to indigenous institutions, ethnic factors, kinship patterns, and other persistent cultural forces. This study analyzes the role of a consequential but largely neglected element in state-building: the military and police services of less-developed countries. Giving primary attention to Ghana, the Congo (Kinshasa), and Ethiopia, it examines the multiple effects of the armed forces and police on the character, direction, and performance of political authority from 1960 through mid-1970. The analysis is not confined to unconstitutional army intervention in the political arena, but covers a wider range of relations between military power and political authority in the states examined. It also studies and evaluates the effects of U.S. military aid and public safety assistance in tropical Africa.

The author, Ernest W. Lefever, is a Brookings senior fellow and an adjunct professor of international politics at the American University in Washington. He has written *Crisis in the Congo: A U.N. Force in Action,* published by Brookings in 1965. His other books include *Ethics and United States Foreign Policy* (1957), *The World Crisis and American Responsibility* (1958), *Arms and Arms Control* (1962), and *Uncertain Mandate: Politics of the U.N. Congo Operation* (1967).

Spear and Scepter reflects the growing attention devoted by the Brookings Foreign Policy Studies Program to the political-military aspects of U.S. activities abroad. The Institution appreciates the assistance of the advisory committee and other readers of the manuscript, many of whom are named in the author's note. The views expressed are, of course, those of the author and should not be construed as being those of persons consulted. Nor do they necessarily reflect the views of the trustees, officers, or other staff members of the Brookings Institution.

KERMIT GORDON
President

August 1970
Washington, D.C.

Author's Note

EFFORTS BY American scholars and statesmen to understand the complexities of politics in tropical Africa have been handicapped by a lack of experience in the area and by the uniqueness of the African situation. In contrast to the long American involvement in Asia and Latin America, U.S. relations with most of central Africa are recent, restrained, and primarily a response to rapid decolonization in the 1960s.

The uniqueness of the African political problem results largely from the precipitous shift of sovereignty from governments in London, Paris, and Brussels to inexperienced African regimes. The burden of presiding over the destiny of 100 million newly enfranchised citizens was suddenly thrust upon leaders who at best had only a brief apprenticeship in political responsibility. The overwhelming majority of their people were and are rural and illiterate. Their fundamental identity and loyalty are largely defined by their membership in one of the 2,000 tribes and linguistic groups of central Africa.

The following analysis seeks to accept the realities of tropical African politics, including what has been called the "trauma of independence," and to recognize the severe limitations of Western political norms, expectations, and analytical categories in understanding the African experience. The first four chapters present the African political setting and case studies of Ghana, the Congo (Kinshasa), and Ethiopia. Chapter 5 compares the effects of the armed forces and police services on the character and direction of political development in the three countries, and Chapter 6 considers the military and public safety assistance they have received from the United States. Several hypotheses and conclusions are developed on the political impact of the army and police, and the influence of American security aid. These observations are applicable in the first instance to the three states. But because the fundamental problems of exercising political authority and ensuring domestic peace are essentially the same throughout tropical Africa, and indeed in large areas of Asia and Latin America as well, the observations may have wider application in the Third World.

In making a study that relied heavily on interviews with knowledgeable persons in the United States and in Africa, I became more widely indebted than is usual. The list of persons who read portions of the manuscript or who were consulted is too long to include here, but I would like especially to acknowledge the contributions of the following: George Bader, William Bradford, Christian Chapman, Victor C. Ferkiss, Richard Geisler, G. McMurtrie Godley, William E. Griffith, William F. Gutteridge, Edward K. Hamilton, Richard T. Kennedy, John Killick, Helen Kitchen, John G. Kormann, Donald N. Levine, Mitchell A. Mabardy, William P. Mahoney, Jr., Robert E. Osgood, John N. Plank, Albert A. Rabida, Arthur Richards, Arthur Tienken, Oliver L. Troxel, M. Crawford Young, and I. William Zartman.

I am grateful for the helpful criticism and encouragement of Henry Owen, director of Foreign Policy Studies at Brookings, and for the research support of Nancy Davis Frame, whose capacity to track down obscure facts deserves special commendation. I also wish to express thanks to Breck Milroy, whose patience and accuracy in typing and retyping the pages eased the burden of all concerned; to Alice M. Carroll, who edited the manuscript; and to Margaret Stanley, who prepared the index.

Parts of Chapter 1 appeared in a different form in my article, "State-Building in Tropical Africa," published in the winter 1968 issue of *Orbis*. Permission to use those passages is gratefully acknowledged.

ERNEST W. LEFEVER

Contents

Spear and Scepter

CHAPTER ONE

Politics in Tropical Africa

One of Africa's most intractable problems is how to integrate different tribes into a modern nation within a democratic framework. All African States have this problem, though its dimensions and urgency vary from State to State.

KOFI A. BUSIA[1]

THE PEACEFUL DISSOLUTION of the European colonial order in most of tropical Africa in the early 1960s inaugurated a turbulent and unpredictable era of political conflict, change, and adaptation in a vast underdeveloped region three times the size of the United States. The hundred million indigenous people living between the Tropic of Cancer and the Tropic of Capricorn belong to more than two thousand tribes and speak twice that many languages and dialects. The great majority of these people are illiterate and live in small villages. Their primary identity is the traditional tribe, which severely limits their social loyalties and their view of the larger world.

The political responsibility for these tribesmen and their kinfolk living in or near the European-built cities was transferred in a massive and precipitous shift of sovereignty from mature, metropolitan governments in Europe to fledgling African leaders with little experience in the art of state politics. These partially Westernized politicians, varying widely in education, political sophistication, and patriotism, have de-

---

1. *Africa in Search of Democracy* (Praeger, 1967), p. 111. A professor of sociology and culture of Africa, Busia was the leader of the parliamentary opposition in Ghana before 1959. In October 1969 he became Ghana's first freely elected prime minister.

clared their determination to maintain and develop the thirty states bequeathed them. Each of them has repeatedly declared his intention to develop a modern welfare state along general Western lines, supported by an expanding economy based on foreign trade and investment, and secured by statewide military and police services.

It has been argued that most new African states are not economically and politically viable and that therefore their boundaries should be redrawn to create larger or smaller units corresponding to tribal lines or economic realities. This abstract argument flies in the face of the determined view of the great majority of Africa's leaders who insist on maintaining present frontiers and oppose any territorial changes by force or subversion, or even by "peaceful" annexation or secession. The new rulers understandably show no disposition to merge their recently attained autonomy into a more inclusive sovereign entity, much less to have their territory emasculated by secession. Even when it looked as though Biafra had a good chance, only four of the forty members of the Organization of African Unity (OAU) recognized the secessionist state. As President Julius Nyerere of Tanzania observed at the founding OAU conference in 1963, we all could agree that "our boundaries are so absurd that they must be regarded as sacrosanct."[2]

To maintain and develop any new state is a formidable task. In tropical Africa this task has been exacerbated by the character of the precolonial societies as well as the ambiguous colonial heritage and the abrupt and premature transfer of sovereignty. Precolonial Africa south of the Sahara was largely an iron-age culture. Unlike the Mediterranean world, it developed no literature, no science, and only the most primitive forms of architecture and artifacts. The wheel and mathematical calculation were unknown. Animism was the dominant religion. The primary social unit was the extended family, the primary source of identity the tribe. The imagination and historical memory of the traditional African were wholly circumscribed by his tribal identity.

The tribe was also the primary political unit. The tribal chief wielded final political authority, though larger kingdoms were established by conquest by the stronger warrior tribes. Tribal wars were frequent and savage by modern Western standards. Ritual cannibalism and indigenous slavery were widespread. The Atlantic trade in slaves was stimu-

2. Quoted by Rupert Emerson, "African States and the Burdens They Bear," *African Studies Bulletin*, Vol. 10, No. 1 (April 1967), p. 2.

lated by Africa, and the "African leadership of the day fought fiercely against" abolition of the slave traffic.[3]

Physically and politically, tropical Africa was passive:

[It] possessed no maps. With eighteen thousand miles of coast, it produced no oceangoing ships, no navies or navigators. It sent no trade missions or emissaries around the world, of which it knew—and contrived to know—nearly nothing. Indeed, before the pan-Africanizing experience of colonialism, each tribe was ignorant of almost all African lands except its own, and those of its neighbors and present or past enemies. A female continent, Black Africa was to be "discovered," penetrated and dominated by others. There were few exceptions to this image of passivity.[4]

The conquest of Africa by the European powers in the nineteenth century had a unifying, not balkanizing, effect upon the continent. The tribes fell under a political system of some fifty administrative territories and six European language zones. The colonial administrators, along with Christian missionaries, brought education, medical care, and better living standards. Law and order were imposed. Tribal fighting was greatly reduced and the cruel excesses of the witch doctors and cannibalism were curbed. Slavery was abolished. The rudiments of Western justice were made available to a large portion of the population.

Most consequential of all, the imperial presence in Africa fostered among a partially Westernized elite a sense of supratribal identity and a desire for political authority and autonomy coextensive with the territorial state. But neither the elite nor the larger population was prepared for wider political responsibility. The ambiguous legacy of the colonial period was a desire for self-determination without the capacity for self-government.

From Colony to State—Tribe to Nation

Political independence came too abruptly and too soon to tropical Africa. States were established by fiat, not by conflict. Statehood was essentially a gift, made in response to an indigenous "demand" generated by the Western conscience and the desire of an increasing number of Africans to enjoy the fruits of industrial society. Authority was

---

3. Russell Warren Howe, "Man and Myth in Political Africa," *Foreign Affairs* (April 1968), p. 585.

4. *Ibid.*

handed over with little struggle, thus delaying the reaction to the "trauma of independence."[5] A people who must fight to control a territory learn more about the exacting requirements of exercising political power than those who simply observe a colonial administration or participate in the civil service of an alien authority. This element of struggle helps to explain President Jomo Kenyatta's strength in Kenya.

The delayed shock of the birth trauma can also be attributed to the apparently smooth and successful early transitions of authority in Ghana and the Sudan. The illusion was shattered within a few years by a spate of mutinies, assassinations, coups, countercoups, and civil-tribal wars in a dozen countries. The severity of the conflict in the Congo, Nigeria, and the Sudan has bred a more sober and realistic recognition of the shock and burdens of independence. The "catastrophic effects" of both colonization and decolonization have been recognized, along with the probability that the effects of the latter will continue "for generations to come."[6]

When the political cohesion and coherence imposed by European conquest were suddenly withdrawn, the endemic forces of tribe, language, and region reasserted themselves. Where these atavistic forces prevailed over the improvised and fragile authority of the new state, chaos and violence were the inevitable result. Two fundamental requirements for the development of an effective state become apparent: a successful political-legal transition from colony to state, and a successful psychological-ethnic-cultural transition from tribe to nation. Under optimal conditions the former can be effected quickly and smoothly, but even under the best of circumstances the transition from traditional tribal identity to a larger national identity is likely to be long and tortuous.

Decolonization in Africa can be described as the fragmentation of sovereignty at the periphery of empire. Under political pressures, large pieces of territory were cut loose, not to fend wholly for themselves, but to become independent and self-determined states that would be sustained in a large measure by continuing cultural, economic, and security ties with the former colonial power. These new states, seriously deficient in the disciplines, habits, and institutions essential to modern eco-

5. The psychological concept of trauma is applied to the African scene by Victor T. Le Vine, "The Trauma of Independence in French-Speaking Africa," *The Journal of Developing Areas* (January 1968), pp. 211–24. See also Emerson, "African States and the Burdens They Bear," pp. 1–13.

6. Alan Paton, "The Yoke of Racial Inequality," *New York Times*, Nov. 30, 1968.

nomic and political development, have been correctly described as weak, fledgling, embryonic, makeshift, and soft.[7]

A major reason for this weakness is the fact that the formal transfer of legal authority is not accompanied by a transfer of power. The shift of sovereignty, symbolized ceremoniously by the lowering of an old flag and the raising of a new one, is a relatively simple transaction involving a commitment by the old government to cease exercising authority and by the new to accept the responsibilities of government. Political power and capacity, in contrast, can only be drawn from the human and material resources within the new state. It is impossible to predict whether a newly installed government possesses that capacity even though it has a firm promise of help from its former metropolitan power or other friendly states.

A small state may be in a perpetually precarious position, but it is not an anachronism. A small, poor, and tribally diverse state with an overwhelmingly illiterate population can survive indefinitely if it is surrounded by friendly neighbors and is sustained by a propitious balance among the great powers. If it also receives trade, investment, and other forms of support from industrial states, it can even prosper. All weak states continue to exist only with the sufferance of more powerful states whose interests may be partially induced by fear of each other. The independence of the Congo in the 1960s, for example, was insured in part by the rivalry between the United States and the Soviet Union, each seeking to limit the other's influence in this mineral-rich and strategically located country.

The most serious barrier to national identity and the most serious internal obstacle to effective statewide government in tropical Africa is the persistence of tribal identity, thought, habits, and social structures. "African countries are distinguished from other Third World clusters by extremely weak national centers" and "a periphery which consists of societies until recently self-contained." Original African "values, norms and structures" have "survived to a significant extent everywhere, even where their existence was not legally recognized" during the colonial era.[8] A 1947–48 survey in Ghana found "intense tribal loyalties" even

---

7. Gunnar Myrdal in *Asian Drama: An Inquiry Into the Poverty of Nations* (Twentieth Century Fund, 1968) uses the word "soft" to describe the regimes of South Asia which can legislate but not govern.

8. Aristide R. Zolberg, "The Structure of Political Conflict in the New States of Tropical Africa," *American Political Science Review* (March 1968), pp. 70–71.

among "those who had been town-dwellers for many years."[9] And a 1965 study of Ghana concluded: "A considerable body of evidence points to the persistence of elements of traditional social structure even within the most 'modern' sectors of Ghanaian society. Ethnic background, kinship affiliation, and traditional residence patterns still play a role even within the urban context and indeed may provide the basis for organizations which appear at first sight to be essentially Western."[10] In some circumstances the tribe can be used to attain statewide objectives, but on balance tribalism is a political liability. Increased attention is being given to the problem of bridging the gulf between the intimate tribe and the remote nation.[11] Tom Mboya of Kenya, who understood this problem and decried "negative tribalism," was ironically the victim of a tribal assassination in 1969.

In terms of present political goals, colonial rule has been criticized for showing too much respect for indigenous institutions. "African societies might now be in a better position for 'take-off' if colonial exploitation had been harder on them—if the colonial powers had done the nasty work of destroying traditional structures and had engendered men socially and psychologically prepared to build a new society."[12] Since the colonial authorities were not "nasty" enough, the new African leaders are in the awkward position of being "nationalists without nations,"[13] presiding over tribally fractured states.

A cohesive national identity is an asset in state-building, but its absence is not an insurmountable obstacle. Though a multiplicity of tribes tends to "retard the process of national unification," it need not be a barrier to the state's survival or "the creation of a broader political nationality. Indeed, the larger their number and the smaller their size, the better are the chances of effective amalgamation. Moreover, it could be argued that such a rich pluralism makes dictatorship less likely by providing countervailing power centers."[14] Rivalry between large tribal communities for leadership and the fruits of power was the primary

9. Busia, *Africa in Search of Democracy*, pp. 117–18.

10. Philip J. Foster, *Education and Social Change in Ghana* (Routledge and Kegan Paul, 1965), p. 301; cited in Busia, *op. cit.*

11. For a summary of the problem, see Douglas E. Ashford, "How Non-Western Are the New Nations?" *World Politics* (January 1962), pp. 364–74.

12. Quoted in Helen Kitchen (ed.), *Footnotes to the Congo Story* (Walker and Company, 1967), p. 161.

13. The term was suggested by the title of a book on Latin America by Victor Alba, *Nationalists Without Nations* (Praeger, 1968).

14. Gabriel A. Almond and James S. Coleman, *The Politics of Developing Areas* (Princeton University Press, 1960), p. 301.

cause of the bloody civil war between Biafra and the Nigerian government.

Every African state, including Ethiopia but excepting Somalia, must confront the stark reality of ethnic fragmentation. In terms of state survival the immediate answer to the problem is a central government strong enough to impose its will on all groups within its territory. In terms of developing a cohesive state, the long-range answer lies in detribalization, the slow, painful process of replacing primordial loyalties and habits with increasing participation in a new and larger social-political community.

Contemporary African leaders, as former Secretary of State Dean Rusk put it, operate from the "premise that the various ethnic groups . . . can and should reconcile their differences within present national boundaries and in the process build national identities reflecting African values and African necessities."[15] But there is no assurance that a larger identity will be realized in all areas of tropical Africa in the foreseeable future. Crawford Young speaks of the "myth" of detribalization and warns that urbanization is not synonymous with Europeanization.[16] Emerson notes that the transition from tribe to modern nation in Africa "is very much more difficult now than it was for the Western peoples and states" which moved "by gradual stages under far easier conditions."[17] In view of the burdens of instant independence and profound cultural deficiencies, it would be foolhardy to assume that the statehood experiment will produce no failures. Any state that fails to meet the minimum requirements of the modern world may well retrogress into the kind of tribal fragmentation and conflict that preceded the colonial era.

The Limitations of Western Norms

The supratribal territorial state in tropical Africa is a pure European import, accepted with little question by the indigenous politicians. It is alien in concept, function, and external manifestation. Nevertheless, the great majority of African leaders, in spite of their ambivalence toward

15. *Department of State Bulletin* (Oct. 7, 1968), p. 353.
16. Crawford Young, *Politics in the Congo: Decolonization and Independence* (Princeton University Press, 1965); see especially "The Challenge of Cultural Pluralism," pp. 232–40.
17. Emerson, "African States and the Burdens They Bear," p. 3.

the West, have declared their intention to develop a modern state based upon a money economy and a universal franchise.

A distinction should be made between maintaining a *minimum state* and developing an *active modern state*. The former, no matter how poor, weak, and economically stagnant it is, manages to survive because its government is not seriously challenged from within and is sustained from without by benign neighbors, foreign assistance, and a balance of power in the area. Its foreign policy is passive, largely confined to rhetoric, vote-trading in the United Nations General Assembly, and efforts to gain external material assistance.

While an active modern state may have many of these attributes, it is characterized by economic growth and political development in the direction of stronger and more broadly based government. Most new states in Africa aspire to become active modern states, but none has achieved this objective. Like many Third World countries they are probably destined to remain minimum states for a long time.

The most immediate and urgent political task is that of "state-preserving,"[18] as distinct from the longer range task of state-building. State-building implies movement from a minimum state to a modern state. Any state, minimum or modern, must have a system of political authority and sanctions capable of protecting its people from internal and external dangers.

Political development may be defined broadly as a process embracing the disciplines of state-preserving and state-building, including all changes that enhance the government's capacity to maintain the security of its people and to enforce the law throughout its territory. The movement toward a more just, responsible, and democratic exercise of power may be defined as democratic political development. The first task of government is to govern. In terms of Western values, the second task is to govern justly, the third to govern democratically.[19] As of mid-1970 few tropical African states had made notable progress in the second and third tasks. Only eleven out of forty countries ruled by blacks or Arabs had an opposition party, and most rulers regarded such an opposition as highly undesirable.

18. Harold K. Jacobson suggested this useful term in "ONUC's Civilian Operations: State-Preserving and State-Building," *World Politics* (October 1964), pp. 75–107.

19. See Gabriel A. Almond, "Political Development: Analytical and Normative Perspectives," *Comparative Political Studies* (January 1969), pp. 447–69.

Since Western values and political institutions are recent and alien influences in tropical Africa, the new states should not be judged by Western norms. "Although we can refer to the existence of 'states' and 'regimes' in Africa, we must be careful not to infer from these labels that their governments necessarily have authority over the entire country, any more than we can safely infer from the persistence of these countries as sovereign entities . . . a sense of community and the ability of authorities to enforce cohesion against a people's will."[20] More modern and complex cultures than that of Africa cannot provide appropriate guides to political development in Africa.

Indigenous and Imported Elements

Because the state is not an indigenous institution in tropical Africa, the new states depend upon the developed world, particularly the Western industrial states, for their survival and development. The extent of their dependence is most evident in the contrast between externally furnished resources and disciplines and the persisting tribal thought-forms and habits of the overwhelming mass of the people.

Tribal identity—expressed in special preferences for tribal brothers—often compromises loyal service to the state. Widespread nepotism, along with the avarice that asserts itself during periods of great political change, contributes to a high level of corruption. This "corruption as a system of government" in tropical Africa has been dubbed "kleptocracy."[21] Another significant political factor, particularly apparent in the Congo during the 1964 rebellion, is superstition and magic.[22]

20. Zolberg, "The Structure of Political Conflict," p. 72.

21. Stanislav Andreski, *The African Predicament: A Study in the Pathology of Modernization* (Atherton Press, 1968), pp. 92–109. He concludes that the "losses caused by corruption by far exceed the sum of the individual profits derived from it, because graft distorts the whole economy" (pp. 108–09). J. S. Nye, on the other hand, maintains that certain types of corruption under certain circumstances can contribute to constructive economic and political achievement. See his "Corruption and Political Development: A Cost-Benefit Analysis," *American Political Science Review* (June 1967), pp. 417–27. Albert O. Hirschman also takes a relaxed attitude toward certain kinds of corruption in societies where "corruption is rampant," in his *Development Projects Observed* (Brookings Institution, 1967). See especially "Latitude for Corruption," pp. 107–12.

22. See "Witchcraft, Sorcery, Magic, and Other Psychological Phenomena and Their Implications on Military and Paramilitary Operations in the Congo" (memorandum prepared by James R. Price and Paul Jureidini, Special Operations Research Office, American University, Aug. 8, 1964).

In sharp contrast to Western culture, traditional African society tends to be static, and strongly resistant to change, innovation, and adaptation. Aimé Césaire celebrates this passivity in his well-known poem in praise of negritude:

> Hurrah for those who never invented anything;
> Hurrah for those who never explored anything;
> Hurrah for those who never conquered anything.[23]

This massive inertia is destined to have a profound and largely negative effect upon political and economic development for a long time to come. "A Fool lies here who tried to hustle the East," Rudyard Kipling's epitaph in *The Naulahka*, is even more appropriate to tropical Africa.

A tiny but slowly growing indigenous elite has some understanding of the requirements of political authority and the disciplines of government, including the necessity to collect taxes.[24] This Westernized vanguard, varying in size and competence from country to country, includes many top politicians, professional people, and businessmen. More detribalized than urban dwellers or educated villagers, they are the chief bearers of rising expectations.

Most of these modernized leaders recognize the need for continuing external resources and are eager to use them. Like H. Kamuzu Banda, president of Malawi, they demonstrate a capacity to do so without compromising their essential political integrity.[25] Many of them, unfortunately, are ambivalent toward the West, suffering something like the identity crisis of an adolescent attempting to establish a separate identity from his parents. Most African leaders simultaneously recognize and resent their continued dependence on Europe and the United States. Many have a profound inferiority feeling which is sometimes expressed in public criticism of Western practices they associate, justifiably or unjustifiably, with racial discrimination or "colonialism." The strident outcry against the Belgian-American mission to rescue some 2,000 foreigners held hostage by communist-supported rebels in the Congo in

23. Quoted by Guy Hunter, *The New Societies of Tropical Africa* (London: Oxford University Press, 1962), p. 324. See also his concluding chapter, "The Quality of African Societies," pp. 316–47.

24. The traditional attitude toward taxes was dramatically illustrated when King Olajide Olayode was beheaded after he urged the residents of Ogbomosho in western Nigeria to pay their taxes. *Washington Post*, July 4, 1969.

25. See his interview, "A Black Ruler Tells Why Africa Needs the Whites," in *U.S. News and World Report* (May 13, 1968), pp. 64–68.

November 1964 was, among other things, a dramatic manifestation of this inferiority complex.[26]

The elite includes a minority who are fully or partially alienated from the values and institutions of the democratic West, but most are committed to the goals of economic development. A few have turned to communist states for economic advice and assistance, but even they find it difficult to avoid substantial reliance on Western aid, talent, and ways of doing things.

Between the elite and the static mass stands the semidetribalized African—the product of European industry or Christian missions. He is a marginal man, semiliterate, confused, and often restless, both an asset and a liability. His precarious identity can be exploited by rabble-rousing politicians or be eased by gainful employment or by fuller participation in the larger nascent political community.

The untapped human and natural resources of Africa are vast. The bulk of the population is engaged in subsistence agriculture. The potential for commercial farming, mining, and light industry is great. Its realization requires external investment of resources and managerial personnel and development of a skilled and disciplined indigenous work force. While such tribal manifestations as communal land tenure, traditional authority, and the economic obligations of the extended family act as deterrents to economic development, modernization in Africa is not impeded by a widespread caste system (like that in India) or imported feudal institutions (like those in Latin America).

Tropical African economies are very poor and growing at a snail's pace. The per capita gross national product increased at a rate of about 1.4 percent a year in constant prices between 1957 and 1966, from approximately $112 to $129.[27]

For economic viability and political stability the African states must import a wide range of human and material resources—capital goods, consumer goods, arms, and technical and managerial skills—through grant aid, loans, trade, private investment, and technical assistance. Their dependence on the two hundred thousand or more Europeans who have stayed beyond independence day is probably without parallel

26. This incident is discussed in Chap. 3.
27. Joseph Palmer II, testimony in *Foreign Assistance Act of 1968*, Hearings before the House Committee on Foreign Affairs, 90 Cong. 2 sess. (1968), Pt. 2, p. 344.

in history. Increasingly, Africans are being educated at home and abroad,[28] and are slowly beginning to provide the requisites of character and skill that may eventually produce a strong and viable state. They are now like the men to whom Prometheus gave the "mechanical arts" and fire, but failed to provide "political wisdom"; with food to nourish their bodies but without the "art of government," they proceeded to destroy themselves.[29]

Inertia and chaos are the greatest obstacles to state-building in black Africa. A lower level of internal and interstate conflict and violence produces a more favorable environment for preserving and strengthening the existing states. Stability is the result of a variety of internal and external factors, including appropriate forms of economic, military, and public safety assistance. Perhaps the single most important contribution to political development in Africa are effective efforts to stabilize the area. The "revolutionary" spokesman who is dissatisfied with the present state structure in Africa or present regimes there is compelled to take a negative view of stability, peaceful change, and legality because he regards "revolutionary" violence and conflict as necessary means to usher in the "new order."

Limited Role in World Politics

Tropical Africa provides an off-center but not inconsequential stage for the drama of world politics.[30] The larger significance of political developments in that vast area has been exaggerated in the recent past by the competition between the West and the communist states for "allies" in the Third World, and the importance of the African actors is often inflated because the United States and the Soviet Union seek to woo their votes on key issues before the UN Security Council and General Assembly.

28. In 1968 several thousand tropical Africans were studying in the United States and more than 370 military and 95 police personnel received special training in the United States.

29. Busia, *Africa in Search of Democracy*, p. ix, quotes the example from Plato's *Protagoras*.

30. The relationship of Africa's emerging states to the larger international system is discussed by C. T. Thorne, Jr., "External Political Pressures," in Vernon McKay (ed.), *African Diplomacy: Studies in the Determinants of Foreign Policy* (Praeger, 1966), pp. 145–75.

The black African states are involved in world politics by necessity and by choice. Liberia and Ethiopia excepted, they were created under the rubric of decolonization, which in the liberal Western view is a fulfillment of the right of self-determination and in the communist view is but the first step toward "liberation from Western imperialism." Since Washington and Moscow were the two most insistent advocates of rapid decolonization, the new states tumbled into the international community as neutrals holding a birth certificate and UN membership card in one hand and reaching out for a U.S. credit card with the other. Officially and formally nonaligned, all these states lean one way or the other in the East-West struggle and shift direction from time to time in response to changing internal or external circumstances. Since 1960 a majority have been moderate and inclined toward the West. A minority have been militant, welcoming a significant degree of political and economic influence from communist states (usually without precluding Western diplomatic recognition or material assistance) and sometimes indulging in strident anti-Western rhetoric. Mali, Guinea, and Ghana have been militant in the past, and more recently Congo (Brazzaville), Tanzania, and the Sudan have assumed that posture. Conversely, moderate governments have been willing to accept substantial Western advice and assistance, though they may receive some communist aid. Liberia, Ethiopia, Senegal, Ivory Coast, Kenya, and the Congo (Kinshasa) have been fairly steady moderates.

African neutralism, like Asian neutralism, is a pragmatic response to the realities of world politics.[31] A neutralist leader seeks to remain aloof from external struggles that do not bear upon his immediate interests; he does not want his state to become a political battleground for two alien adversaries. President Jomo Kenyatta of Kenya once said: "When two elephants fight, it is the grass that suffers; and when East and West are struggling in Africa, it is Africa that suffers."[32] Kenyatta's observation is selectively valid. Peaceful competition between Washington and Moscow, for example, has doubtless increased economic aid to Africa.

The foreign policy of African states, like that of the great majority of

31. See Ernest W. Lefever, "Nehru, Nasser, and Nkrumah on Neutralism," in Laurence W. Martin (ed.), *Neutralism and Non-Alignment* (Praeger, 1962), pp. 115–20; Arnold Rivkin, *The African Presence in World Affairs* (Free Press of Glencoe, 1963), pp. 131–98.

32. *New York Times*, April 12, 1961.

poor countries, is strongly oriented toward getting from the developed world all the material assistance possible, consistent with their political integrity. Some of their leaders have become adept at persuading Washington and Moscow, sometimes simultaneously, that a voluntary and noncommercial transfer of economic or military resources is in the interest of the donor state; this valuable state-building asset might be called "temporary alliance potential." The new African states have developed ephemeral and more enduring caucuses and blocs to lobby with the big powers or to marshal votes at the United Nations; such groups were particularly active during the first years of the Congo crisis.[33]

Policies of Moscow and Peking

In this arena of competition, new to both superpowers, Moscow has had a more turbulent experience than Washington. In the first years of independence, communist propaganda exploited the African ambivalence toward the West, accusing the United States and the former colonial powers of "racism" and "neocolonialism." In Ghana and the Congo, where Moscow made its greatest efforts, it attempted to "radicalize" the political situation by the classic communist tactics of subversion, through trade, loans, military aid, and bribery.[34] According to a former U.S. ambassador to Guinea and Kenya, the activities of the "Soviet KGB and other Communist intelligence services . . . are both far-flung and intensive. Between 60 and 70 percent of all Soviet-bloc diplomatic personnel in Asia and Africa are intelligence agents in disguise. And among Communist newsmen, the proportion is even higher."[35]

Heavy-handed Soviet penetration resulted in the expulsion of the Russian diplomatic mission from the Congo in 1960 and again in 1963 and was one of the key factors that prompted the military and the police to overthrow President Kwame Nkrumah in Ghana in 1966. These

33. See Ernest W. Lefever, *Uncertain Mandate: Politics of the U.N. Congo Operation* (Johns Hopkins Press, 1967), pp. 157–71; Thomas Hovet, Jr., *Africa in the United Nations* (Northwestern University Press, 1963).

34. See Fritz Schatten, *Communism in Africa* (Praeger, 1966).

35. William Attwood, "A Few Kind Words for the CIA," *Look* (April 18, 1967), pp. 70–71. See also Attwood's *The Reds and the Blacks* (Harper & Row, 1967), pp. 17–19 and 296–97.

severe political setbacks, together with the widening Sino-Soviet rift, forced the Kremlin to downgrade its expectations in tropical Africa and to reappraise its policy and tactics accordingly.[36] Since 1965 Moscow has not overtly supported direct subversive activity against tropical African regimes, but has channeled its weapons and training assistance to guerrilla groups, primarily those seeking to overthrow "white regimes."[37] Though they are more pragmatic and less doctrinaire than they were in 1960, the Russians still supplement their diplomatic and trade relations with quiet, long-range infiltration efforts. Substantial investments of rubles and prestige have been replaced by behavior approximating traditional diplomacy, though there is no hard evidence that Moscow's long-range goals have been significantly altered.

In sharp contrast, Peking has adopted the revolutionary tactics Moscow has abandoned. China (sometimes with the help of Cuba, Algeria, or the United Arab Republic) supported the 1963–65 rebel movement in the Congo. It has been active, sometimes with the support of the regime, in Nkrumah's Ghana, Guinea, Mali, Congo (Brazzaville), Burundi, Kenya, Tanzania, and Zambia. Red China provides material support and some political direction to the more militant guerrilla groups. It regards the Soviet Union and the United States as its principal adversaries and as the chief obstacles to its version of "national liberation" north and south of the Zambezi.[38] Peking has encountered serious difficulties with the governments of Kenya, Burundi, and post-Nkrumah Ghana. It is the only one of the big powers that appears to have increased its political and economic investment in tropical Africa in the 1965–69 period.[39]

36. See Zbigniew Brzezinski (ed.), *Africa and the Communist World* (Stanford University Press, 1963); Robert A. Scalapino, "Sino-Soviet Competition in Africa," *Foreign Affairs* (July 1964), pp. 640–54; Helmut Sonnenfeldt, "Soviet Strategy in Africa," *Africa Report* (November 1960), pp. 5 ff.; and Marshall I. Goldman, *Soviet Foreign Aid* (Praeger, 1966), pp. 168–84.

37. See Donald H. Humphries, *The East African Liberation Movement*, Adelphi Paper No. 16 (London: Institute for Strategic Studies, March 1965).

38. See Colin Legum, "Peking's Strategic Priorities," *Africa Report* (January 1965), pp. 19–21; "China: A Revolution for Export," *Mizan* (London, March–April 1967), pp. 80–86; George T. Yu, "China's Failure in Africa," *Asian Survey* (August 1966), pp. 461–68. See also John K. Cooley, *East Wind Over Africa: Red China's Offensive* (Walker and Company, 1965).

39. The Zambia-Tanzania railroad in East Africa is the most dramatic example of Peking's interest. The Chinese are building a thousand-mile rail line from Lusaka to Dar es Salaam at an estimated cost of $688 million in accordance with an agreement with Tanzania and Zambia signed in 1967. See *New York Times*, July 21, 1970.

Washington's Recent Interest

The U.S. posture and commitment in tropical Africa, as was evident in the Congo in 1960, is in part a response to the behavior of the communist states and their allies. The states of that still "female" region are often the residual legatees of larger decisions. "The cold war has been the sinews of African diplomacy: if the U.S. and Russia were 'on the same side,' Africa's leverage on them would sink toward the pathetic level of its economic and military power."[40]

In terms of American political, strategic, and economic interests, Africa ranks below Europe, Asia, and Latin America, and Central Africa below the states bordering on the Mediterranean and located south of the Zambezi, particularly the industrialized Republic of South Africa.[41] U.S. policy seeks to augment the forces of stability and peaceful change as a means of maintaining the balance of power in the larger world and as a prerequisite to constructive economic and political development in Africa. To discourage conflict within African states, Washington opposes military intervention by other governments, African and non-African. The United States opposed secessionist Katanga and Biafra, staying out of both conflicts. It did provide military equipment and logistical support for the UN Force that ended Katanga's secession in January 1963. Biafran secession was crushed in January 1970 with substantial military aid from the Soviet Union.

American diplomatic and aid policies are designed to strengthen the new states and encourage the development of moderate governments capable of responding to the needs of their people and of sustaining

40. Russell Warren Howe, "China as the Trump in the African Pack," *New Republic* (Sept. 5, 1964), p. 16.

41. See Noel Mostert, "High Stakes Southeast of Suez," *The Reporter* (March 7, 1968), pp. 17–20; and E. S. Virpsha, "Strategic Importance of South Africa," *NATO's Fifteen Nations*, Vol. 12, No. 1 (February–March 1967), pp. 37–43. For an earlier assessment see James M. Gavin, *War and Peace in the Space Age* (Harper, 1958), pp. 274–77. Economically South Africa is more important than tropical Africa. U.S. private investment in the republic in 1966 was $601 million, compared to $1.5 billion for the rest of the continent combined. South Africa produces 95 percent of all the gold mined in Africa and approximately 75 percent of that produced outside the communist world. An industrialized state, South Africa has a per capita GNP of $530, about three times higher than the average for Africa. It generates more than half of Africa's electrical power with a per capita consumption equal to that of Western Europe. It produces ten times as much steel as all other African countries combined.

mutually beneficial relations with one another and with the industrial states of the East and West. To this end the United States has provided a modest amount of economic, technical, and security assistance, the last named including both military and public safety aid.

While the political and strategic interest of the United States in a particular region cannot be quantified, both economic and security assistance are significant indicators of the importance of the region as seen by Washington. "The U.S. foreign assistance program," according to an official statement in 1969, "is the primary means of expressing U.S. interest in Africa."[42] The following comparison of economic aid (1946–68), military aid deliveries (1950–68), and the congressional authorization for military aid for fiscal 1970 in millions of dollars illustrates the relatively low U.S. interest in Africa.[43]

	Military aid		Economic aid,
	1950–68	1970	1946–68
World	$33,260.7	$434.0	$94,726.0
Europe	14,201.7	2.1	27,011.2
East Asia	9,747.3	214.3	12,154.1
Near East and South Asia	5,645.5	149.6	20,866.1
Latin America	687.0	21.4	13,087.8
Africa (whole)	218.0	20.5	3,923.4
Africa (tropical)	152.8	14.1	2,044.0

Except for Western Europe, which received the largest portion of military aid in the earlier period, the relative ranking of the regions is the same for the eighteen-year period as for fiscal 1970.

The volume of U.S. economic and security assistance to Africa has leveled off since the mid-sixties, reflecting the more clearly seen realities in the larger world and especially in Africa. Like Moscow, Washington has been chastened by the intractability of the African political problem and the severely limited political and economic capacity of its new states. Both superpowers now operate under a more sober assessment of tropical Africa's strategic value, the reduced interest and commitment of each reinforcing the other.

42. U.S. Agency for International Development, *U.S. Foreign Aid in Africa: Proposed Fiscal Year 1970 Program* (1969), p. 1.

43. Department of Defense, International Security Affairs, *Military Assistance Facts* (May 1969), pp. 8, 16, and 17; Agency for International Development, *U.S. Overseas Loans and Grants* (May 29, 1969).

Neglect of the Military Factor

In the early years of African independence, economic development was commonly seen as "the natural way of adjusting a traditional society to the exacting demands of a modern democratic way of life."[44] But there are too many intangible and unpredictable variables in the complex formula for political development to establish reliable correlations between measurable economic factors (such as gross national product, per capita income, annual growth rate, or the percentage of the population in industry) and political behavior. Politics is more an art than a science.

In the past few years the significance of noneconomic elements in the politics (and even of the noneconomic factors in economics) of developing states—tribal, kinship, and identity questions; literacy and education; elite-mass relations; and the persistence of traditional behavior—has been recognized. The impact of religion, superstition, magic, nepotism, and corruption has been examined. Political parties, political elites, political communication, and the formal instruments of government inherited from the colonial power have also been studied.

The postcolonial rash of coups and upsurge of conflict and chaos in tropical Africa has belatedly focused attention on the army and the police as consequential and hitherto largely overlooked actors in the unfolding political drama. A principal reason for this neglect is the fact that these legal instruments of coercion were not a political problem in the colonial period; they were necessary to maintain law and order and with very few and temporary exceptions were loyal to the metropolitan power. No armies in tropical Africa played a "liberating" or revolutionary role and none had a discernible effect on the pace or character of decolonization. Yet, by mid-1970 there had been more than thirty coups or abrupt changes of government in which the army played a major role.

On independence day the African armies were essentially nonpolitical and nonconspiratorial. Their European and African officers fully expected to continue serving the new regime as they had the old. The African officers accepted the Western doctrines of civilian supremacy and a nonpolitical army, learned by example of the colonial powers and by precept at Sandhurst and St. Cyr.

44. Chief H. O. Davies of Nigeria, quoted in Rivkin, *The African Presence in World Affairs*, p. xvii.

Virtually all African armies continued to be heavily dependent upon European officers and advisers and on material support provided by the former metropolitan power. Even in such countries as Ghana and Nigeria, where the Africanization of the officer ranks was most advanced, European officers continued to predominate in top command and training positions during the first several years of independence. All officers and most noncommissioned officers in the Congo were Belgian on independence day. As late as the end of 1968 all the top command positions in Zambia's army were held by British officers; the highest Zambian officer was a major. Though the top positions in the armies of Kenya and Tanzania had been Africanized by 1968, both governments employed high-level British officers as military advisers. Tanzania also employed Canadian officers.

During and following the transition to statehood in most African countries the army was the strongest symbol of continuity between the old and the new orders. When the frail and inexperienced regimes could not withstand the centrifugal forces unleashed by the withdrawal of externally imposed restraints, the military in a dozen states moved in to fill the vacuum. The circumstances varied widely, but in those where military intervention appeared justified to save the state from disintegration, as in the Congo, or from dictatorship, as in Ghana, the officers were obviously uncomfortable in their unexpected role. Even in the islands of relative political stability, such as the Ivory Coast and Kenya, the army came to realize that simply by performing its classic function it was in fact acting politically by siding with the regime against its active or latent opponents.

Until recently, it had "occurred to few students . . . that the military might become the critical group in shaping the course of nation-building"; scholars had assumed "the future of newly emergent states would be determined largely by the activities of their Westernized intellectuals, their socialistically inclined bureaucrats, their nationalist ruling parties, and possibly their menacing Communist parties."[45] In retrospect, the increasing political significance of the army and the police should have been more fully anticipated. Military intervention should

45. Lucian Pye, "Armies in the Process of Political Modernization," in John J. Johnson (ed.), *The Role of the Military in Underdeveloped Countries* (Princeton University Press, 1962), p. 69. Other writers who have related the instruments of coercion to political development are S. E. Finer, Morris Janowitz, Edwin Lieuwen, J. M. Lee, and William Gutteridge. Only the latter two have discussed the African scene.

have come as no surprise. With the grim backdrop of bloody turbulence in many places in Asia and Latin America, why should the less plausible states of Africa have been immune from conflict, coups, and chaos? In Africa, more than in any other region, the army is a "heavy institution" in a light society with a weak government. In such a "porous civilian-political order the military have a capacity to act with authority and force. As the army modernizes, a dangerous 'competence gap' grows between it and the rest of the community. The influx of technical training and ideas from industrialized countries underlines this point and widens the gap."[46] As long as the central political symbols and institutions are weak and national cohesiveness is elusive—a condition that may persist for generations in most African countries—the politics of force will frequently supersede the politics of persuasion.

Army, Police, and Politics

The government of an independent territorial state must, by definition, have reliable instruments of coercion at its disposal to protect its people against internal and external dangers. No state can long endure unless it has an army or police force or their equivalents, or unless it is sustained by propitious equilibrium of internal and external forces. The scepter, a symbol of sovereign political authority, must be upheld by the men who wield the spear. This does not mean that governments are maintained on the points of spears, but that governments, sustained by the passive or active consent of their people, also must enjoy a monopoly of the legitimate use of violence within their territory. In any state—old or new, past or present—the military establishment by its very existence cannot avoid having a significant impact on political affairs, even when it refrains from acting.

In view of these classic political postulates, confirmed in everyday events, the scholarly neglect of the military (and police) in new states must be attributed to the modern movement away from classic political theory, an academic prejudice against the military as an institution, and a preoccupation with the more familiar noncoercive factors.

African armies tend to be the most detribalized, Westernized, mod-

46. Fred Greene, "Toward Understanding Military Coups," *Africa Report* (February 1966), p. 10. See also Zolberg, "The Structure of Political Conflict," pp. 73–87.

ernized, integrated, and cohesive institutions in their respective states. The army is usually the most disciplined agency in the state. It often enjoys a greater sense of national identity than other institutions. In technical skills, including the capacity to coerce and to communicate, the army is the most modernized agency in the country. It is the "best organized trade union,"[47] a potent pressure group competing for its slice of the meager state budget.

A more vivid symbol of sovereignty than the flag, the constitution, or the parliament, the army often evokes more popular sentiment than a political leader. The officer corps is an important and conspicuous component of the tiny ruling elite. In trim and colorful uniforms the army marches in independence day celebrations and its top brass stand with the head of state and prime minister on the reviewing platform. The political leaders understand only too well their dependence on the loyalty and effectiveness of the army in upholding their authority and in putting down any major challenge to the regime.

The military behavior of Africa's new states has been significantly affected by two factors that are commonly overlooked or underemphasized. One is the progressive, occasionally rapid, Africanization of the officer corps that has sometimes brought with it an erosion of professional skill and discipline. In some places it has led to a diminution of loyalty to the regime, a development that can be seen as positive or negative, depending upon one's view of the legitimacy and competence of the government in question. Some politicians, particularly in East Africa, have deliberately slowed the pace of Africanization, not only to maintain professional standards, but to assure military loyalty through the continued employment of British officers in command posts or as advisers.

The other phenomenon is temporary regression to earlier forms of tribal warfare. In the Congo, Nigeria, the Sudan, and elsewhere, Western rules of war—respect for civilians, fair treatment for prisoners, etc. —have given way to atavistic and brutal behavior that shows no mercy for civilians or prisoners and is more intent on ravishing the countryside for booty than achieving military objectives. This deterioration of discipline, usually associated with the breakdown of civil order, has occurred in part because of the absence of European or African officers

47. Zolberg, "The Structure of Political Conflict," p. 75.

trained in a tradition of civility. In the Western democratic world the chief function of the military is to deter and prevent war, while in the tribal tradition—particularly of the more aggressive tribes—the vocation of the warrior is to make war, to "wash his spear" in blood as it is sometimes put. The extent of this "spear washing" for revenge or for booty is determined in part by the remoteness of the area of combat from central civilian and military control, the intensity of the tribal hostility involved, and the professional quality of the government's junior officers and noncommissioned officers. In view of the deeply embedded warrior tradition that contemporary African armies must both build upon and restrain, it is fortunate that there have been no large interstate wars in Africa since independence.

Three Case Studies

This study is concerned with the total impact of the military and police services upon the unfolding political drama of central Africa. Since it would be impossible to deal with each of the thirty-two states, case studies of three are presented.[48] Ghana, the Congo (Kinshasa), and Ethiopia were selected to represent a wide range of diverse elements and because of their importance in the area and their significance to the United States relative to other states in the region. The interest of the African states in their own political development and the U.S. interest in furthering this objective in a context of regional stability provide the normative points of reference for the analysis.

Central Africa has many common elements that distinguish it as a region from Latin America, the Middle East, or Southeast Asia. Transcending geographical and state frontiers, these common attributes are more important politically than the differences, making it possible to generalize about the political situation in most of the black African states regardless of their variety in size, location, or economic situation. This basic political similarity is rooted in the essentially homogeneous culture of the indigenous peoples and their common experience of a recent and superficial intrusion of Western culture and political control.

48. The studies are based upon the few documentary sources available on African armies, and on interviews by the author with knowledgeable persons in the United States, Britain, Belgium, and Africa. See Ernest W. Lefever, *Crisis in the Congo: A United Nations Force in Action* (Brookings Institution, 1965), and *Uncertain Mandate.*

The character and organization of the army bear a striking resemblance from state to state. Derived from its basic task of maintaining order and security, its similarity is reinforced by a persistent, transcultural military tradition. Probably the most clearly defined institution of statehood, the armed services, even in states with profoundly differing histories and cultures and with widely differing relations to the external world, constitute a system of command and obedience. The character and functions of the police services are similar, if more limited. These two are the only agencies legally authorized to employ violence against persons and property. Hence, the basic relationships between political authority and the legal instruments of coercion, between scepter and spear, are similar in any state, though the modalities of interaction may vary widely.

Ghana, the Congo, and Ethiopia not only embrace the geographic, climatic, economic, cultural, anthropological, and political diversity of tropical Africa, but the whole range of political-military relationships found in the area. During the past decade in these three countries there have been four successful coups, two abortive coups, tribal conflict, civil war, two attempts at secession, and a peaceful transfer of power from a military to a civilian government. These states thus provide a rich laboratory for examining the multiple relations between spear and scepter.

A former British colony, Ghana is one of the most advanced states in tropical Africa, economically, educationally, and politically. Like other West African leaders, Ghana's first president, Kwame Nkrumah, was strongly influenced by Western political ideas and institutions and sought to detribalize Ghanaian society and politics. His regime became increasingly corrupt, confused, and authoritarian, a striking contrast to that of the National Liberation Council whose army and police leaders overthrew Nkrumah in 1966 and returned the country to constitutional civilian rule three years later with Kofi A. Busia as prime minister.[49]

With a significantly different colonial experience, the former Belgian Congo was torn by tribal and civil strife for the first seven years of its independence but by mid-1970 appeared to be relatively stable under

49. A more complete description of the land, people, and political situation in each country is provided in the case study chapter devoted to it. Appendix A gives comparative political, demographic, economic, educational, and security information on Ghana, the Congo, and Ethiopia.

the moderate military rule of President Joseph D. Mobutu. On independence day the Congo had virtually no Westernized elite and its
leaders had had no apprenticeship for political responsibility. Because
the Congo is less developed and less Western than Ghana, traditional
identity and enmity have had a much greater impact on internal politics
in the Congo, though General Mobutu in his several military and political roles has sought to build upon and at the same time weaken traditional patterns of authority. The country's deep tribal and regional fis-
sures have been major factors in causing the succession of regimes that
has plagued the new state. The two major challenges to central authority have been the rebel movements, largely in the northeast, and the
two-year secession of the copper-rich province of Katanga which was
brought to an end by the military action of a sizable UN Force. The
Congo achieved a unique distinction, not only in Africa but in the entire
world, by playing host, often grudgingly, to a four-year UN expeditionary force.

Ethiopia falls into an entirely different category. An ancient feudal
land with a long oral and written tradition, it is governed by an authoritarian but gradually modernizing emperor. Located in East Africa on the
Red Sea, Ethiopia faces toward the Arab world. It is less developed economically and educationally than the Congo. Though Ethiopia has
never been a European colony, it has been subjected to considerable
invited and uninvited European influence. The five years of uninvited
Italian occupation had some modernizing effect, though it was less consistent, humane, or widespread than the African legacy of Britain and
Belgium. Despite its tribal diversity and backwardness, Ethiopia has a
sense of pride and identity that the new African states have not
achieved. The role of the military in this semifeudal and constitutional
monarchy has been quite different from that of any other tropical African state. The Italian conquest and occupation and the abortive coup of
1960 have made a deep imprint on the armed forces. Because of Ethiopia's strategic location, its politically moderate and relatively stable
regime, and the presence of a U.S. Army communication facility in the
country, Ethiopia has received more than three times as much U.S. bilateral military assistance as all the other tropical African states combined.

In terms of American military assistance, Ethiopia and the Congo are
the two most favored tropical African states; Ghana is less so because of
the Nkrumah period and the fact of British security assistance. The vol-

ume of military hardware and training provided to tropical Africa by
the United States from 1950 through fiscal 1968 was as follows:[50]

Ethiopia	$118,000,000
Congo (Kinshasa)	19,900,000
Ghana	100,000
Eleven other tropical African states	14,800,000
Total	$152,800,000

The combined aid to Ethiopia, the Congo, and Ghana was more than
nine times greater than that to all of the other eleven recipient states.
Of these, Liberia received $6 million in aid, reflecting its historic Ameri-
can ties.

The same general pattern of interest is shown by U.S. economic
assistance, though the higher proportion going to Ghana, the Congo,
and Ethiopia is not as pronounced. In the 1946–68 period, all economic
transfers, including grants, loans, and food, but excluding military aid,
were as follows:[51]

Ethiopia	$ 228,900,000
Congo (Kinshasa)	405,400,000
Ghana	240,100,000
Other tropical African states	1,243,900,000
Total	$2,118,300,000

The combined total of economic aid to the three countries was
$874,400,000 or approximately 60 percent of the total received by all
the other tropical African states. The selective interest of Washington is
explicit in the priority states identified in AID's presentation to the
Congress in 1969—Ghana, Congo, Nigeria, Ethiopia, and Liberia.[52]

Seven Areas of Inquiry

Focusing on the impact of the coercive instruments on politics, this
study is concerned with the spectrum of significant relationships and
interactions between spear and scepter, not only with the unconstitu-

50. U.S. Department of Defense, International Security Affairs, *Military Assistance Facts* (May 1969), p. 17.
51. U.S. Agency for International Development, *U.S. Overseas Loans and Grants*
(May 29, 1969), pp. 80–120.
52. U.S. Agency for International Development, *U.S. Foreign Aid in Africa*
(1969), p. 2.

tional intervention of the military in the political realm. It seeks to assess the variety, intensity, and consequences of the multiple effects of the army and police upon the instruments, process, and direction of politics, including domestic and foreign policy.[53] What effect do the security instruments have upon state-building and state-preservation? The character, extent, and impact of U.S. military and public safety assistance are also analyzed to ascertain their effect upon the army and police and through them upon political development and stability. Ultimately, have the programs of military and public safety assistance effectively served U.S. objectives in the three states?

The central presupposition of this study is that political stability is a necessary though not sufficient prerequisite for constructive political development, except in severe crises that may warrant temporary political disruption or even military intervention to correct a nonviable political situation. A minimal degree of order is essential so the constructive forces in these emerging societies can operate without constant attention to or fear of political violence and other forms of turbulence. One distinction between turbulence that initiates constructive action and turbulence that postpones constructive action is made explicit in the four types of military intervention identified below. This fundamental and nonrevolutionary premise is expressed by a strong preference for stability and peaceful change.

The multiple interrelationships between spear and scepter are examined through a series of questions regarding (1) maintaining the state, (2) building a nation, (3) upholding the regime, (4) replacing the regime, (5) domestic policy, (6) foreign policy, and (7) structure and process of politics.

1. Maintaining the State

How effectively have the army and police performed their basic security function of defending the territorial and political integrity of the state? Have nonsecurity functions or activities impaired the performance of their primary task? To what extent do symbolic and other

---

53. The analysis is not concerned, except incidentally, with the covert intelligence apparatus of the state, whose task is to gather information on the intentions, capabilities, limitations, and vulnerabilities of actual or potential threats to the central government. The army and police act on this intelligence and perform some intelligence functions themselves.

noncoercive attributes of the services contribute to the security function? Have the services been loyal to the central government when it confronted serious internal or external challenges? On balance, have the security forces enhanced political stability?

2. Building a Nation

What contribution have the armed services and police made to the organic process of developing national identity and pride? To what extent are the services detribalized? Have they achieved a positive and cohesive national identity? How Westernized are they in terms of military doctrine and political orientation? Has the example of a national army encouraged detribalization in the government and other civilian institutions?

As the most modern and technically oriented statewide institution in tropical Africa, what impact have the armed forces had on economic modernization through example, by transmitting skills, by stimulating the growth of a communication and transportation infrastructure, or by engaging in civic action projects? To what extent have skills taught by the armed services been utilized in the civilian economy? What has been the impact of the army literacy and educational program? Have there been significant civic action projects? Has the army's "efficiency" spilled over into the civilian sector?

3. Upholding the Regime

Have the services been loyal to the regime, even when it was under severe pressure from tribal, regional, or factional elements seeking to overthrow it? Have they been effective? Have the services been divided during a crucial challenge to an effective and legitimate regime? Has the army or elements within it ever sought to overthrow a viable regime?

4. Replacing the Regime

Military intrusion into the political sphere has occurred in tropical Africa under a variety of circumstances that can be classified into four recurring elements reflecting the dominant motivation of the leaders of a particular coup. Military intervention, of course, may be the result of multiple motivation, though in actual practice one or two of the elements noted below tend to predominate.

The security coup is undertaken to replace a regime judged incapable of defending the state from internal or external challenges. Seeing the state threatened by disintegration, the plotters are chiefly interested in restoring order and security. The regime may have been weakened by corruption or subversion. The army intervenes temporarily to arrest chaos and keep the administration going until the crisis is past and the political processes can return to a situation approximating normality. The military may take sides to restore order, but intervention is not motivated by fundamental dissatisfaction with domestic or foreign policy or with the political or constitutional system which, in fact, they pledge to preserve and restore. The security and survival of the state is the primary objective. The security coup is sometimes called a custodial coup.

The reform coup is prompted by dissatisfaction with the character or policies (as opposed to competence) of the existing regime. The army insists that the old, corrupt, and wrong-headed ruling group be replaced by a new, clean, and right-headed regime. The old regime is frequently accused of being under the influence of domestic or external subversive forces. The new interim regime, usually a military or a military-civilian elite, insists on new domestic and foreign policies that conspicuously, though often only superficially, differ from those of the discredited leaders. Frequently the reform includes cleansing and streamlining the bureaucracy. The new rulers promise to return to constitutional government as soon as conditions permit. The reform of domestic or foreign policy is the primary objective. The reform coup also has a custodial aspect.

The new elite coup is little concerned with security or policy and is motivated primarily by ambitious men who use the army to gain power and its rewards. The plotters may be civilians or soldiers or both, but after the coup the officer corps enjoys an enhanced position whether or not it participates directly in the new ruling group. This changing-of-the-guard coup is often motivated by deep-seated class or tribal rivalries and hence invites a countercoup.

The punitive coup is motivated by real or pretended grievances in the military establishment against the regime and is not concerned with security or policy. The regime is accused of slighting the status, prestige, or desired amenities of the army and is punished by expulsion. The army may ally itself with a civilian faction seeking to oust the regime for other reasons, and it may or may not become a part of the new ruling group. The new regime must confer status and material benefits on the officer corps and ranks if it expects to remain in power. One version of the new elite coup, the punitive putsch, has little policy significance unless civilian elements associated with it are seriously reform-oriented.

With these four types of coups in mind, what has been the basic character and motivation of the intrusions of the military into the political arena in Ghana, the Congo, and Ethiopia? In each instance, what immediate and longer range impact did the coup or attempted coup have on internal security and political development? An analysis of the aftermath of a coup often gives clues to its motivation. In this connection the five sequels of military intervention identified by Dankwart A. Rustow are helpful:

> (1) At one extreme the soldiers may retain power for a minimum of time, quickly returning to their barracks and restoring the government to civilian hands. (2) At the opposite extreme, the soldiers may stay in power permanently, inaugurating a stable military oligarchy. Among the intermediate possibilities there are those (3) of a series of military coups leading to a condition best characterized as praetorianism, (4) of a prolonged twilight situation between civilian and military rule, and (5) of a social and political revolution under military aegis which, by removing the conditions that led to the coup, establishes civil government on a new and more secure basis.[54]

5. Domestic Policies

On the African scene domestic policy may be characterized as generally moderate or militant. Moderate policies are those reflecting a pragmatic and experimental approach as opposed to a rigid, ideological, and militant approach. Moderate policies emphasize continuity with the past without sacrificing innovation and adaptation. This means continued cooperation with Western states and the adaptation of Western governmental forms to local requirements. In economic terms, moderation permits a variety of forms of ownership, management, and investment, tailored to meet African realities rather than the specifications of

---

54. Dankwart A. Rustow, *A World of Nations: Problems of Political Modernization* (Brookings Institution, 1967), p. 190. The five sequels are elaborated in pp. 190–206.

any imported model from the East or West. Militant policies tend to reflect the Russian, Cuban, or Red Chinese models.

To what extent has the army supported moderate as opposed to militant policies? What is the political orientation of the officer corps and how fully is it consulted by the political elite on domestic nonsecurity questions? What is the net impact on domestic questions of the army as a pressure group competing for a slice of the meager state budget? Is the army a conservative or moderating influence on state economic policies?

6. *Foreign Policy*

Foreign policy, like domestic policy, may be described as moderate or militant and for the same reasons. In tropical Africa, where all states are formally nonaligned, the moderate regimes have welcomed substantial Western aid and advice without precluding normal diplomatic and economic relations with communist states. Conversely, militant regimes seek or accept a significant degree of political and economic influence from communist states and sometimes engage in strong anti-Western rhetoric. Does the officer corps have a pro-Western orientation? To what extent does the security function itself predispose soldiers and policemen against communist policy and tactics in Africa? What role does the officer corps play in foreign policy deliberations? What impact has the government's foreign policy of the last decade had upon the outlook of the military? Do the security services believe that communist or other militant states have supported or are likely to support subversive activities against their country?

7. *Structure and Process of Politics*

In exercising or departing from its security role, what influence has the army had upon the structure of the government, the separation of powers, the instruments of franchise, or any other forces that mold statewide political agencies or processes? Has the army engaged in tribal, party, or factional politics? Has it provided the minimal security essential to constructive politics?

The questions enumerated above determine the range of information treated in the case studies of Ghana, the Congo, and Ethiopia. The answers are not given in the case study chapters, but in Chapter 5 in a comparison of the interrelationships between spear and scepter in the three countries. The analysis of the role of U.S. military and public safety aid, including hardware, training, and the presence of American advisers in the host country, is dealt with separately in Chapter 6. In each area of inquiry the summary of factual observations and judgments is followed by hypotheses that may be useful in examining other states in Africa or elsewhere in the developing world.

UPPER VOLTA

Kulungugu

Bolgatanga ★

UPPER

White
Volta

NORTHERN

★ Tamale

GHANA

—··—··— International boundary
—·—·— Region boundary
National capital
★ Region capital

0   25   50
├───┼───┼───┤ miles

DAHOMEY →

IVORY
COAST

Black
Volta

BRONG-AHAFO

LAKE
VOLTA

TOGO

Sunyani ★

ASHANTI

Kumasi ★

EASTERN

Ho ★

VOLTA

Akosombo ●

Volta River Dam

WESTERN

Koforidua ●

Volta

LOME ⊛

Teshie ●

CENTRAL

ACCRA ⊛ ● Tema

Elmina ●
Sekondi ★ ● Cape Coast
● Takoradi

GULF OF GUINEA

CHAPTER TWO

Ghana

*An officer in the armed forces [must possess] the best and
noblest traits of character: integrity, efficiency and
unquestionable loyalty.*

KWAME NKRUMAH[1]

THE BIRTH of independent Ghana on March 6, 1957, after
113 years of British rule, was celebrated in a mood of great expectation
buttressed by the country's considerable material and human resources.
Not the least of these was American-educated Kwame Nkrumah, tropical Africa's best known nationalist leader and prime minister of the
Gold Coast during the last five years of British rule. Nkrumah, who became president of Ghana in 1960 with the official title of *Osagyefo*
(variously translated to mean brave leader in war or adversity, or re-
deemer in a nonreligious sense), was an ambitious and charismatic
leader, but certain character flaws led to his downfall six years later.

Nkrumah's legacy to Ghana is ambiguous. As the unchallenged ruler
of a one-party state, he helped to forge a supratribal consciousness and
a sense of national pride, but his increasingly despotic and corrupt
regime eroded the institutions and the ideal of democracy bequeathed
by the British. After the National Liberation Council ousted him in
1966, the only solid political foundation to build on was the "non-
Nkrumahist Ghanaians trained at Sandhurst and the British Police
Training School at Hendon" and other "incorruptible elements in the
civil service, the judicial service, and at the universities."[2] In the economic realm he left behind the Volta River Dam and Hydroelectric
Scheme with its great potential, a number of lesser development proj-

1. Press release no. 46/62, Embassy of Ghana, Washington, D.C., Oct. 17, 1962.
2. Henry L. Bretton, *The Rise and Fall of Kwame Nkrumah: A Study of Personal
Rule in Africa* (Praeger, 1966), p. 146.

ects, and an expanded school system, but he had squandered a large portion of the national purse in unsound, prestige projects and uneconomic state corporations, as well as by bribery and kickbacks and a vast party patronage network designed to insure his tight personal control of the country. Under his erratic rule the economy slowed down, unemployment rose, and the $0.5 billion in foreign reserves in 1957 had been transformed into a national debt of $1.2 billion by 1965.

Nkrumah's failure as a political leader can be attributed largely to his arrogance and his fondness for ideology. He thought of himself as a philosopher like Jefferson or Lenin, but the ideology he evolved was a hodgepodge of slogans and clichés from divergent sources. Though he successively described himself as an "orthodox Marxist," a "Marxist socialist," and a "Christian Marxist," he was neither a consistent socialist nor anything else. He did, however, voice one persistent theme—anti-imperialism—but this was directed mainly toward the West and did not prevent him from inviting alien advisers and security agents from communist states whose influence over important political decisions was eventually as great as that of the British during the last days of their rule. "Nkrumahism was not an ideology," but "an indigestible brew concocted by a cynical assembly of mercenaries, 'hit-and-run' experts, sincere but frustrated political theorists, and charlatans," and included "unrelated fragments from Stalin's Russia, Hitler's Germany, from Marcus Garvey, Malcolm X, and Lenin."[3] Even when Nkrumah was closest to the East, he was quite prepared to accept material support from the West.

In the end Nkrumah fell victim to his inflated ego and his strange susceptibility to bad advice, both of which militated against sound economic and political policies for dealing with the fundamental needs of his people. As a statesman, he was not in the same league as Emperor Haile Selassie or President Nasser, whom he regarded as archrivals for pan-African leadership and whose superior talents were demonstrated by political longevity. Nkrumah fostered a shameless cult of personality to match his grandiose designs at home and abroad. The *Osagyefo*[4]

3. *Ibid.*, p. 164.

4. Other titles given Nkrumah included: "His High Dedication, The Aweful, The Achiever, The Ruthless, The Valorous, The Quencher of Fires, The Fount of Honor, The Father of the Nation, The Brave Warrior, The Renewer of All Things" (Henry Tanner, "Nkrumah Steps Up Nkrumahism," *New York Times Magazine*, Jan. 14, 1962, pp. 12–23). Tanner says, "The personality cult that he has built up around him is more extravagant than anything ever tried by Stalin."

sought to become the George Washington of a united Africa. As he surrounded himself with his strange and unreliable crew of foreign and domestic confidants, he isolated himself from his regular civilian and military advisers who were capable of recommending sound decisions.

As time passed, his self-imposed isolation turned into fear and he no longer trusted his own army and police service. To protect his person and defend his regime he built up a secret security structure that was largely administered and supplied by communist regimes. This counterpoise to the regular military and police establishments demoralized their officers. The army and police were further weakened by equipment shortages, reduced functions, and the infiltration of Nkrumah's informers. The unfolding drama between Nkrumah and his security services, which eventually led to the successful army-police coup against him, can best be understood in light of certain basic facts about the country and the character of the internal security forces before independence.

People, Land, and Economy

Situated on the Gulf of Guinea in West Africa, the Republic of Ghana covers 91,843 square miles, an area slightly smaller than Oregon or West Germany.[5] It has a 340-mile coastline in the south and shares frontiers with the Ivory Coast in the west, Upper Volta in the north, and Togo in the east. About 70 percent of Ghana's 8.4 million people live in the southern half of the country where most of the wealth is concentrated. The capital, Accra, and the other major urban centers are found along the coast. The tropical rain forest belt, extending northward from the shore, produces most of the cocoa, timber, and minerals.

The predominantly agricultural economy is based primarily on cocoa, which provides almost 70 percent of Ghana's export earnings. Since 1957 the balance of payments has shown a deficit almost every year because of declining cocoa prices, increased imports of capital goods, and mismanagement of resources. Ghana's per capita income, averaging about $214 per year, is one of the highest in Africa.

5. Political, economic, ethnic, educational, and military information about Ghana is included in a comparative table which also carries similar facts about the Congo and Ethiopia. See Appendix A.

The Volta River Dam, which started to produce electric power in 1965, was financed largely by the United States in conjunction with Britain and the International Bank for Reconstruction and Development. It was made economically feasible by an agreement to build an American-owned aluminum smelter at Tema, presently in full operation, that purchases a substantial percentage of the electricity produced.

Economically and educationally Ghana is one of the most developed states in tropical Africa. About 25 percent of the people over fourteen years of age are literate. Approximately 13.3 percent of the population is in primary and secondary schools compared to 11.5 percent in the Congo and 1.4 percent in Ethiopia. There are some 4,800 students in Ghana's three universities located at Legon (near Accra), Kumasi, and Cape Coast. About 16,400 students are enrolled in teacher training institutions.

There are many ethnic divisions in Ghana; over 50 different languages or dialects are spoken. The major tribal groups are the Ga, Ashanti, Ewe, and Fanti. The official language is English.

Ghana's budget for 1969 was $460 million of which $48 million was allocated for the military services and $19.9 million for the police. The armed forces number 17,000 men, or one serviceman for every 500 inhabitants. There are 18,600 men in the National Police Service.

The government of Prime Minister Busia, installed in October 1969, is politically moderate and formally nonaligned, but it leans toward the West from which it receives economic and military assistance.[6] Since 1962 the United States has provided approximately $100,000 in military assistance to Ghana and since 1966 has trained 25 police officers. From 1962 through 1968 it made available approximately $214 million in all forms of economic assistance.

The present U.S. policy of cooperation with and support of Ghana is based on the assumption that this country can become a bastion of stability and constructive development in West Africa, an objective made all the more important by the bloody tribal conflict in Nigeria. President Kennedy, operating on this assumption in 1961, decided to go ahead with $133 million in loans for the dam and smelter despite a spate of anti-American and procommunist statements from Nkrumah.

6. *New York Times*, Oct. 17, 1969.

From Gold Coast Regiment to Army

On independence day the Gold Coast Regiment, until then a part of the British West Africa Frontier Force, became the Ghana Army. The regiment had developed during the ninety years of conflict, 1807–96, between the British, who were protecting their traders in the coastal areas, and the Ashanti tribes farther inland. The British relied largely on Fanti troops along the coast until 1873 when the governor turned to Europe and neighboring Nigeria for additional manpower.

In response to continuing Ashanti restiveness and French colonization in West Africa, the British in 1898 established the West Africa Frontier Force (WAFF). Commanded by some 100 British officers and noncomissioned officers, this force of about 2,000 African soldiers included constabulary units from the Gold Coast, Nigeria, Gambia, and Sierra Leone. From 1900 until World War I, these units were organized to operate jointly to support imperial defense objectives.

During World War I thousands of indigenous soldiers from British Africa fought in Togoland and the Cameroons against German troops and served in East African transport units,[7] but none qualified for advancement to officer status. In contrast, in World War II troops from British Africa served outside of Africa, notably in Burma, and a small number of Africans became officers under Britain's "slow and gradual process of developing indigenous officer cadres, when political conditions permitted."[8] The new conditions included pressures generated by the expansion of the WAFF from 6,500 to 176,000 men and a recognition that some experienced soldiers met the minimal standards for junior officer positions.[9]

The British approach to Africanization of the officer corps differed from that of the French, reflecting their respective colonial policies. In broad terms, French policy was based on the premise of a "civilizing mission" that sought to create as many "black Frenchmen" as possible

7. Frederick D. Lugard, *The Dual Mandate in Tropical Africa* (London: William Blackwood & Sons, Ltd., 1923), p. 610.

8. Morris Janowitz, *The Military in the Political Development of New Nations* (University of Chicago Press, 1964), pp. 13–14. See also William Gutteridge, *The Military in African Politics* (London: Methuen, 1969), pp. 14–19.

9. F. M. Bourret, *The Gold Coast* (2nd ed., Stanford University Press, 1952), p. 151.

—Africans who spoke, acted, and thought like Frenchmen and who eventually would assume the rights and duties of French citizenship. The British premise was more protective and paternalistic and sought to transmit British culture and morals primarily to a small African elite.

Performance, Morale, and Discipline

The record of the African troops in the Gold Coast Regiment in World War I was uneven. The soldiers did well in a familiar tropical climate, but less than satisfactorily in the cold highlands of East Africa. During World War II they served only in tropical areas and performed well.[10] Generally morale in 1941–45 was good. The adverse effect of the color-cultural bar which was expressed in differences in pay, food, accommodations, and leave from European troops in the same area was partially offset by the advancement of some Africans to the officer ranks.[11] Military service, including travel, the opportunity to meet foreigners, and the acquisition of useful skills, enhanced the morale, self-confidence, and pride of the African troops, though there is no evidence that the war experience altered significantly the political consciousness of the African soldier or his view toward the eventual independence of his country.

Recruiting, Training, and Benefits

In the nineteenth century, troops for the regiment were recruited largely from the more warlike tribes in the northern territories. Primitive, illiterate, and Moslem, these people made reliable soldiers. The Ga, Ewe, and other coastal people who had the benefit of British education never joined the regiment in significant numbers, choosing instead the civil service, business, or the professions. In the later years some two-thirds of the enlisted men came from the more sparsely settled, backward northern areas where military service continued to be the quickest way for a man to better his status. Most of the Africans who qualified for officer positions came from the south.

In 1953 the British began to admit Africans regularly to the Royal Military Academy at Sandhurst and the officer cadet schools at Alder-

10. E. E. Sabben-Clare, "African Troops in Asia," *African Affairs*, Vol. 44, No. 177 (October 1945), p. 155.
11. General Sir William Platt, "Studies in War-time Organization: East Africa Command," *African Affairs*, Vol. 45, No. 178 (January 1946), pp. 32–33.

shot and Chester. By 1957 about 10 percent of the regiment's officers were Africans who had attained that position by training or experience or both. A military officer was highly respected in West Africa and a young man selected for Sandhurst training was held in special esteem.

The British had a broad educational program for the enlisted men that included intensive instruction in the English language, the lingua franca of the army and government. The army also provided training and experience in a wide range of skills, most of which had direct application to civilian life. For most young men the army was an opportunity for immediate self-advancement and preparation for a future civilian vocation. For several years before and after independence the salary of the enlisted man was about 50 percent higher than the civilian minimum wage. In 1961, for example, the minimum civilian wage was slightly less than $1.00 per day while an infantry soldier received almost $1.50. Further, the army provided the soldier and his family with food, shelter, clothing, and medical care.

Identity and Political Orientation

The African officers, particularly those trained in England, were thoroughly immersed in the British military tradition of civilian supremacy and a nonpolitical army. They were among the most British of the Westernized elite in their political and cultural outlook and even in their manners, reflecting the conservatism of the British officers and cadets with whom they were trained. The curriculum at Sandhurst placed heavy emphasis on constitutionality and the rule of law. That training had a strong, enduring influence on many Ghanaian and other African officers, as one cadet's appraisal indicates:

> Now I look back on Sandhurst with nostalgia. It is one of the greatest institutions in the world. Through its doors have passed famous generals. kings and rulers. I can now remember men like King Hussein of Jordan and Ayub Khan of Pakistan. It is an institution that teaches that all men are equal, that the profession of men-at-arms is essential, and a peaceful one. It shows the stupidity of racial conflicts, and the joy of the communion of all men in the service of peace. . . . I left Sandhurst, crossed the Wish Stream, looked back at my old school, and was filled with boundless gratitude. Sandhurst deepened my understanding of the world and also opened to me a new world of adventure and tolerance.[12]

12. A. A. Afrifa, *The Ghana Coup: 24th February 1966* (Humanities Press, 1966), pp. 51–52.

With this background it is not surprising that the officer corps (which remained primarily British for several years after independence day) and the troops (wholly African) made the transition from the Gold Coast Regiment to the Ghana Army with scarcely a ripple. The gradually increasing number of Ghanaian officers played no significant political role in the events leading to independence. Nor did they identify with any political faction in the first years of independence.

Though the officers and their men were wholly nonpolitical, after several years of independence the mood of some Ghanaian officers began to change in response to Nkrumah's downgrading of the army and his increasingly arbitrary and demagogic behavior. No doubt the nonpolitical and nonconspiratorial tradition was a major reason why the Ghanaian officers did not move against Nkrumah before they did. Not only the officers but the noncommissioned officers and the enlisted men held this professional and instrumental view of the military. One observer with wide contact with African officers in the British areas believes that the armed forces of Ghana absorbed Western modes of thought and behavior more fully than those of any other tropical African country.[13]

Ghana Armed Forces: 1957–59

The principal change from Gold Coast Regiment to Ghana Army was one of nomenclature. The army was organized, trained, and armed to fulfill a largely domestic role in Commonwealth defense. The chief of the new Ghana Defense Staff was British and he and his British assistants exercised decisive control and influence over strictly military matters. British officers also held all the top command positions and the great majority of junior officer posts. In March 1957 there were 220 British officers and about 25 Ghanaian officers, all in lower ranks (by April 1961 there were 150 Ghanaians and 230 Britons in the officer corps).[14]

The African officers were competent, but the majority lacked the experience, tradition, and training for promotion to higher command

13. William F. Gutteridge, *Military Institutions and Power in the New States* (Praeger, 1965), pp. 100–05.
14. Jon Kraus, "The Men in Charge," *Africa Report* (April 1966), pp. 17–18.

and staff duties. The army had to compete with the civilian economy for men of officer caliber. The noncommissioned officers and enlisted men were well trained and effective.

Recruitment during this period was entirely voluntary and the men seeking long-term enlistments far exceeded the number required. Though there were no formal tribal quotas, inducements, or impediments, the armed forces were not a balanced cross section of Ghana's ethnic diversity. The combat units continued to come largely from the more backward north, the officers almost exclusively from the educated groups in the south. Technicians for the army and specialists for the embryonic navy and air force, both established in 1959, were also recruited from the south because a middle school leaving certificate was required.

The relationship of the Ashanti to the armed forces is unique and ironic. A proud, self-conscious, and cohesive people with a strong warrior tradition, they were prohibited from enlisting in the regiment because of their conflict with the British. Even after the prohibition was withdrawn, the Ashanti never joined the armed forces in large numbers. During World War II they provided less than 10 percent of the total Gold Coast military enlistment, though they were and are slightly more than 20 percent of the population. In 1956 only 5 percent of the army was Ashanti. Resentment against the army continued among the Ashanti until at least 1960.[15]

During the first years of independence the Ghana armed forces numbered some 8,000 men, a figure approximating the military strength of Nigeria with a population six times larger.[16] This disparity which persisted through 1966 reflected two historic factors. The first was London's policy of considering the military requirements of British West Africa as a whole rather than country by country and recruiting accordingly; the second was the transfer of the West Africa regiment headquarters from Freetown to Accra about 1940. In financial terms, Ghana's defense expenditures in 1957–58 were $9.5 million, or 5.3 percent of the total state budget.

With headquarters at Burma Camp, Accra, the army field forces were

15. Gutteridge, *Military Institutions and Power in the New States*, p. 60.
16. In 1966 Nigeria had one serviceman for every 4,956 inhabitants, and Ghana had 844, according to Charles S. Stevenson, "African Armed Forces," *Military Review* (March 1967), pp. 107–12.

organized into two brigade groups, each with two infantry battalions, an independent reconnaissance squadron, an engineer field unit, and attached signal and medical elements, all supported with central installations near Accra. The battalions were spread widely throughout the country, located at Accra, Takoradi, Tema, and Tamale. A recruiting center was located at Kumasi, the Ashanti "capital." In 1960 the Ghana Military Academy along Sandhurst lines was established at Teshie, near Accra, with a British commandant.

During the first three years of independence the relationship between the army and the new government was generally smooth, except for one event in December 1958 which seemed to indicate that Nkrumah did not fully trust his officer corps. Preoccupied with recruiting and training cadets, the British and Ghanaian officers behaved professionally and did not become involved directly or indirectly in partisan politics. The one celebrated exception involved Major Benjamin Awhaitey, a Ghanaian who commanded Giffard Camp in Accra, who was accused of failing to report conspiratorial conversations he allegedly had with R. R. Amponsah, a principal figure in the opposition United Party. It was also alleged that Amponsah had sought to bribe Awhaitey, then second in seniority among all Ghanaian officers, to gain support among noncommissioned officers for a coup against Nkrumah. Awhaitey was convicted and cashiered for neglect of duty. Amponsah and other United Party officials were imprisoned.

Shortly after the trial a government commission was convened, headed by a British justice, Granville Sharp. The other two members of the commission were a Ghanaian judge and a West Indian jurist. The Ghanaian and Indian found that Amponsah and others had been involved in a revolutionary conspiracy and had used Awhaitey to get army support. Dissenting, Justice Sharp found no conspiracy and strongly implied that Amponsah had been trapped and Awhaitey framed.[17]

The evidence on this affair is still inconclusive, but it appears that Awhaitey did engage in secret and unprofessional political discussions with the United Party leader, but that he had no intention of becoming

17. Government of Ghana, *Report of the Commission Appointed Under the Commissions of Enquiry Ordinance*, CAP. 249 (Accra: The Government Printer, 1959). See also Dennis Austin, *Politics in Ghana: 1946–1960* (Oxford University Press, 1964), pp. 380–82.

involved in plans for military action against Nkrumah. As viewed by Nkrumah such conversations were "conspiratorial," while from the more impersonal perspective of Justice Sharp they could be imprudent without being subversive. The incident demonstrated that Nkrumah was alert to the possibility of a plot involving army officers. He used the affair to discredit and neutralize the United Party which he regarded as intrinsically conspiratorial and to make it clear he would tolerate no disloyalty in the army or elsewhere. However interpreted, the affair was a harbinger of future strains between Nkrumah and the officer corps.

The Army and Nkrumah: 1960–63

The four years from 1960 through 1963 were marked by rising but subdued tension between the armed services and Nkrumah. Military and police officers and other elements in the Westernized elite became increasingly concerned by Nkrumah's successful efforts to arrogate political power to himself, his ruthless methods of dealing with opposition, his grandiose pan-African dreams, and his growing dependence on the Soviet bloc for security advice and assistance. Both the army and the police were demoralized by Nkrumah's interference in their affairs and the restrictions he placed upon them, but they remained loyal.

Though there was no overt effort on the part of the army or police to topple the regime or even to change the fundamental political direction of the government, there were quiet rumblings of criticism and disaffection, muted in part by the benefits the army and police received by their service in the Congo. One of the first Ghanaian officers to become politically conscious was A. A. Afrifa whose misgivings were certainly shared by others.

In 1961 when Afrifa was only 25 years old he was sent to Britain for the second period of military training, this time to the infantry schools at Hythe and Warminster. A previous tour of duty in the Congo had awakened him to politics. While in the United Kingdom he both heard and expressed misgivings about Nkrumah's violations of the democratic institutions. When he returned to Ghana, he later recalled, he "became interested in the political situation."[18] By August 1962 when he re-

18. Afrifa, *The Ghana Coup*, pp. 72 and 75.

turned as a captain from his second stint in the Congo, he had become "convinced that Kwame Nkrumah had failed the country" and he actually contemplated storming Flagstaff House with his 300 men to overthrow the president by "quick and decisive military action."[19] For prudential reasons he did not act until four years later, and then in collaboration with other military and police officers in the successful February 24 coup.

Toward a One-Man Regime

Through legal and parliamentary manipulations, supported by the largely illiterate mass of his Convention People's Party, Nkrumah managed to consolidate virtually all power in his own hands and effectively destroy the United Party and other opposition elements. One of his major instruments was the Preventive Detention Act of 1958 which he applied with increasing frequency.[20] In 1962 Nkrumah persuaded the Assembly to extend from one day to twenty-eight the period a suspect could be held under the act without a formal charge. Another instrument of control was the 1960 constitution which was railroaded through Parliament without adequate debate and had the effect of endowing Nkrumah with almost absolute power and of laying the foundation for making him president for life, an honor conferred on him two years later by the Assembly. Afrifa says Nkrumah tore the old constitution "into shreds" and then foisted the new one on the country to aggrandize his personal ambition; the president "and his lieutenants, under the guise of ensuring political calm, worked to consolidate their own future. The Head of State, armed with all his powers, dismissed members of the Armed Forces and the Judiciary, when and how he liked, every time he suspected a threat to his position, or throne."[21]

Armed with laws to suppress his opponents and supported by a rubber-stamp majority in the Assembly, Nkrumah appeared to have a free hand to fulfill his goals of African socialism at home and to pursue his pan-African ambitions abroad. But his weakness for bad advice and

19. *Ibid.*, p. 85.
20. See Austin, *Politics in Ghana*, pp. 376–95, for a summary of the various control measures designed to neutralize the opposition, including the 1960 constitution. See also, "Recent Developments in Ghana," *Bulletin of the International Commission of Jurists* (Geneva, Switzerland, March 1964), p. 13, which concluded: "Ghana has now unmistakably chosen the path of centralized personal rule."
21. Afrifa, *The Ghana Coup*, p. 63.

his growing paranoia bred creeping opposition among the elite and precipitated a number of incidents that challenged the security of the regime. Two such events in 1962 convinced Nkrumah that both the army and the police were potential sources of serious opposition.

The first was an assassination attempt against Nkrumah on August 1 while he was being driven through Kulungugu in northern Ghana. A bomb was thrown at his car. He escaped unhurt, but four persons were killed and more than fifty injured. This led to a purge of his own Convention People's Party, the chief victims being the foreign minister, the information minister, and the party secretary, all of whom were imprisoned. When the men were acquitted of complicity in the incident in a "trial" by the Special Criminal Division of the High Court, Nkrumah declared the decision null and void, fired the chief justice, and forced the other two judicial representatives of the division to resign.[22] He also assumed personal control over the civil service, a move designed in part to tighten his surveillance over the police.

On September 9, just two days after Nkrumah was proclaimed president for life and during a celebration of his escape at Kulungugu, another bomb exploded a few hundred yards from Flagstaff House. One person was killed and sixty-three injured. In response, Nkrumah initiated further emergency measures, including the recruitment of security personnel from Soviet bloc states to supervise the troops guarding him and his residence.

The internal security situation continued to deteriorate. On September 18 an army warrant officer, Edward Tetteh, jumped to his death from the Accra police headquarters where he was being held for his alleged involvement in the Kulungugu assassination attempt. Tetteh, who was stationed at the Burma Camp armory, was accused of supplying the army grenade used at Kulungugu. This suicide exacerbated the tension and mutual suspicion between Nkrumah and the security services. Apart from the possible guilt of Tetteh, there appeared to be no army or police personnel involved in the known plots of this period.

Ill-Fated Expansionist Efforts

Ghana's military officers were only marginally involved in Nkrumah's abortive efforts to expand his influence in Africa, though they

22. William Burnett Harvey, *Law and Social Change in Ghana* (Princeton University Press, 1966), p. 341.

necessarily played a major role in the UN Congo effort which Nkrumah considered an opportunity to give substance to his pan-African dreams.[23] Regarding himself as the heir apparent to a united Africa, Nkrumah launched a series of moves toward this end. Replete with flowery rhetoric he formed the Ghana-Guinea union in 1958, adding Mali in 1960, but instead of enhancing his power the abortive union turned Togo and Nigeria against him. His grandiose scheme for a United States of Africa with a common citizenship, currency, and foreign and defense policy, was rejected by other African leaders. Nkrumah can, however, be given credit for helping to create the sentiment that in 1963 materialized in the modest Organization of African Unity (OAU) whose charter stressed the principles of state sovereignty and noninterference. The OAU Defense Commission, meeting in Accra in November 1963, refused to accept Nkrumah's proposal for an African high command to "liberate" by military means the remaining colonial territories.

His earlier effort to establish an African military command, launched at the Casablanca Conference of six African states with troops in the Congo in January 1961, also came to nought. Eighteen months after his proposal for a joint command had been accepted, headquarters were set up in Accra with Mohammed Fawzi of the United Arab Republic as commander. This ill-conceived endeavor provided high Ghanaian Army officers with the opportunity to travel, to meet foreign officers, and to gain military information about the African states they visited. But soon they realized that the joint command had no viable mission and was being used by Nkrumah to extend his influence and by President Nasser to gain political support in tropical Africa for his ambitions in the Middle East. With their disillusionment and the disinterest of the other Casablanca governments the effort was quickly and quietly laid to rest.

Military Experience in the Congo

In terms of professional competence and morale, the Ghana Army and its officer corps gained substantial benefits by providing a contingent for the UN Force in the Congo, in spite of Nkrumah's political designs. "His one ambition was to see a United Independent Congo which would eventually be a part of the Ghana-Guinea-Mali Union,

23. See W. Scott Thompson, *Ghana's Foreign Policy, 1957–1966: Diplomacy, Ideology, and the Nkrumah Period* (Princeton University Press, 1969).

with himself, Kwame Nkrumah, as the head—an embryo of the future Empire of Africa."[24]

As early as 1958, two years before the Belgian Congo was given independence, Nkrumah and Patrice Lumumba had become friends. Nkrumah regarded the less experienced Congolese leader as a protégé and Lumumba was quite prepared to accept the role. A few weeks before independence day, June 30, 1960, Ghana established a special office in Leopoldville (now Kinshasa) headed by Andrew Djin, who served as his personal link with Lumumba. On July 12 a six-man Ghanaian delegation, including Colonel S. J. A. Otu, the senior Ghanaian in the officer corps, arrived in the Congo to ascertain how Ghana might help Lumumba to reassert control over the Congolese Army (which had fallen apart when Lumumba dismissed its Belgian officer corps). On July 14 the Security Council voted to dispatch a UN Force to the Congo. On the same day Major General H. T. Alexander, Nkrumah's chief of staff, arrived in Leopoldville with a platoon of Ghanaian soldiers in response to Deputy Prime Minister Antoine Gizenga's request for interim aid until UN troops arrived. The Ghanaian unit, later integrated into the UN Force, was augmented by a much larger contingent the following day in response to Secretary-General Hammarskjold's call for peacekeeping forces, especially from African states.

In terms of its resources, Ghana made one of the heaviest manpower contributions to the Congo effort, this in the face of serious political complications in the early days. By August 20, 1960, there were 2,394 Ghanaian officers and men in the Congo and the contingent remained for three of the four years of the UN mission, contributing a total of almost 40,000 man-months. During this time approximately one-third of the army was in the Congo.[25] Only India, Ethiopia, Nigeria, and Tunisia provided more man-months than Ghana and none of the 34 contributing states sent as high a percentage of its armed forces. Nigeria was second with 26.7 percent.

When the conflict between Lumumba and Hammarskjold erupted over the proper role of the UN Force, particularly toward secessionist Katanga, the governments of the militant African states with units in the Congo were confronted with a serious problem. They were all pro-

---

24. Afrifa, *The Ghana Coup*, p. 69; see also pp. 65–74.
25. Ernest W. Lefever, *Uncertain Mandate: Politics of the U.N. Congo Operation* (Johns Hopkins Press, 1967), pp. 158, 228.

Lumumba and anti-Tshombe, and they frequently charged Hammar-skjold with being anti-Lumumba and pro-Kasavubu, if not pro-Tshombe. The Kasavubu forces prevailed in Leopoldville in September 1960, and the Kasavubu delegation was seated by the UN General Assembly on November 22. At the Casablanca Conference in early January 1961, Guinea, Mali, and the UAR, in protest against Hammar-skjold's policies, declared they would withdraw their units and they subsequently did.[26]

Though a participant in the Casablanca Conference, Ghana argued against the troop recall and urged that the UN Force be given one more chance, even though the previous August 11 Ghana had said its unit "would be justified in taking independent action."[27] This moderate stance is remarkable in view of Nkrumah's continued political support of Lumumba's heirs as well as several incidents reflecting the ambiguous position of Ghanaian troops in the Congo. One event will illustrate the problem. In September 1960, President Kasavubu, angered by Nkrumah's special political ties with Lumumba, accused Ghanaian troops of supporting Lumumba to the detriment of the central government. Evidence does not support this charge. On the contrary, Ghanaian troops took part in the UN Force action on September 12, 1960, to deny Lumumba entry into the Leopoldville radio station which had been closed by UN authorities. Lumumba made a strong protest to Nkrumah, who replied that the troops behaved properly because they were "for the moment under the orders of the United Nations."[28] Several high UN officials insist that the Ghanaian unit was loyal to the UN Command, in spite of the political pressure its officers were under from Accra.[29] Subsequently, the Ghana unit was moved out of Leopoldville to quiet the controversy and to mitigate political pressures on the unit from agents of its own government.

General Alexander asserts flatly that Nkrumah "failed to understand that troops placed under United Nations command cannot take orders

26. *Ibid.*, pp. 162–66.
27. UN Security Council, *Official Records* (SCOR), Supplement for July, August, and September 1960, A/4427 (Aug. 11, 1960), p. 93.
28. Jules Gérard-Libois and Benoit Verhaegen, *Congo: 1960*, Vol. II (Brussels: Les Dossiers du CRISP, n.d.) p. 909.
29. Author interviews with Rajeswar Dayal, UN officer in charge at the time, in New Delhi, Feb. 22, 1965; and with Major General Indar Jit Rikhye, the Secretary-General's military adviser, in New York, April 27, 1965.

from their parent country" and that this caused "a great deal of friction between him, myself, and other senior Ghanaian officers."[30] This may have been true of the early days, but for most of the time Ghanaian troops were in the Congo, Nkrumah's relations with the UN Command were essentially correct.

Ghana's substantial and constructive contribution to the UN Force was marred by a mutiny and massacre in early 1961. In January the Third Battalion of the Ghana Army, stationed at Tshikapa in South Kasai, mutinied. Its commander Colonel David Hansen, a young Ghanaian who later commanded the Ghana Navy, was inexperienced and rather unpopular among the troops. This, combined with the troops' separation from their families and easy access to liquor and Congolese women, led to a breakdown of battalion discipline. The Ghanaian officers lost control and Hansen was severely beaten by some of his men. After about 36 hours of turbulence, involving some 200 men and several noncommissioned officers who acted as leaders, order was restored by British officers of the Ghanaian units. Ninety of the mutineers were sent by plane to Ghana, where an unspecified number of them were later court martialed and severely punished.[31]

On April 28, 1961, at least 47 Ghanaian soldiers were murdered by Congolese troops in Port Francqui and thrown into the river for no discernible military motives.[32] A high Ghana Army officer has said that the incident might have been prevented if the British officers of the men involved had taken more adequate security precautions. This was the most serious of several atrocities committed against UN troops by ill-disciplined Congolese soldiers. This tragedy, Nkrumah's disillusionment over the course of Congolese political events, and other factors led to the gradual withdrawal of Ghana's troops (then numbering some 1,600) over the following six months. By February 1962, however, a Ghanaian battalion was back in the Congo and remained there until September 1963.

Afrifa, who views Ghana's involvement in the Congo primarily as an extension of Nkrumah's pan-African ambitions, criticizes the "constant

30. H. T. Alexander, *African Tightrope: My Two Years as Nkrumah's Chief of Staff* (Praeger, 1966), p. 34.
31. *Ibid.*, pp. 68–70.
32. See Lefever, *Uncertain Mandate*, pp. 233–34. Alexander says that "120 Ghanaian soldiers with their British officers were murdered" (Alexander, *African Tightrope*, p. 66).

interference by Kwame Nkrumah and his aides in the internal problems of the Congo" which caused great difficulties for General Alexander and UN officials.[33] "By August 1960 all our forces and equipment were concentrated on the Congo to the detriment of our own country. . . . We had lost lives in a struggle which was not ours."[34]

But there is no evidence that the security situation in Ghana suffered because one-third of the army was in the Congo. The troops received what amounted to free training and experience. They were fully supplied, with food, clothing, shelter, and medical care, by the UN Command while out of the country. Each officer and man regardless of rank or nationality received a daily allowance of $1.30 from which he could purchase items in the UN's post exchange. Ghana continued to pay the regular salaries. Transportation to and from the Congo was paid from UN funds. The Ghana Army acquired in the Congo free or at low cost a quantity of modern military equipment, including helicopters, ground vehicles, and communications gear. Added to these material benefits, the troops had the broadening experience of meeting their counterparts from other countries in Africa, Asia, and Europe.

In political terms, Nkrumah earned some much-sought prestige in Africa and beyond for Ghana's substantial contribution to the UN effort. Among moderate governments where his reputation was sagging, his refusal to go along with the Casablanca pullout won him a measure of respect.

The performance of Ghana's contingent speaks well for the professional quality and nonpolitical character of the army. The officers and men were steadfastly loyal to the UN Command despite unusual political pressures and the Tshikapa mutiny which was directed not against the UN Command, but against a few Ghanaian officers.

Turn toward the Communist States

Nkrumah's attitude toward his officer corps vacillated between pride and apprehension. He sought to improve and strengthen the army. At the same time, he pursued policies that undercut the authority and prestige of his top officers. The 1960–63 period saw the Africanization of the officer corps, the abrupt dismissal of General Alexander, and an increasing dependence upon communist states for military training and

33. Afrifa, *The Ghana Coup*, p. 71.
34. *Ibid.*, p. 70.

advice, each reflecting and increasing the tension between the president and his army.

In January 1960 General Alexander became chief of the Defense Staff, succeeding Major General A. B. V. Paley, also a Briton, who had had the post since 1956. Alexander and the other British officers serving with him supported the Africanization of the officer corps as rapidly as Ghanaians could be trained. In fact, Alexander drew up plans for turning over the armed forces entirely to Ghanaian officers by late 1962. By mid-1961 the military academy had graduated its first class and three of the four infantry battalions were commanded by Ghanaians. One of the two brigade commanders was Ghanaian. There were forty company-grade Ghanaian officers, making a total of about 120 with officer posts.[35] Everyone seemed pleased with the steady pace of transferring the leadership of the army to young Ghanaian officers.

On September 22, 1961, suddenly and without notice, Nkrumah dismissed Alexander, replacing him with Brigadier S. J. A. Otu, and Africanized the remainder of the officer corps. This meant the dismissal of some 80 British officers from command positions. In his abrupt letter of dismissal to "Major General H. T. Alexander, CB, CBE, DSO," the president implied that Africanization was moving too slowly and added: "I have been greatly disturbed by the attitude which the British Government have taken over the question of Katanga" and insisted it was "politically imperative that in present circumstances, direct command of the Ghana Armed Forces should be held by Ghanaians."[36] Nkrumah, who in the same letter proclaimed himself supreme commander of the Ghana armed forces, did not mention pledges of economic and military aid he had received during his extensive July–August tour of the USSR, Poland, East Germany, Czechoslovakia, Hungary, Yugoslavia, and Red China. Under these circumstances it was embarrassing for Africa's foremost "anti-imperialist" to depend on 80 British officers. Communist diplomats and agents, as well as the Marxists in his own entourage, probably also advised him to expel the British from command positions.

Nkrumah's ouster of the British officers had been contemplated for some time. In June 1961 he had reached an informal agreement with Canada to provide military technicians and training officers, the first of

---

35. William F. Gutteridge, "The Armed Forces of Ghana Today," *Canadian Army Journal*, Vol. 15, No. 3 (Summer 1961), pp. 47–48.
36. The full letter is found in Alexander, *African Tightrope*, p. 149.

whom arrived in September 1961. On January 8, 1962, he concluded a formal agreement with Ottawa for 30 Canadian officers to perform functions previously in British hands.[37] The following May, London agreed to provide a joint services training team of British officers to advise Ghana's armed forces but to have no command responsibilities. The cost of these two programs, except for pay and allowances for the officers, was to be borne by Accra.

While he was decreasing Western military advice and assistance, Nkrumah for the first time turned to the communist states for security aid. During his summer trip to communist states he ordered Alexander to select 400 cadets immediately for officer training in the Soviet Union. In a "cry from the heart," a letter to Colonel J. A. Ankrah who five years later became the first chairman of the National Liberation Council, Alexander expressed the misgivings of the officer corps, British and Ghanaian alike. It was written September 22, 1961, the day he was dismissed:

> ... The President proposes to send 400 potential officers to the Soviet Union for training. I have done all I can to persuade him that such action is neither necessary nor prudent. It is not necessary because it will in no way speed up the rate of Africanization which by doubling the size of the Academy I have already put at a gallop. . . . It is unwise for several reasons. Firstly, it splits the training and outlook of the Officers into two camps, and can breed neither contentment nor efficiency. Secondly, I consider that such action may in the long-term prove dangerous to the President himself.[38]

Alexander's judgment was ratified by subsequent events. In October 1961, Ghana sent 68 cadets who had been rejected by its own academy to the Soviet Union for military training. The men returned within six months, dissatisfied with their training and disillusioned by their total experience in Russia. After careful screening, many of them were admitted to the Ghana Academy. Eventually one-third of the group became officers. It was a disaster from the beginning and, perhaps more than any other single development, demoralized ranking Ghanaian officers.[39] Alexander's warning that the opening to the Soviet bloc "may in

37. Canadian Department of External Affairs, "Military Training Assistance to Ghana," *External Affairs* (April 1962), pp. 136–37.

38. Alexander, *African Tightrope*, p. 147.

39. This demoralization was evident in the views expressed during author interviews in Accra, Feb. 1, 1965, with Air Commander M. A. Otu and Lieutenant Colonel E. K. Kotoka, the latter an original member of the National Liberation Council who was killed in the abortive countercoup of April 17, 1967.

the long-term prove dangerous to the President himself" was elegant prophecy.

During this period Nkrumah started to recruit security personnel from Eastern Europe to supervise the troops guarding him and his residence. By 1963 he had converted the President's Own Guard Regiment (POGR), established by Alexander some years before as a relief tour from Congo duty and a post for older officers, into an elite bodyguard supervised in part by foreign communist agents. That Nkrumah entrusted this most sensitive security task to European communists rather than to his own countrymen just as he ousted the last British officers, whose loyalty was beyond question, is an irony that was not lost on the Ghanaian officers who continued to encourage the president to rely more on the British and less on the Soviet bloc.

Nkrumah's ambivalence toward the armed services was eloquently though indirectly expressed in his speech before the Ghana Military Academy on September 29, 1962, in which he repeatedly emphasized "unquestionable loyalty" to the regime as the preeminent virtue of an officer:

> To become an officer in the armed forces is a matter of great distinction and pride. It also demands of you the best and noblest traits of character: integrity, efficiency and unquestionable loyalty. . . . Maintain and cherish the confidence which the people, the Party and the Government have in you.
>
> Loyalty must transcend all personal interests and ambitions, all tribal or regional considerations. The basic requirement is to be loyal in your thoughts. . . . Loyalty demands of you that you place the interests of the State above all others. . . .
>
> Ghana is passing through a revolutionary period. . . . [There are among us] detractors and reactionaries . . . who represent imperialist interests. . . . It is your bounden duty to bring to the notice of the authorities the slightest trace [of subversive activity among them].[40]

Deepening Crisis and the Coup: 1964–66

The momentum of untoward developments of the early sixties accelerated during 1964 and 1965. Among the elite groups there was a growing uneasiness, a mingled sense of fear and hope that the downward spiral could be halted only by a drastic event. The deteriorating eco-

---

40. Press release no. 46/62, Embassy of Ghana, Washington, D.C., Oct. 17, 1962.

nomic situation bore more directly on the common people than did Nkrumah's increasingly arbitrary rule and his deepening reliance on communist assistance which affected primarily the Westernized elite.

The unfavorable balance of payments worsened, consumer buying power declined, and unemployment rose. Though the Volta River Dam was in operation by the end of 1965, the Tema Harbor had been improved, and the Valco aluminum smelter was about to open—all having largely future rather than present benefits—there was growing criticism of uneconomic projects like the 18-mile Tema motorway ("the road to nowhere") and the Palace of African Unity (built for a one-week conference at a cost of almost $30 million and having no other practical use); unproductive "socialist" enterprises on the Russian pattern; and outright kickbacks and bribery in government contracts. These economic developments demoralized the people at home and made it virtually impossible for Ghana to get credit from Western sources abroad.

The Downward Spiral

Acutely aware of the mounting disaffection, Nkrumah cracked down even harder. The elite suffered most; dissenters or alleged dissenters were dismissed, arrested, or imprisoned. One of the victims was a celebrated foreigner, Conor Cruise O'Brien of Ireland, who had become vice chancellor of Ghana University after he was dismissed from UN service in the Congo in late 1961. An admirer of Nkrumah's "African socialism" and "anti-imperialism," O'Brien gradually became disillusioned with the president's political use of the university and left the country at the end of his contract in 1965.

Moving ever closer to the communist world, Nkrumah drifted from Moscow toward the more militant Peking. The Soviet Union continued economic and military aid. Though his heart was with Peking, his stomach was with Moscow. Under his Bureau of African Affairs, Nkrumah operated four "freedom fighter" camps to train foreign nationals in the ideology and tactics of guerrilla warfare for eventual military operations against Rhodesia, the Portuguese provinces, and South Africa. These camps, begun in 1960 with the help of Russian and Chinese agents, were operated by Red Chinese instructors.

There appears to have been a second type of "freedom fighter" camp, designed to train black Africans to overthrow black "reactionary" governments. Whatever the political aims of this communist-operated guerrilla training, a number of Ghana's neighbors, including Senegal, Togo,

Nigeria, and the Ivory Coast, felt threatened by "yellow-trained Peking Communism."[41] They had good reason to be apprehensive because of Peking's well publicized subversive efforts against black regimes in Kenya, Zanzibar, and Congo (Brazzaville). Moscow disassociated itself from this "black" subversive effort, fearing it would undermine Soviet objectives elsewhere in Africa, though it continued to assist other African "freedom fighter" efforts designed to overthrow "white" regimes.

Nkrumah continued to be plagued by ambivalence toward the regular armed forces and the police. Proud of his army, he had encouraged its development. He saw the armed forces as a symbol of national integration, a necessary bulwark against a serious threat to internal security, and a tangible earnest of his right to leadership in Africa. By 1965 the army numbered 14,000 men, double its strength in 1960. It had ten battalions—six infantry, two POGR, one paratrooper, and one reconnaissance. The air force and navy had about 1,000 men each. All his officers were Ghanaian, most of them were well trained, and most of the senior officers had served in the Congo. Even after the Ghana Academy was in operation, some of the best officer candidates were sent to Sandhurst, and a few to India and Pakistan. The Ghana Army in 1964 probably had 50 Sandhurst graduates and its top naval candidates were still trained at the Royal Naval College in Dartmouth. The made-in-Britain imprint was strong.

At the same time, Nkrumah continued to take measures that seriously subverted the morale and effectiveness of his regular security services, notably creating counterweights by transferring security functions to special agencies under his personal control, depriving the army of necessary equipment and facilities, and politically manipulating army officers.

In July 1965 the enlarged POGR, consisting of 50 officers and 1,100 men, was detached from the army and made directly responsible to the president. It was secretly trained by foreign communist officers and provided weapons whose firepower was superior to that of the regular forces. Under his so-called Presidential Detail Department, in addition to the POGR, was the Civilian Wing (including bodyguard, protection, functions, and comptroller units), the Counter Intelligence Unit, and the "secret camps" division which operated sites at Elmina Castle, Akosombo, Afienya, and Okpongle.[42]

In June 1964 Nkrumah introduced military training into the Workers

41. Paris, Agence France Presse, 17:30 GMT, Jan. 8, 1965.
42. See *Nkrumah's Subversion in Africa* (Accra: Ministry of Information, 1966).

Brigades which had been created in 1957 to give socially useful work to young men and to mobilize political support for the regime. This was seen by officers as a threat to the army but Nkrumah never armed the brigades, which numbered 7,000, and they never became a serious paramilitary force.

Nkrumah further demoralized the officer corps by abrupt changes among senior personnel. On July 28, 1965, Major General S. J. A. Otu, Defense Staff chief, and Major General J. A. Ankrah, deputy chief, both fifty years old, were summarily retired from active service. Two brigadiers were promoted to major general to replace them: Nathan A. Aferi as defense chief and Charles M. Barwah as his deputy. Barwah had been serving as Nkrumah's unofficial adviser for several years. Reasons for the abrupt change were not given, but some observers believe that Aferi, who was a key prosecution witness in the Awhaitey case in 1958, was considered more loyal than Otu. It has also been suggested that Otu and Ankrah had dared to protest Nkrumah's detachment of the POGR from the army.

Three months after getting rid of Ankrah and Otu, Nkrumah proposed the formation of a "people's militia," ostensibly to be trained for an invasion of Rhodesia, but thought to be a counterweight to the regular army. Whether or not Nkrumah really intended to set up such a force, he at least convinced some officers that he was serious. Against this backdrop Afrifa described the mood of the army in 1965:

> Our clothes were virtually in tatters. We had no ammunition. The burden of taxation was heavy. The cost of living for the ordinary soldier was high. The Army was virtually at the mercy of the politicians who treated it with arrogance and even open contempt.
>
> We were also aware that members of the President's Own Guard Regiment were receiving kingly treatment. Their pay was higher and it was an open fact that they possessed better equipment. The men who had been transferred [to the POGR] from the Regular Army no longer owed any allegiance and loyalty to the Chief of Defence Staff, but to Kwame Nkrumah who had become their commanding officer.[43]

It was in this atmosphere of apprehension that fleeting thoughts of ousting Nkrumah began to take concrete form in the minds of several army and police officials. "In November 1964," recalls Afrifa, "when I was Acting Brigade Major at the 2nd Infantry Brigade Headquarters at Kumasi, I quietly conceived a plan for the coup" and discussed the idea

43. Afrifa, The Ghana Coup, pp. 99–100; see also p. 103.

with Lieutenant Colonel Cofie-Crabbe, commander of the First Battalion at Elmina. "There were approximately one thousand men under his command. I assured him that if we made a quick dash for Accra in the night we could arrest Nkrumah and topple" the regime. Retrospectively he noted that "at that time security guard was not as formidable as it was by the 24th of February, 1966." The plan was abandoned when Crabbe fell under the suspicion of the army intelligence chief.[44]

Some top police officials were also disturbed for many of the same reasons that caused anxiety in the army. The police were more involved in the regime than the army because they were called upon to make many illegal arrests. Hence, the police service under Nkrumah became corrupt and demoralized, though some officers tried to maintain their integrity. J. W. K. Harlley, who is regarded as the co-author of the 1966 coup, says that the increasing number of arbitrary arrests instigated by Nkrumah when Harlley was intelligence chief led him to the conviction that the overthrow of the president was necessary and morally right. Upon his appointment as police commissioner in January 1965, he recalled, his "first consideration" was how he could "effect the arrest of the arch criminal, Kwame Nkrumah, or dispose of him."[45] He kept the idea to himself until April 1965 when he discussed it with Colonel Kotoka, then a general staff officer in the Defense Ministry, and other army colonels and majors.[46]

By mid-1965, Ghana was ripe for a coup. The ferment in the army, the police, the courts, and a significant slice of the civil service could not be neutralized by the external manifestations of loyalty on the part of the Convention People's Party (CPP) faithful who profited from a vast patronage system. One observer said "the ballot box was emptied of meaning, and the hapless electorate was offered instead the mythology of Nkrumahism. The CPP . . . was held together only by the power of graft."[47] Major General J. A. Ankrah blamed Nkrumah and the CPP for "maladministration, mismanagement, the loss of individual freedom, and economic chaos."[48]

44. *Ibid.*, p. 96.
45. J. W. K. Harlley, "The Decisive Role of the Police," an address to members of the police service, March 10, 1966 (Accra: State Publishing Corporation, 1966), p. 2.
46. Author interview with J. W. K. Harlley, Accra, Oct. 13, 1966.
47. Dennis Austin, "The Ghana Coup d'Etat," *Survival* (London, May 1966), p. 169.
48. Quoted by Kraus, "The Men in Charge," p. 17.

Inadvertently Nkrumah wrote his most appropriate political epitaph three weeks before the coup in an address to Parliament while explaining and in part justifying the recent "unfortunate military intrusions into the political life of several independent African states." If one reverses Nkrumah's ideological rhetoric, his words were prophetic:

> [The root cause of military coups] can be found not in the life and tradition of the African people, but in the maneuvers of neocolonialism. . . . Corruption, bribery, nepotism, shameless and riotous and ostentatious living become rife among the leaders of [a neocolonialist] regime. This brings untold suffering on the workers and people as a whole. . . .
>
> The masses have then nowhere to turn for redress. They therefore have no choice but to organize to isolate the army from the corrupt regime, if the army itself is free from the taint of corruption.[49]

The Coup: February 24, 1966

Nkrumah's "political kingdom" came to an abrupt and inglorious end on February 24, 1966, while he was flying from Rangoon to Peking on a mission to bring peace in Vietnam. This was just three months after General Joseph Mobutu took over for the second time in the Congo. Nkrumah became the victim of a military-police coup, engineered by a handful of concerned men who had served him well, who believed in parliamentary government, and who had not previously intruded into the political realm. They all had to overcome their strong inhibitions against seizing power by unconstitutional means.

The conversations about a coup, initiated in 1965 between Harlley and Kotoka, had grown to include Afrifa, a major in the Second Infantry Brigade Group under Kotoka's command at Kumasi. These three felt it essential to include Colonel A. K. Ocran, commander of the crucial First Brigade Group in Accra. They decided to overthrow the regime by a combined military-police operation, replacing it with a temporary National Liberation Council to be headed by Major General Ankrah, the deputy defense chief dismissed in 1965. They assumed that Chief of Staff Aferi and Deputy Chief Barwah would support Nkrumah since each had profited from Ankrah's dismissal.

The timing of the coup was determined by Nkrumah's Asian trip which began on schedule on February 21, 1966. The planners concluded there would be less bloodshed if he were not in the country and in a

49. *Parliamentary Debates, Official Record* (Accra: Government Printer), Feb. 1, 1966, columns 2 and 3.

position to order or rally loyalist forces. On February 23 the 600-man garrison at Tamale, 350 miles north of Accra, began to move south under cover of a continuing alert occasioned by the uncertainty arising from Rhodesia's unilateral declaration of independence. Joining with elements of Kotoka's Second Brigade, they moved on Accra from Kumasi while Harlley's police were rounding up cabinet ministers and other CPP officials. At 4:45 in the morning of February 24, the first insurgent units reached Flagstaff House whose 400-man POGR unit was commanded by Colonel David G. Zanlerigu, who had eluded capture in his home. The attackers were pinned down by an accurate barrage from POGR guards. Another rebel unit seized the nearby Ghana radio station and broadcast the fall of Nkrumah about 6:00 a.m. Osu Castle (Government House) fell without a fight.

At 9:00 o'clock Kotoka issued an ultimatum to the Flagstaff House defenders to lay down their arms by 11:30 a.m., but it was not until late afternoon that Colonel Zanlerigu surrendered. The POGR guards were taken by surprise and put up a good fight in the early hours, though their morale was undercut when they learned the identity and purpose of the attackers. Some of the men are said to have persuaded Zanlerigu to surrender.

The coup was not bloodless, but there was little loss of life. The insurgents showed deliberate restraint. Colonel Kotoka, for example, refused to use armored car guns against Flagstaff House to avoid needless casualties. The National Liberation Council (NLC) announced that the insurgents had lost seven men.

The number and identity of the casualties among the defenders of Flagstaff House is clouded by rumor and conflicting testimony. According to unofficial reports 27 men died, not including Major General Barwah, the highest ranking victim, who was shot at Burma Camp when he resisted arrest. The evidence is not conclusive, but it appears that several East Europeans were killed at Flagstaff House, but fewer than the 11 mentioned in the press.[50] It was the habit of some foreign communist advisers to remain in Flagstaff House through the night. Whatever their role on February 24 may have been or how many may have died, the fact remains that Russian security advisers were

50. See Donald H. Louchheim, "Soviets Lost Lives in Army's Ghana Coup," *Washington Post*, March 1, 1966, p. A–10; and Lloyd Garrison, "Coup in Ghana: Elaborately Organized Upheaval," *New York Times*, March 5, 1966, p. 2.

employed by Nkrumah and that after the coup the NLC chose not to comment officially on the alleged foreign casualties.

The coup was a masterpiece of timing, secrecy, and efficiency. This was due primarily to the discipline of the regular army units involved, and the excellent cooperation between the top army and police officials. The police were crucial because it was their intelligence that made possible not only the arrest of key government and CPP officials in Accra, but the apprehension of members of Parliament and other Nkrumah supporters throughout the country.

The immediate, spontaneous, and widespread support for the NLC and the quick collapse of the supposedly popular and deeply embedded CPP came as a surprise to many observers. It soon became apparent, however, that the CPP had already lost whatever genuine support it had once had and that it had never really captured popular loyalty. Magnified by the propaganda of a one-party press and inflated by Nkrumah's charisma, the CPP turned out to be an empty shell when the life blood of patronage was cut off and when the sanctions for "disloyalty" were removed.

Nkrumah never reached Hanoi. In the tradition of Chinese courtesy, the news of the coup was withheld from him by hosts in Peking until after he had been received as Ghana's head of state with a 21-gun salute. Offered political asylum by Guinea's president, Sekou Touré, Nkrumah arrived in Conakry on March 2. The following day, in the tradition of African courtesy, Touré gave his old friend the honorary title of co-president of Guinea.

The Army-Police Regime: 1966–69

In Accra the victorious soldiers and police established a ruling National Liberation Council with General Ankrah as chairman. Composed of four military men and four policemen, including all the chief planners, the NLC maintained formal parity between the two security services. By design the members, listed below, reflected the tribal, regional, and religious diversity of Ghana (army members are listed with their post-coup rank):

1. Lieutenant General J. A. Ankrah, chairman, Ga from Accra area, Methodist, 50 years old. (Resigned in a scandal in April 1969.)

2. Major General E. K. Kotoka, Ewe from the Volta Region, reared a Presbyterian, now Roman Catholic, 39 years old. (Killed in the abortive countercoup of April 17, 1967.)

3. Police Commissioner J. W. K. Harlley, deputy chairman, Ewe from the Volta Region, Presbyterian, 46 years old.

4. Colonel A. A. Afrifa, Ashanti from Manpong north of Kumasi, Presbyterian, 29 years old. (Replaced Ankrah as chairman in April 1969.)

5. Brigadier A. K. Ocran, Fanti from the Central Region, Roman Catholic, 36 years old.

6. J. E. O. Nunoo, assistant commissioner of police, Ga from Accra, Church of England, 49 years old.

7. A. K. Deku, deputy commissioner of police, Ewe from Denu, Roman Catholic, 43 years old.

8. B. A. Yakubu, deputy commissioner of police, from Gushigu in the Northern Region, Moslem, 40 years old.

The average age of the NLC was 40; Ankrah was the oldest and Afrifa the youngest. Because the air force and navy were comparatively very small and none of their officers were involved in planning the coup, it was not felt necessary to have these two branches represented. Colonel E. A. Yeboah was added to the NLC to replace Kotoka. As events unfolded, General Ankrah, Commissioner Harlley, and Colonel Afrifa emerged as the three strongest leaders.

Political Reconstruction

The NLC suspended the 1960 constitution and announced it would govern by "decrees which shall have the force of law" until a new constitution was promulgated. Nkrumah was dismissed as president and commander-in-chief, and a common criminal-wanted poster was issued for his arrest, which read in part: "Armed, May be Dangerous!" His ten ministers were arrested and subsequently deprived of their properties. The national Assembly and the CPP were dissolved. The courts and other government agencies were continued, though key political appointees were detained.

In his first major speech, Chairman Ankrah asserted that the NLC would "run the affairs of this country until true democracy" has been "fully restored."[51] The "overthrow of the old government," he added, was necessary and the only way to restore the "blessings of liberty, justice, happiness, and prosperity" to Ghana. Nkrumah, he said, had

51. Radio broadcast, Feb. 28, 1966. The text is in *The Rebirth of Ghana: The End of Tyranny* (Accra: Ministry of Information, April 1966), pp. 22–30.

"completely lost the trust and confidence of the people" by his "capricious use of power and the Draconian measures he resorted to at the expense of our national institutions." The "maladministration" of Nkrumah and his "lackeys, cronies, sycophants, and political renegades" would be replaced by leaders dedicated to a democratic "welfare state," which would be genuinely nonaligned in foreign policy and would respect the integrity of other African states. The NLC, he said, had no "ambition whatsoever to rule . . . indefinitely."

Committed to the restoration of justice and social order, the NLC confronted three chief tasks—to prevent national bankruptcy, to develop a viable interim government, and to prepare for a legitimate and constitutional successor regime. For the first year it focused major attention on the desperate economic situation. Relying heavily on Ghanaian and foreign experts, the NLC undertook austerity measures and sought and received emergency economic aid, primarily from London and Washington. The situation improved slowly, aided by devaluation and a reasonably good world cocoa price. By 1969 domestic prices had stabilized and trade was in balance, but the economy remained stagnant and Ghana still was burdened by a debt of more than $820 million.[52]

On the political front the NLC moved to destroy Nkrumah's far-flung control apparatus by punishing the beneficiaries of gross corruption and eliminating top government and party officials of the old regime. Most ministers and ranking national and regional CPP functionaries were placed in "protective custody" for an unspecified period. Between 550 and 600 persons were arrested, many of whom were released after screening. As of December 1967 some 270 remained in custody, including some POGR personnel not listed among the original arrests and many persons involved in the abortive April 17, 1967, countercoup.

Immediately after the 1966 coup some 900 persons then being held without trial under the Preventive Detention Act of 1958—a few for as long as eight years—were released. On April 5, 1966, the act was repealed.

To curb active opposition, the NLC on March 2 banned all political activity. Some former officials of the United Party were given positions of responsibility.

52. *Washington Post*, Oct. 21, 1969.

The government-owned Guinea Press (named for the Gulf of Guinea) accommodated literally overnight to the new regime. One day it was pro-Nkrumah, the next it was supporting the NLC. The *Ghanaian Times, Evening News, Weekly Spectator,* and other journals of the Guinea Press were encouraged by the NLC to be responsible critics. The *Legon Observer,* an unofficial fortnightly published at the University of Ghana, was loyal to the new regime but more critical than the popular press.

Though the press under the NLC was far more free than under Nkrumah,[53] in a number of instances the new regime cracked down. Four editors of government-owned newspapers were dismissed in 1967, for example, because they denounced as unfair to Ghana an agreement between the NLC and Abbott Laboratories, an American pharmaceutical firm. The agreement was abrogated in December 1967.[54]

On January 8, 1968, twenty-nine persons associated with the *Legon Observer* went on trial in the Accra High Court on charges stemming from criticism (in the December 8, 1967, number) of the court for delays in hearing cases. Attorney General Victor Owusu argued that the article tended to bring the High Court into contempt and thus prejudice the public against the government. On January 22 the defendants pleaded guilty and apologized. In November 1968 the University of Ghana was closed for two weeks during protests over the suspension of five students charged with writing "obscene" articles in the campus paper, *Siren.*[55]

As an earnest of their pledge to return to constitutional rule, the NLC on November 4, 1966, appointed a constitutional commission of distinguished civilians chaired by Supreme Court Chief Justice Edward Akuffo-Addo. The NLC also established a political commission to give advice on immediate questions ranging from tribal affairs to foreign policy. Both bodies included respected and well-known opponents of Nkrumah.

On January 26, 1968, the constitutional commission presented its draft constitution for a democratic successor government embracing the

53. The Ghana press in 1966 and 1967 was characterized as "transitional" by the *Freedom of Information Center Report* (May 1968), University of Missouri School of Journalism. This designation means that the Ghana press was half way between a high degree of freedom (United States and Guatemala) and a high degree of control (USSR and Ethiopia).
54. *Financial Times* (London), June 10, 1968.
55. *Africa Report* (February 1969), p. 36.

principle of the separation of powers. It called for a president with strictly limited authority; a prime minister as head of government; a unicameral parliament of 140 members to be elected by universal adult suffrage; and a strong and independent judiciary. It also provided for a cabinet, whose ministers must be approved by parliament, and which is "responsible for the general policy of the Government."[56]

The constitution stipulates that the armed forces operate "under the effective control of the Executive, without prejudice to the command structure of the Forces" and provides "that no person should have power to raise any armed force in Ghana without the authority of Parliament," a clause designed to prevent the creation of special security forces such as Nkrumah's POGR.

The Abortive Countercoup

From the outset the NLC was not seriously threatened by any civilian group or interest—tribal, regional, economic, or political. Like any other military regime, however, it constantly lived under the potential threat of a countercoup by disaffected officers, or by a falling out among its members. The CPP was banned and the other parties had ceased to function before the coup. The trade unions were weak, the press supine; the tribal chiefs had been reduced to largely ceremonial and pastoral functions by Nkrumah. There was, however, some labor unrest, including a railway strike in September 1968, but the NLC was not shaken.[57]

The University of Ghana under the NLC, as in the Nkrumah era, was the center of sharpest criticism, but it did not present a "clear and present danger" to the regime. Unlike General Mobutu in the Congo, the NLC did not turn to the academic community for special help because some of its faculty and students had been compromised and the intellectual resources in Ghana were far richer than those in the Congo. CPP and Marxist sentiment gained strength at the university after Nkrumah silenced opposition there. In the appointment of commission members, academics were considered along with lawyers, civil servants, businessmen, and other professionals.

Though feared in some quarters, no effective opposition was generated by the deposed Nkrumah from his exile in Guinea. At first,

56. See *The Proposals of the Constitutional Commission for a Constitution for Ghana* (Accra-Tema: State Publishing Corporation, January 1968).
57. *Africa Report* (February 1968), p. 38, and (November 1968), p. 33.

Nkrumah was permitted to broadcast anti-NLC appeals to his country-men. But in an effort to improve his relations with neighboring states, Touré severely restricted Nkrumah's activities and by late 1967 no longer permitted him to broadcast or speak or write for publication. All of Nkrumah's correspondence was monitored by Guinean officials.[58] He was virtually a prisoner in Elephant House, his seaside residence. In April 1968 Touré sent home 35 Ghanaians who had accompanied their leader into exile.[59]

That the NLC did not take seriously enough the only plausible source of opposition—disaffected army officers—was eloquently demonstrated on April 17, 1967, when a poorly organized, nonpolitical countercoup led by a disgruntled lieutenant came dangerously close to toppling the regime. On that day 120 troops of Squadron B of the Reconnaissance Regiment at Ho, 90 miles northeast of Accra, entered the capital unchallenged at 3:15 a.m. and attempted to overthrow the government. The coup was led by Lieutenant Samuel B. Arthur, a young Fanti, and two other lieutenants.[60] Arthur had been left in charge of the unit while its regular commander, a captain, was in Britain for advanced military instruction.

After arrival in Accra, the troops were divided into separate units to attack Flagstaff House, Osu Castle (headquarters of the NLC), and the radio station. They gained quick entry into Flagstaff House, guarded then by other elements of the Reconnaissance Regiment who were reluctant to challenge their friends. At Osu Castle the rebel unit led by Second Lieutenant Emmanuel Osei-Poku blasted off the gates but failed to capture General Ankrah. General Kotoka was less fortunate. He was wounded and captured at Flagstaff House. When he requested medical treatment, his captor, Lieutenant Moses Yeboah, reportedly asked: "Did you know me when you were promoting yourself?"[61] Kotoka was later shot to death at the airport by Yeboah and became a national hero. Before long his picture adorned yard cloth used for making homemade garments.

The rebels took the radio station and announced at 6:00 a.m. that the NLC had been replaced by Lieutenant Colonel J. Y. Assasie, Major S. M.

58. *Sunday Times* (London), Dec. 24, 1967, p. 5.
59. *New York Times*, April 28, 1968.
60. Claude E. Welch, Jr., "Ghana: The Politics of Military Withdrawal," *Current History* (February 1968), p. 97.
61. *Daily Graphic* (Accra), May 6, 1967, p. 10.

Asante, and Major R. A. Achaab, who were not involved in the rebel operations. The plotters acted as though the coup had succeeded. After killing Kotoka, Yeboah fell asleep and later went to visit a lady friend, and Osei-Poku did not press the attack at the castle. More determined, Arthur tried in vain to rally support. The fumbling of the insurgents gave the NLC time to regroup. The Accra troop commanders had been initially confused and their units slow to respond. On the second day the loyal forces prevailed, chiefly because they were less disorganized than the rebels. The three lieutenants and their men surrendered and the countercoup was over.

The abortive attempt appears to have been a punitive coup generated by the personal frustrations of a handful of junior officers who felt they were not being promoted rapidly enough. They drew up no bill of particulars against the NLC, nor did they reflect Nkrumahist sentiment, though they were reportedly influenced by rumors that NLC members were feathering their own nests.[62]

The near success of the coup revealed serious weaknesses in the command structure, readiness, and initiative of the Ghana Army. How did one hundred and twenty soldiers pass undetected and unreported in their four-hour move to Accra? Part of the answer lies in the fortuitous coincidence of the move and an army exercise to combat smuggling on the Togo border begun on April 15. But why was the capital garrison in such a low state of readiness? Why the confusion in the loyal forces? The basic answer lies in the failure of the NLC to anticipate a challenge from within the army and to take appropriate precautionary steps.

The untoward events of April 17 reflected very unfavorably upon the NLC. It felt compelled to take strong disciplinary measures, unprecedented in Ghana for harshness. After a hurried investigation and military trial the two principal conspirators, Arthur and Yeboah, were publicly executed by firing squad on May 9, 1967, at Teshie.[63] Osei-Poku received a thirty-year sentence. Although the two service chiefs were held formally responsible for the failure of the loyal forces to respond quickly to the April 17 challenge, it was the unit commanders who displayed lack of initiative. The Ho Reconnaissance Squadron was disbanded; a hundred enlisted men were placed under protective custody and later released. Nine of the squadron's noncommissioned officers were sentenced to prison terms of seven to forty years.

62. *Ibid.*, May 2, 1967, p. 3.
63. Welch, "Ghana: The Politics of Military Withdrawal," p. 98.

The speed and harshness of the punishment, particularly the two executions, were criticized in some quarters, but were amply justified by the seriousness of the crime and the fact that military men were pronouncing judgment on military men guilty of high treason. This swift justice was not lost on future would-be plotters. The NLC took immediate steps to improve intelligence and tighten command and control procedures in the armed forces.

Role and Status of the Armed Forces

Under the three and one-half year rule of the NLC the armed forces were given no special benefits, privileges, or status. On the contrary, they were restored to their classical role as the coercive instruments of constituted authority. The irregularities of political interference in the command structure and the creation of counterpoise security agencies were eliminated. With the full range of traditional security functions restored, the morale and efficiency of the officers and men rose. The army gained a new position of public esteem because it had helped "liberate" the country from Nkrumah.

Committed to civilian and constitutional rule and regarding itself as an interim regime, the NLC deliberately did not create a military government, that is, one in which most key posts are held by military men. The overwhelming majority of posts below the NLC level were filled by civilians. Paradoxically, in significant respects the NLC operated more like a traditional civilian government than did the civilian Nkrumah regime in its latter years.

The strength of the armed forces since 1966 has remained relatively constant and there has been little recruitment of new officers. In 1968 the army had about 15,000 men, and the air force and navy about 1,000 each. The austerity-minded NLC approved $42 million for defense, about 10 percent of the state budget. In contrast to Nkrumah's arbitrary interference in developing the military budget, the NLC followed regular procedures.

Officer training has gradually improved and an increasing number of officers have been trained abroad. Since the coup 41 Ghanaian officers have been trained in the United States. Britain and other Commonwealth countries have continued to provide training facilities. In the fall of 1968 an annual two-week training exchange program between Ghanaian and British infantry units was initiated. Britain and Canada continue to supply most of Ghana's military hardware, though U.S. military aid includes some equipment as well as training.

Missions of the army and the police given by Nkrumah to the POGR and other presidential units were automatically restored when these irregular agencies were eliminated by the NLC. With the sudden demise of the POGR, the traditional military ceremonies in Accra were returned to the army, a significant function in a developing state where the security functions are necessarily limited. The Reconnaissance Regiment has provided the ceremonial and guard duties at Flagstaff House. Policemen have shared with soldiers guard duty at Osu Castle, headquarters of the NLC, symbolizing the fusion of police and military power. On September 3, 1968, an NLC commission recommended that the Workers Brigade be restored to its original purpose of providing constructive work for the unemployed and be "divested of all its military pretensions."[64]

Frontier security has also been returned to the army, navy, and police. Under Nkrumah this task was given to special border guards who were not accountable to the armed services or police. Coastal areas, for example, were patrolled by four Russian boats stationed at Tema.

There is no evidence that either the officer corps or the armed forces acting as a pressure group had any extraordinary influence on the political, economic, or legal decisions of the NLC, or that the military establishment as such became involved in politics. Military influence on nonmilitary matters was exercised by the army members of the NLC who, like their colleagues from the police service, regarded themselves as temporary custodians of the state.

Foreign Policy

Under the NLC the mood and substance of Ghana's policy toward its immediate neighbors, Africa as a whole, and the larger world underwent a sudden and profound change. The tone was set by General Ankrah: "Ghana's primary responsibility is to tackle her internal problems with vigor and realism" and we "pledge to abstain absolutely from interfering in the internal affairs of other States."[65]

The NLC moved quickly to improve relations with neighboring Togo, Upper Volta, and the Ivory Coast and concluded agreements with them

64. *Africa Report* (November 1968), p. 33.
65. *The Rebirth of Ghana*, p. 28.

that opened the borders and restored trade. Volta Dam power was sold to Dahomey and Togo.

On the broader African scene the early reluctance of the more militant states to recognize the NLC was dissipated and relations with all of them except Guinea improved with time. The moderate African states quickly granted recognition and were relieved that Nkrumah's strident pan-African rhetoric and lopsided "neutralism," which relied heavily on the support of the Soviet Union, had come to an end. They welcomed the level-headed stance of the NLC which unequivocally renounced the use of force between tropical African states. The regime's dedication to peaceful solutions was demonstrated by its efforts to help mediate the Nigerian civil war.

Though the NLC joined in the general OAU declaration to "liberate" Africans under "white rule," it provided no material support for this cause. In view of its immediate destruction of Nkrumah's communist-led "freedom fighter" camps and public and private statements of NLC members, it was highly unlikely that the regime would support military measures against Rhodesia or any other area. Of Rhodesia, Afrifa said, "It would be criminal and purposeless to lead . . . an army of excellent soldiers ill-equipped to fight an unnecessary war"; if all that the "four million Africans" there could do "at the time of the unilateral declaration of independence" was to "throw a few petrol bombs," why should Ghana become involved?[66]

In its relations with the larger world, the NLC returned to a more genuinely neutral position and restored Ghana's historic Western ties. London and Washington recognized the new regime one week after the coup. In his February 28 address, Ankrah said, "The people of Ghana set considerable store by their membership in the Commonwealth."

Over 1,000 Russians, East Europeans, and Chinese were promptly expelled after the coup. They included 665 Soviet and 52 Chinese technicians, security advisers, and "freedom fighter" instructors.[67] The technicians included men in fishing and construction. The reaction against communist penetration was harsh but stopped short of a diplomatic break with the Soviet bloc. It did result in suspending relations with Cuba on September 27, 1966, and with China on October 20, after

66. Afrifa, The Ghana Coup, p. 104.
67. W. Scott Thompson, "New Directions in Ghana," Africa Report (November 1966), p. 19.

neither had granted recognition. Suspicion of the communist states persisted and relations remained cool. Nevertheless, long-term trade agreements were signed with Poland and Bulgaria in November 1966 and with Czechoslovakia in March 1967. Trade was continued with Russia, though at a lower level than in the latter Nkrumah years.

In spite of slowly improving relations with the Soviet Union, a deep-seated suspicion of Russian motives and behavior persisted in the NLC. These suspicions came to the surface in a strange incident in October 1968 when Ghana seized two Soviet fishing trawlers in its coastal waters because the crews were suspected of smuggling arms in a plot to restore Nkrumah to power. The crewmen were interrogated and detained for over four months. Such a crude subversive intrusion by the Russians into Ghana only two years after 665 of their technicians and advisers had been unceremoniously expelled seems implausible, especially in view of Moscow's general normalization of relations with moderate African regimes since the mid-sixties. Yet the possibility of a subversive move on the part of the KGB, designed perhaps to propitiate old friends in Ghana, cannot be dismissed out of hand, according to one observer.[68] The theory that the KGB and the Soviet Ministry of Trade may have been working at cross-purposes is given some substance because at this very time Ghana's air marshal, M. A. Otu, was being detained for his part in an alleged plot to restore Nkrumah. "The connection between the Otu case and the trawler incident is only speculative," but "the stern handling of the straying trawlers served as a clear warning to the Soviet Union that Ghana was in no mood to tolerate Soviet probes."[69] There have been no further untoward incidents involving the Russians.

The NLC's relations with the Western powers have been much easier, but not without occasional tensions. The new leaders' request to Britain and the United States for emergency aid to ease their desperate economic plight was promptly and positively answered. For largely historical reasons Britain soon reestablished a preeminent position in Ghana, even though its material assistance was necessarily small. Washington was quite prepared to play a secondary and supportive role. Along with other creditor governments, London agreed to a moratorium on interest

68. W. Scott Thompson, "Ghana's Foreign Policy Under Military Rule," *Africa Report* (May–June 1969), pp. 10–11.
69. *Ibid.*, p. 11.

payments. But because of her own economic problems, Britain was unable to provide $24,000 worth of desperately needed military uniforms and boots requested by the NLC.

Immediately after the coup the United States extended debt rescheduling assistance, encouraged private American investment, and resumed or substantially increased various economic aid programs to Ghana. During the NLC period Washington transmitted about $75 million in aid, $13.2 million in grants and $61.8 million in loans. The major American private enterprise in Ghana is the Valco aluminum smelter at Tema which has made the Volta River Dam economically feasible. As of 1968 the smelter was producing 104,000 tons of high-grade metal a year.

United States security assistance to Ghana has been small, a total of approximately $100,000 from 1962 through 1968,[70] including three Nkrumah years when no aid was given. Since 1966, 41 military officers and 25 police officers have been trained in the United States. Even this modest program of economic and security assistance places Ghana among the eight U.S. priority states in tropical Africa that together receive two-thirds of aid to the area.

The openly pro-American posture of the NLC, particularly the outspoken support of General Ankrah for U.S. policy in Vietnam, plus the increased visibility of the American presence in the early post-coup days, disturbed the professionals in the Foreign Ministry and provided the backdrop for several outbursts of anti-Americanism among the more militant and socialist-minded intellectuals. The most celebrated case was the Abbott affair occasioned by the NLC's effort to secure responsible foreign investors and managers to salvage and operate the better of the uneconomic state enterprises begun under Nkrumah. Abbott Laboratories of Chicago in June 1967 signed an agreement to rehabilitate a Hungarian-built pharmaceutical plant. Abbott was to hold only 45 percent of the new firm's shares, but the deal generated hostile and emotional criticism in sectors of the press. The *Ashanti Pioneer* and the *Legon Observer* bitterly attacked Abbott, but their real target was the military-police regime. As a result, four editors were fired and in December Abbott canceled its contract. After this incident, which prompted some new but moderate restraints on foreign investment, NLC-American relations returned to normal.

70. The basis for this assistance is found in an agreement between Ghana and the United States which entered into force on Feb. 12, 1958. See Appendix B.

Orderly Transition to the Busia Regime

By any reasonable standards the NLC made a solid contribution to a viable, just, and democratic state. Its performance is all the more remarkable when compared with the corruption, mismanagement, and demagoguery of the Nkrumah era. In the economic sphere, the NLC curtailed widespread corruption, improved the balance of payments, increased foreign aid and private investment, and generally put the economy on a sound footing. Under the Council, Ghana remained secure at home and regained its respect abroad. In spite of the abortive coup and occasional incidents of wrongdoing, the performance and morale of the armed forces and the police improved measurably.

A temporary and unconstitutional regime forced to suspend political competition, the NLC ironically showed more respect for the rule of law, permitted greater latitude of speech and press, and encouraged far freer development of voluntary associations than its predecessor. The courts and the civil administration had greater freedom than during the last five Nkrumah years. The NLC also restored a balance among the various interests and groups that had been destroyed or neutralized by Nkrumah's one-man, one-party system.

But the NLC's most noteworthy contribution was its achievement of a peaceful and orderly transition to a constitutional and democratic civilian regime. From the very outset the coup leaders made careful and extensive preparations for a return to competitive politics. Their repeated promises to do this were fully redeemed.

On August 29, 1969, Ghana, the first tropical African country to gain independence, became the first one to accomplish a peaceful transition from a military to a civilian government. On that day the Progress Party headed by Kofi A. Busia won 105 of the 140 seats in the national Assembly under the terms of a new constitution promulgated a week before. The next largest party, the National Alliance of Liberals, gained 29 seats. One disquieting aspect of the election was a partial reversion to voting along tribal lines, a problem that must be kept in bounds if the destructive character of tribal politics in Nigeria, Kenya, and elsewhere is to be avoided.

The new 161-page constitution, embracing all the major elements in the 1968 draft, has drawn upon the American separation of powers and the British parliamentary system and has incorporated ideas from Indian and Scandinavian models. It restricts "preventive detention" to extreme emergencies and provides for a strong independent judiciary and for a prime minister elected by a majority of the Assembly. At the last minute, under NLC pressure, the constitution was altered to have the presidential office filled by the NLC's three ranking leaders, pending the election of a president in 1972. A House of Chieftains, largely a ceremonial institution, was created to symbolize modern Ghana's ties with traditional authority. As in the original draft, the armed services and the police are restricted to their classic role as instruments of civilian authority.

In appearance, manner, style, and political orientation, Prime Minister Busia stands in sharp contrast to the Nkrumah he long opposed. The fifty-six-year-old scholar is quiet and gentle, the author of several books on African culture and sociology. He studied philosophy and economics at London University and at Oxford. A pragmatic democrat, his goal for Ghana is a multiparty "democratic welfare society," one in which "everyone is his brother's keeper." This biblical language comes easily to the prime minister who is an active Methodist layman.

Busia has said he will concentrate on building the economy at home and being a good neighbor abroad. "We are very pragmatic" in African affairs, he has said, and "our first consideration is our own country. We leave the theorizing to those who have the time and inclination to do so."[71] At his first press conference on November 8 he indicated his desire to have some interchange with the Republic of South Africa, a view he subsequently reconfirmed. This suggests that Busia is determined to pursue a pragmatic foreign policy, formally neutral but inclined toward the West. Three weeks after his installation as prime minister on October 1, Busia visited President Nixon in Washington and requested further aid in arranging a stretch-out of Ghana's remaining debt of more than $820 million, virtually none of which is owed the United States. Acknowledging the strong American interest in cutting its foreign assistance, Dr. Busia said, "we are prepared to see that aid is properly used" for its intended purpose.[72]

71. *New York Times*, Oct. 17, 1969.
72. *Washington Post*, Oct. 21, 1969.

The Ghana Police Service

Like the armed forces, the Ghana Police Service has deep roots in the British Gold Coast. The development of the two instruments of coercion is similar in important respects because they shared the same cultural, domestic, and foreign influences and political authority. The differences between the two are inherent in their respective functions.

Before Independence

Until 1901 the Gold Coast constabulary embraced both police and military functions. That year the British assigned military duties to the Gold Coast Regiment and police duties to a reorganized constabulary. Parallel with and antedating the constabulary were the local Native Authority Forces which the British used to uphold their system of indirect rule in West Africa. To facilitate control and legitimize authority, the British worked through traditional chiefs to whom they gave authority in certain spheres, including the maintenance of local law and order. The Native Forces were limited largely to enforcing traditional laws and the directives of the local chiefs whose authority was circumscribed by the colonial administration.

The Native Authority Police were permitted to wear a uniform, but not to bear arms. The Gold Coast police were armed and served the townships (native quarters on the outskirts of urban areas) rather than villages where their presence would undermine the authority of the Native Police. Within the townships the regular police were used as escorts and guards as well as for normal police duties.[73] The parallel existence of the Native Forces and the constabulary has continued into independence, but since the early 1950s the functions of the Native Forces have been increasingly restricted to the more remote areas of the country.

During a three-year modernization campaign initiated in 1950 to enlarge, centralize, and Africanize the police, the service was expanded from 4,000 to 5,000 men. Communications, transportation, and mobility were improved and new police posts were built. In an effort to phase out eventually the Native Police, their functions were more clearly de-

73. Lugard, *The Dual Mandate in Tropical Africa*, pp. 205–06.

fined and they were renamed the Escort Police. In contrast to the regular police, the Escort Police had no literacy requirement so members of the Native Forces were able to retain their positions. In the regular police Africans were given all noncommissioned positions and began to replace British officers in the higher ranks.

In preparation for independence a number of police officers were trained in Britain and were promoted to assistant superintendent on their return. The average age of newly commissioned African police officers in the 1950s was about 35 years compared to 25 years for second lieutenants in the army. The police were generally promoted from the ranks rather than from a selected category of officer cadets. By independence day most of the higher posts had been Africanized, and the police service gave every indication that it would serve Ghana as effectively as it had the Gold Coast.

Though centrally administered, the police were essentially a local organization. Unlike a soldier, a constable was generally recruited from the area he served. Living in towns and villages, the police were in closer touch with the population than the soldiers who lived in barracks. The police were not controlled from London by the Colonial Office or the War Office, but by the colonial governor who was more aware of local problems. In contrast to the army, advancement to commissioner status in the constabulary became available as early as World War I.

While the army was neutral and uninvolved during the movement for independence, the police acquired a mild taint by their association with occasional acts of discipline by colonial authorities. During the Accra riots of 1948, for example, a British police superintendent fired on a group of discontented army veterans, supported by the pro-self-government United Gold Coast Convention, when they attempted to march to Christianborg Castle to deliver a petition to the governor.[74] Such incidents tended to reflect on the police, but there is no evidence that African policemen ever fired on African demonstrators agitating for independence.

The Nkrumah Years: 1957–66

In structure, function, and doctrine, the Ghana Police Service was patterned after the British police system. This was also true of the

---

74. Austin, *Politics in Ghana*, p. 74.

criminal code until it was distorted by Nkrumah's various emergency measures. Ghanaians are a generally peaceful and law-abiding people who respect authority and recognize the necessity of police. Indoctrinated in the British approach, the police have been firm but not harsh and have resorted to force only as a last resort.

In addition to the traditional functions of preventing and detecting crime, apprehending offenders, upholding law and order, and protecting persons and property, the Ghana police were given the responsibility for licensing vehicles and drivers, registering firearms, and enforcing immigration and customs laws. The largely illiterate Escort Police, dressed in distinctive khaki uniforms with red fezzes, usually performed sedentary guard functions, routine patrol, prisoner escort, crowd control, riot duty, and ceremonial functions. Though they did not routinely carry arms, they were issued staves or light firearms for emergency duties.

The police service was organized into nine regional commands and a half dozen special branches, the largest and most important branch being the Criminal Investigation Department (CID) administered by an assistant commissioner. In 1961 the CID had an authorized strength of 585 men. A special branch directly under the national headquarters dealt with subversive activities.

During the Nkrumah era the police service grew from 6,000 to about 12,000 men, including approximately equal numbers of regular and Escort Police. For budgetary, training, and other reasons, plans for significantly reducing the proportion of Escort Police did not materialize. As in the army, the regular police were recruited primarily in the more literate south, the Escort Police from the more backward north.

The British training program for new recruits and for serving officers was continued, though it languished in the latter Nkrumah period. Regular recruits were trained in the Police Training School in Accra, and Escort Police were trained at Elmina Castle. In 1959 the Ghana Police College was opened with a six-month course (including law, criminal investigation, administration, map reading, etc.) for training commissioned officers, a function formerly entrusted to Britain. The Africanization of the officer ranks proceeded apace. In late 1958 the first Ghanaian was appointed to command the service. By 1960 about 90 percent of the commissioned officers were Ghanaian, and shortly thereafter the British officers were reduced to a handful of technicians and advisers.

The police service, like the armed forces, both benefited and suffered from the Nkrumah regime. In the early years Nkrumah strongly supported professional training and other efforts to modernize the force, but as his rule grew increasingly arbitrary and repressive the police service was compromised and the quality of its performance fell. In 1960 police morale was temporarily boosted when a mobile emergency detachment of Escort Police sent to the Congo to maintain order in Leopoldville performed well.

Required to enforce the Preventive Detention Act and other such emergency measures, the police necessarily became identified with the increasingly unpopular regime. Some police officers became involved with the bribery and kickbacks that were a hallmark of Nkrumah's patronage system, but many officers tried to maintain their professional standards under extenuating circumstances.

Again, as in the army, police morale received a blow when some of their assigned functions, including immigration control and border patrol, were arbitrarily given to Nkrumah's special security agencies. Both the military and police suffered from status deprivation.

A dramatic incident on January 2, 1964, both illustrated and deepened the growing tension between Nkrumah and the police service. On that day a constable on duty at Flagstaff House fired five shots from close range at Nkrumah for reasons that are still obscure. The bullets went wild but killed Assistant Police Superintendent Salifu Dagarti. Within a week Nkrumah purged the top ranks of the service. Police Commissioner E. R. T. Madjitey was fired, along with his assistant and eight regional police commanders. The assistant commissioner, a police superintendent, and six other senior police officials were placed under detention. Nkrumah totally disarmed all police and withdrew from the vicinity of Flagstaff House the police who had served there under the supervision of communist "advisers" since the fall of 1962. He then named J. W. K. Harlley, head of the Criminal Investigation Department, commissioner of the police service which had been cut back to 9,000 men. Concurrently, he placed his personal security wholly in the hands of the POGR.

These drastic disciplinary measures, plus the cutback in strength, appropriations, and missions; Nkrumah's increasing use of informers within the service; and the competitive secret police and internal security agencies under direct presidential control led to the demoralization that induced Commissioner Harlley to join with the army officers in the 1966 coup.

Army-Police Regime: 1966–69

As coauthor of the February 24 coup and the ranking police officer in the ruling National Liberation Council, Commissioner Harlley represented the interests of the police in the coalition regime and soon became one of the NLC's three most influential leaders.

Under the NLC the police, like the military, were given no special benefits or favors, but were restored to their traditional status and functions. Though the police service has not fully recovered from the trauma of the Nkrumah regime, its strength has been increased to 15,000, training has improved, and to a considerable measure morale has been restored. The strength of the service in 1970 was 18,600 men.

The Ghana Police Service in late 1968 was organized into 10 regions that were subdivided into 61 districts, 215 stations, and 209 posts. The regular and Escort Police continued to be the two chief branches, the latter for the first time employing a minimal literacy test. The specialized branches attached to the Accra headquarters approximated those of the early Nkrumah years. The nonuniformed CID had a strength of 875 men. The special branch that deals with subversive activities, though under one of the two police commissioners, operated largely autonomously. Riot control capability was strengthened by the creation of a reserve force of emergency units whose noncommissioned officers and ranks are drawn from the Escort Police and officers from the general police. The police resumed the mission of frontier control with a border guard of 3,350 men manning 102 posts in addition to the airports at Accra and Kumasi and the ocean ports at Tema and Takoradi.

Training facilities were strengthened to accommodate the heavier flow of new recruits and cadets. Regular recruits were trained at the Accra Police School by a faculty of 21 officers. The standard 24-week course was broad and included instruction in English and riot control. A few Escort Police attended the school, but most were trained in regional depots. The regular six-month officer course at the police college was augmented by shorter and more specialized courses. In 1967 two

U.S. police specialists taught a course in riot control for Ghana police instructors under the public safety program of the Agency for International Development.

The majority of Ghanaian police officers who take advanced training abroad attend the British Police Academy at Hendon, but since the coup 25 have had U.S. training, most of them at the International Police Academy in Washington.

Under the NLC the police were loyal, did not intrude in the political arena, and enhanced their professional competence. Evidence suggests that they will continue in the same direction under the regime of Prime Minister Busia.

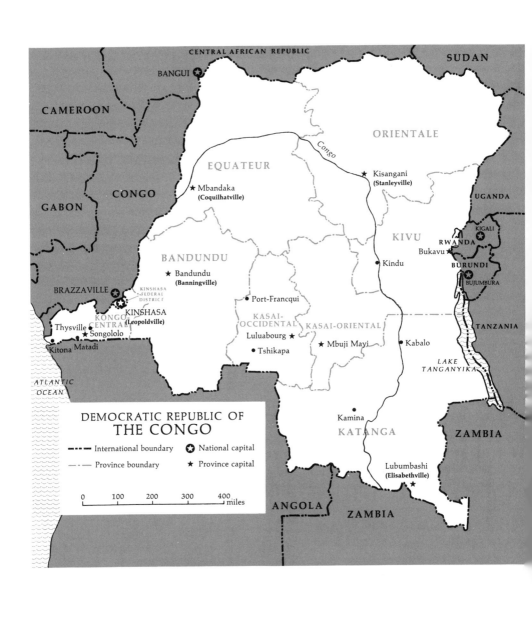

CENTRAL AFRICAN REPUBLIC

SUDAN

BANGUI ✪

CAMEROON

ORIENTALE

CONGO

EQUATEUR

★ Mbandaka
(Coquilhatville)

★ Kisangani
(Stanleyville)

UGANDA

GABON

BANDUNDU

★ Bandundu
(Banningville)

KIVU

KIGALI ✪

RWANDA

Bukavu ★

BURUNDI

BUJUMBURA

Kindu ●

BRAZZAVILLE ✪

KINSHASA
FEDERAL
DISTRICT

KINSHASA
(Leopoldville)

KONGO
CENTRAL

● Port-Francqui

TANZANIA

Thysville ●

● Songololo

KASAI-
OCCIDENTAL

KASAI-ORIENTAL

Kitona

Matadi

Luluabourg ★

● Mbuji Mayi

● Kabalo

● Tshikapa

LAKE
TANGANYIKA

ATLANTIC
OCEAN

DEMOCRATIC REPUBLIC OF
THE CONGO

●—●—● International boundary   ✪ National capital

—●— Province boundary   ★ Province capital

● Kamina

KATANGA

ZAMBIA

0   100   200   300   400
└────┴────┴────┴────┘ miles

Lubumbashi
(Elisabethville)
★

ANGOLA

ZAMBIA

Congo

CHAPTER THREE

The Congo

Though there is political discontinuity in the Congo,
there must be military continuity.
JOSEPH MOBUTU[1]

PRESIDENT Joseph-Désiré Mobutu, more than any other man, has symbolized the meager cohesion the Congo has managed to retain during its first ten chaotic years as an independent state. During all the crises that convulsed the Congo, Mobutu was intimately involved in the key political and military decisions of the central government. In two fateful emergencies he rescued his country from almost certain disaster.

Mobutu is young, intelligent, politically astute, and proud. An African nationalist, he is pragmatic and patriotic and professes an equal distaste for communism and "big business." His two chief heroes are said to be John F. Kennedy and Kemal Ataturk.

Thirty years old when the Congo became independent on June 30, 1960, Mobutu had a deep interest in politics and the army. In 1956 he had ended his seven years in the Force Publique as a sergeant-major in the Leopoldville headquarters. Just before independence he studied journalism in Brussels for a year. Though active in Patrice Lumumba's Mouvement Nationale Congolais, he did not stand in the May 1960 elections, but was appointed Lumumba's secretary of state. After the July mutiny he was given the rank of colonel and made chief of staff of the National Congolese Army (ANC).

He first pulled the Congo back from the precipice on September 14, 1960, by "neutralizing" the bitter conflict between Prime Minister Patrice Lumumba and President Joseph Kasavubu and installing for five months a council of commissioners. His second and more substantial

1. Interview with the author, Leopoldville, September 1962.

intervention, also a bloodless coup, came five years later, on November 25, 1965, when he assumed executive control of the government to end the political stalemate dramatized by President Kasavubu's dismissal of Prime Minister Moise Tshombe. As of mid-1970, Mobutu, as president, was still governing the Democratic Republic of the Congo by decree. As a soldier and statesman, Mobutu has symbolized continuity in the Congo and personified the inescapable dependence of political authority on military power.

For its first ten years the Congo has been the stage for a tragic drama of violence, intrigue, conspiracy, and external interference. Plots and counterplots, rebellions, secessionist efforts, and coups have been played out against a backdrop of tribal conflict, political incompetence, widespread corruption, and atavistic superstitions. Elements of the population have frequently been killed and terrorized by tribal groups, communist-supported rebels, spear-wielding fanatics, or rampaging bands of Congolese soldiers. White mercenaries have fought for the central government and against it. Belgian paratroopers carried out two rescue missions, one invited by the government and the other uninvited. For sheer chaos, confusion, and complexity, the Congo is difficult to match, but the volume of violence and bloodshed there does not begin to equal that of the civil war in Nigeria which lasted almost three years.

Two central realities have dominated the tortured Congo—for the first seven or eight years the central government was not able to exercise effective authority throughout the vast territory and did not have at its disposal a unified and dependable army. It was legally sovereign but not politically sovereign. The scepter was not consistently upheld by a reliable spear. The central government even in early 1970 did not enjoy a firm monopoly on the use of violence within its domain, the fundamental prerequisite for exercising sovereign authority.

The abrupt and premature abdication of Belgian authority in the Congo is not sufficient explanation for the chaos. The breakdown was precipitated largely by internal forces, and principally the behavior of one man, Prime Minister Patrice Lumumba, whose instability and recklessness have cast a long shadow across tropical Africa. Key Belgian and Congolese leaders knew that the Congo was not prepared politically, educationally, or psychologically for assuming the full burdens of self-government.

The transfer of sovereignty made sense only on the widely held assumption that the great majority of the 100,000 Belgians in the Congo —of whom some 10,000 were administrators, technicians, police inspectors, and army officers—would continue to serve indefinitely until trained Congolese could replace them. Thus it was not implausible to anticipate an orderly transition similar to that then taking place in the French areas of Africa.

The fragmentation of the Congo was not inevitable, but it became so primarily because of the political ambivalence of Lumumba, his erratic overreaction to the original barracks disturbance, and his susceptibility to communist manipulation. Lumumba was a complex and charismatic man. Embracing the aspirations of the other Congolese leaders, he had serious character defects that made it impossible for him to work effectively with them. The fact that he was one of the most detribalized and Westernized Congolese may have made him all the more vulnerable to external communist influence. In the few short weeks that he led the Congo he became both the chief cause and symptom of the new state's dilemma. Now, ten years later, President Mobutu still finds it useful to invoke the memory and myth of Lumumba, the great nationalist, the man and politician Mobutu did so much to undermine.

People, Land, and Economy

Strategically located in the heart of Africa, the Democratic Republic of the Congo is almost 80 times larger than Belgium, or equal in area to the United States east of the Mississippi. Its 904,747 square miles stretch from the South Atlantic in the west to Lake Tanganyika in the east. It shares borders with eight states—Congo (Brazzaville), Central African Republic, Sudan, Uganda, Rwanda, Burundi, Tanzania, and Zambia—and Portuguese Angola.

The Congo's 17.5 million indigenous people are divided into about 200 different tribal and language groups. The Bantu, the Sudanese, and the Pygmies are the three major ethnic divisions. The chief indigenous languages are Lingala, Swahili, Kikongo, and Tshiluba, but French is the official language and the only common tongue. From 15 to 20 percent of the adult Africans are literate, and 11.5 percent of the population is in primary and secondary schools, compared to about 13.3 percent in Ghana and 1.4 percent in Ethiopia. There are about 3,500 students in the three universities located at Kinshasa, Lubumbashi, and Kisangani, about 2,000 in teacher training and other post-secondary institutions, and 1,200 to 1,500 students abroad, including 700 in Belgium. The fluctuating European population numbers from 35,000 to 50,000, largely Belgians employed in industry, education, and government.

Rich in natural resources, the Congo is the world's largest producer of cobalt and industrial diamonds. It also exports large amounts of copper, zinc, tin, manganese, and other metals as well as timber, coffee, cocoa, tea, rubber, palm products, and sugar. The Congo has continually had a trade surplus. With a gross national product of $1.5 billion, it has a per capita income of $86 compared to $214 for Ghana and $64 for Ethiopia.

The Congo government's expenditures for 1969 were $370 million, including $54 million for the armed forces and $19.8 million for the police. The army, whose integrity was destroyed when the Belgian officer corps was dismissed by Lumumba in 1960, has been reconstituted largely with Belgian and U.S. assistance and now numbers about 37,000 men or about one soldier for 470 inhabitants. The air force has 600 men, including 150 foreign advisers and technicians. There is an embryonic navy of about 100 men. The National Police Service has 20,800 men.

The Congo's strategic geopolitical position and its vast economic potential have invited the interest of the United States, the Soviet Union, and other powers. From 1960 through 1968 U.S. aid to the Congo, given directly or through UN agencies, totaled about $592 million, of which $198.5 million was military assistance.

The Belgian Force Publique

The present National Congolese Army is the direct successor of the Force Publique established in 1888 when the Congo was still the royal domain of King Leopold II of Belgium. The character and mission of the Force changed little after the sovereignty of the Congo was transferred to the Belgian government in 1908. The Force performed the dual functions of an army and police establishment, maintaining internal order and defending the borders of the state, until after World War II. Throughout its history it numbered 15,000 to 24,000 men and all its officers were Belgian.

In contrast to British and French policy in Africa, the Belgians sent no metropolitan troops to conquer the Congo. The vast expanse was "conquered" by African soldiers commanded by a small number of Belgian officers. During the difficult Arab wars of 1892–94, there were only 120 Europeans with the Force, then numbering about 15,000. By 1905 there were 26 active companies commanded by 360 Europeans and dispersed throughout the country, each serving a district commissioner.

During World War I the Force was strengthened by manpower, equipment, and weapons from the Belgian Army. Detachments of the Force served with the French troops that invaded the Cameroons, with Rhodesian forces in Tanganyika, and with the British West African Frontier Force elsewhere.

After World War I the Force was reorganized into garrison troops and territorial service troops. Stationed at key points, the garrison troops were organized into infantry and artillery battalions supported by reconnaissance, signal, engineer, transport, and commando units and by antiaircraft weapons and transport planes. Each of the six provinces had a territorial service company in each district. These companies were a part of a battalion in the provincial capital whose commander was also the governor's military adviser. World War II had little impact on the Force.

The character and function of the Force changed very little between 1945 and 1959, though the role of the territorial troops was restricted somewhat by the establishment of independent police services after World War II. During this period the Force was responsible for the defense of the small, adjoining Belgian trust territory of Ruanda-Urundi.

In 1959 the Force was divided into gendarmerie and regular army units organized into three regional detachments, each under the command of a colonel. Elisabethville (now Lubumbashi) was the headquarters of the first detachment covering the provinces of Katanga and Kasai. The second was in Leopoldville (now Kinshasa) and was responsible for that province and Equateur. The third detachment, headquartered in Stanleyville (now Kisangani), served Orientale and Kivu. All command positions were held by Belgians. As of May 1960, there were 1,135 Belgian officers, including 21 chaplains and 6 doctors. The 24,000 soldiers and noncommissioned officers were Congolese. Lingala was the command language of the Force.

After World War II, Brussels moved a portion of its armed forces to the Congo where they could be called upon if Europe were ever again threatened by conquest. About 3,000 men were sent to three permanent bases: a small naval installation at Banana on the Atlantic, a land and air base at nearby Kitona, and a large land and air base at Kamina in Katanga. These troops were under direct control of the minister of defense in Brussels, though in a crisis the governor general of the Congo could request them to assist the Force Publique. The Banana base enabled Belgium to control the mouth of the Congo River. Kitona served as the headquarters for both naval and air defense in the eastern Congo. By 1960, the Kamina base had an excellent landing field, a battalion of paracommandos, and two aviation schools. The base buildings covered more than 60 acres. By that date the widely dispersed units of the Force were served by a reliable and extensive communications network.

The Belgians, as a result of three tribal mutinies between 1895 and 1900, followed a policy of integrating tribally all units of the Force down to the squad level. This ethnic scrambling secured unity and loyalty in the army until 1944 when there was a mutiny at the Luluabourg garrison. The eruption was blamed on a nonchalant application of integration policy and led to a reaffirmation of the practice of having at least four tribes represented in each platoon. By 1960 the Force embraced a more balanced cross section of the population than any other Congolese institution. "The Congo army was more a national body than other tropical African military forces."[2]

Performance, Morale, and Discipline

Measured against other African troops, the performance and discipline of the Force Publique after World War I ranged from good to excellent. By 1960 it was widely regarded as the best trained and disciplined fighting force in central Africa. It had "fought with distinction in both world wars" and deserved its "reputation for toughness, efficiency, and some brutality."[3]

As the coercive instrument of Belgian policy in the Congo, the Force since 1908 was characterized by obedience, discipline, and high morale. The Congolese soldier accepted stern discipline and carefully regulated life because the army had replaced tribal ways with a new system of

2. Crawford Young, *Politics in the Congo: Decolonization and Independence* (Princeton University Press, 1965), p. 443. Also see pp. 182, 282–84, and 441–42.

3. Catherine Hoskyns, *The Congo Since Independence: January 1960–December 1961* (London: Oxford University Press, 1965), p. 59.

authority and identity. A proud member of an elite "tribe," his primary loyalty was to the Force, not to the Congolese people or to Belgium, though Belgian symbols, such as King Leopold II, were used to inspire loyalty in the ranks.

The Congolese soldier would fire upon other Congolese if ordered to do so and if they were not of his own tribe. Troops employed in operations against dissident groups were drawn from other parts of the country to eliminate the element of fratricide. The Force was feared and respected by the civilian population and in most cases its presence was sufficient to deter disorder.

The Force Publique operated under an adapted form of the Belgian civilian penal code which was applicable to both Congolese and Belgians. Offenses committed by military personnel were always tried in a military court. There was a higher court for the rank of major and above; a lower court handled the cases of Belgian captains and noncommissioned officers as well as all Congolese. Punishment ranged from small fines to imprisonment and death, but there was an appeal system. The most common offenses were absence without leave, desertion, thievery, fighting, mayhem, and murder. Summary punishment by unit commanders was usually administered on the spot for minor infractions such as drunkenness and failure to clean one's rifle. Punishment by flogging, administered only by Congolese upon Congolese privates, was ended about 1949.

Recruiting, Training, and Benefits

Though recruiting practices varied during the colonial period, the elements of coercion and voluntary enlistment were always present. As elsewhere in tropical Africa, the Force drew most of its troops from the more remote areas. The usual period of service was seven years. Annual quotas were established by decree and allocated to the provinces and districts. Before 1950 draftees were selected from a roster, including an undetermined number of volunteers, compiled by the tribal chief and the local Belgian administrator. After 1950 recruits were chosen from direct volunteers and draft lists. By 1959 the entire annual quota was filled by reenlistments and volunteers.

The military training program was slow, thorough, and methodical, and advancement was determined by frequent tests. After a year of basic training, men with special aptitudes were sent to the Central School at Luluabourg for an additional year, after which some were selected to become sergeants, sergeants major, and first sergeants major. The others were sent to schools or workshops for further specialization. Though attractive incentives were offered for seven-year reenlistments, many men returned to civilian life where their skills in construction, maintenance, etc., were in great demand.

Enlisted men of all ranks received the same basic pay. After World War II, this amounted to about $12 a month and was augmented by an allowance for length of service and for the number of years in grade. The $65 monthly salary of a first sergeant major with eighteen years of service in the Force and ten years in grade was good in a country with an annual per capita income of $60 to $80.

The living standards and educational opportunities of the soldiers placed them in a privileged position, alienating them from their tribal culture. Each married man received a family hut, served by common sanitary and cooking facilities, and rations for his wife and children. Good food, organized physical education, and competitive sports raised the health standards of the troops and their families well above the civilian average.

Each soldier could pursue his education along military or trade lines. Reading, writing, and arithmetic were taught daily. There were evening classes for wives and elementary instruction for children. A secondary school at Luluabourg for the sons of soldiers, veterans, and civil officials had a ten-year program to prepare a man to become a warrant officer, the highest noncommissioned rank and the top position available to Congolese. On independence day there were fewer than ten native warrant officers. Qualified Congolese were first admitted to the Royal Military School in Belgium for officer training in 1957, but none had been graduated by mid-1960.

A bimonthly paper with a circulation of 22,000 was published in Lingala and French to broaden the cultural horizon of soldiers, veterans, and their families. The religious preference of the Force was estimated at 59 percent Roman Catholic, 21 percent Protestant, and 20 percent unaffiliated.

Identity and Political Orientation

Members of the Force Publique, especially those who had served a second seven-year term and had become noncommissioned officers (NCOs), found in it a new sense of identity and esprit de corps. For this reason, reenlistment was relatively high, and desertion and dismissal were very low by African standards. After World War II, when civilian jobs were plentiful, a reenlistment bonus of $36 was instituted that by 1954 induced 47 percent of the men to remain in the Force for an additional three years.

Soldiers returning to civilian life were generally held in high esteem, particularly NCOs whose close association with white officers conferred status and prestige upon them. Because a soldier's new outlook, way of life, and material expectations made him "unfit to return to his village,"[4] the Belgians in the 1920s established special villages for veterans, appointing a former sergeant as chief. The veterans were unable to sustain European standards and the artificial villages became crime centers. They were discontinued in 1959 when urban employment opportunities became available.

Congolese soldiers and NCOs did not think of themselves as Congolese because there was no Congolese nation, but they were probably more loyal to Belgian political authority than was any other sector of Congolese society. Their patriotism was directed to the Force, the supertribe, and their tangible loyalty to the Belgian officer corps. The degree of their detribalization was determined by the length of their service, the intensity of their identification with the army, and the extent of their Christian education before and during military service. The troops were essentially nonpolitical and nonconspiratorial. Some had served elsewhere in Africa in both world wars, and a few in Palestine and Burma, but there is "no evidence that this experience had had any noteworthy influence on their political perspective."[5] Contact with political stirrings in Africa did lead to a small, insignificant increase in political awareness within the Force.

The Force Publique played no role in the two-year nationalist movement that preceded Brussels' abrupt grant of independence, though in early 1960 some soldiers began to ask what independence had to offer them. Like the lower level civil servants, they saw little opportunity for advancement. The political sector was to be completely Africanized, but Belgians were expected to remain both in the army and in the civil administration until qualified Congolese could replace them. The first Congolese cadets training in Belgium were scheduled to get their commissions in 1963. This frustration was deepened by the projected slow

4. Raymond Lester Buell, *The Native Problem in Africa*, Vol. II (Macmillan, 1928), p. 498.
5. Young, *Politics in the Congo*, p. 280.

pace of Africanization that Lumumba, who had special responsibility for defense matters, had endorsed. Shortly after the Brussels round-table conference in 1960 he declared that independence did not mean "we can turn a private into a general," a statement greeted with a campaign of anonymous critical letters in Congolese papers.

There was no danger that Brussels would use the Force to block the Belgian commitment to independence, but some Congolese politicians took the precaution of establishing contacts with NCOs and other leaders of their tribe in the Force. Their motive was not to insure the reliability of the Force, but to develop military support for themselves. As early as 1959, for example, Joseph Kasavubu had secured the support of Adjutant Nkokolo, a fellow Mukongo, who later became a colonel and commandant of Camp Leopold II, where he was able to provide military support for Kasavubu.

Three Regimes the First Year: 1960-61

During its first turbulent year the Congo had three regimes, suffered the disintegration of its statewide army, and became the grudging host to an internationally authorized foreign legion of 19,000 men from 30 different countries. Prime Minister Lumumba served until September 1960 when he was "dismissed" by President Kasavubu and replaced by a council of commissioners installed by Colonel Mobutu. In February 1961 Kasavubu appointed Joseph Ileo as prime minister; he replaced the council and served until August. Moise Tshombe, president of Katanga province, and Deputy Prime Minister Gizenga were also major actors in the drama, along with the diplomatic representatives and agents of Belgium, the Soviet Union, and the United States. UN Secretary-General Dag Hammarskjold was more a broker than an actor. The Congo story can be understood only against the backdrop of the initial crisis whose character had a profound impact on subsequent developments. The sequence of events in the first few days is significant.

The Initial Crisis

The Congo crisis was ignited by a small and isolated incident at the Leopoldville barracks of the Force Publique on July 4 by a handful of discontented Congolese soldiers and NCOs whose prospect for quick promotion looked dim beside the instant prestige conferred on the new cabinet ministers who were being driven about in Cadillacs. On that day one Congolese NCO told some soldiers they no longer needed to obey Belgian officers and at 5:00 p.m. the Force commander, Lieutenant General Emile Janssens, went to the camp to demote him.

The next morning Janssens charged that Prime Minister Lumumba's emotional and irresponsible speeches were the chief cause of restlessness among the troops. At 8:00 a.m. Janssens told the officers, NCOs, and troops at the Force headquarters that he expected absolute obedience and wrote on the blackboard: "Before independence = after independence." At a 6:00 p.m. protest meeting at Camp Leopold II the mutinous troops demanded that Janssens be recalled and that the officer corps be immediately Africanized. When they began to sack the canteen, Janssens alerted the Thysville garrison, 95 miles away, but when the Belgian officers there tried to form a convoy, the soldiers refused to obey. That night Janssens advised Lumumba to call upon the Belgian troops at the two Congo bases to preserve order under the terms of the treaty of friendship signed by the two governments on the eve of independence. Lumumba refused. This was a fateful error because the Belgian troops could have ended the immediate security crisis.

At 7:30 on the morning of July 6 Lumumba and Janssens went together to Camp Leopold II and the prime minister abruptly announced that all the Congolese troops would be promoted one rank. The soldiers hissed him and there was some shoving. Janssens reportedly stood between the angry soldiers and Lumumba to protect him. The mutinous soldiers took off their belts and went into town where they demanded that Kasavubu dismiss Lumumba and that Lumumba dismiss Janssens. They threatened to kill both Lumumba and Janssens, but most reports indicate their hostility was directed primarily against Lumumba. In an emotional broadcast at noon Lumumba declared that Europeans, specifically mentioning Janssens, were behind the "rebellion of Congolese soldiers." Thereafter the cabinet demanded that Brussels replace Janssens with a more progressive Belgian officer.

On July 7 the discontented troops in Leopoldville, still small in number, demanded the removal of all Belgian officers; this time Lumumba, reversing himself, appealed to a high Belgian officer to maintain order in Leopoldville at all costs.[6] The next day the mutiny spread to Katanga,

6. Colonel Louis Marlière, a Belgian officer attached to the Congolese Defense Ministry, says Lumumba in the beginning wanted to replace only Belgian NCOs, except in a few special cases. Author interview, Brussels, June 29, 1965.

Matadi, and elsewhere. In a mood of desperation Lumumba persuaded his cabinet to rubber-stamp his decision to dismiss all Belgian officers. At the same time, the Force was renamed Armée Nationale Congolaise (ANC). Victor Lundula, a civilian who had been a medical orderly in the Force during the Burma campaign and was a tribal cousin of Lumumba, was made a major general and commander of the ANC. Mobutu, also a civilian who had been a clerk in the Force from 1950 to 1956, was given the rank of colonel and made chief of staff.

Instant Africanization and instant chaos followed. By appointment and "election" all Belgian officers and NCOs were replaced by untrained Congolese soldiers, fewer than ten of whom had risen to the noncommissioned rank of warrant officer. Many Belgians panicked and hundreds fled across the Congo River to Brazzaville. Like the army, the civilian administration started to disintegrate. Acting erratically, Lumumba sought advice and aid from the Belgians and Russians simultaneously, and alternately begged and forbade the Belgians to restore order.

Finally on July 10 the Belgians intervened with paratroopers flown from Brussels to the Belgian bases at Kitona and Kamina. They acted without a clear mandate from Lumumba, though Foreign Minister Justin Bomboko declared they intervened at his request. Within nine days the troops peaceably restored order in 26 widely separated places, including several in Katanga. It looked as if the worst were over.

The fateful Matadi incident on July 11, the second day of the intervention, moved the crisis to a high pitch of emotional intensity. The Belgian show of force to restore order in the port city of Matadi broke out into a fire fight in which 12 to 20 Congolese were killed and 13 Belgians wounded. It is not clear how the shooting started, but exaggerated reports of the incident spread quickly and had a great political and psychological impact inside and outside the Congo. In an atmosphere of chaos and rumor, the Matadi reports triggered Tshombe's declaration of independence for Katanga later the same day. Though the province had a long history of separatism and virtual economic autonomy, Tshombe might well have stopped short of secession had it not been for the crisis in Leopoldville. In his move, Tshombe had substantial Congolese support in southern Katanga as well as from the province's European population and economic interests. He was supported abroad by certain Belgian civilian and military officials, but not by the Foreign Ministry.

Neither Brussels nor any other government ever accorded Katanga diplomatic recognition.[7]

Communist and militant African spokesmen seized the Matadi incident and the concurrent Katanga secession as proof that Brussels was attempting to reimpose its authority upon the Congo, a wholly unsubstantiated allegation which some Western observers at the time accepted at face value.[8] In a climate of confusion and misinformation, these charges made it virtually impossible politically for the Belgians to complete the task of restoring order which they were quite capable of doing militarily and which many, perhaps most, Congolese leaders wanted them to. Had the Force Publique officers been more decisive in disciplining the Congolese NCOs in the very beginning, or had the Belgian troops intervened between July 5 and 8, the Congo crisis might well have been nipped in the bud.

The UN Force

Having rejected the one indispensable agency of security—the Belgian officer corps—the Congo was faced with the problem of providing a substitute which, under the circumstances, meant the recruitment of up to a thousand qualified foreign officers and NCOs. It would have been impossible to import a thousand French-speaking non-Belgians who were familiar with the Belgian military establishment. And reinstatement of the Belgians appeared politically infeasible, though selective reinstatement was precisely what Mobutu and others wanted from the outset. Subsequent events suggest that this would have been the most responsible course of action.

Some Congolese leaders suggested that the Belgian troops already in the Congo serve as a temporary substitute for, or a supplement to, the ANC. Here again Lumumba balked, and on July 12 he and Kasavubu appealed to Hammarskjold for UN security assistance. The same day, unknown to Lumumba, Bomboko and several other cabinet ministers requested 3,000 U.S. troops to restore order. Russia and Ghana also received vague aid requests from Congolese officials. Washington turned down the request and supported the appeal for a UN Force.

---

7. For a thorough and objective study, see Jules Gérard-Libois, *Katanga Secession* (University of Wisconsin Press, 1966), especially pp. 277–89.

8. Ernest W. Lefever, *Uncertain Mandate: Politics of the U.N. Congo Operation* (Johns Hopkins Press, 1967), pp. 131–48.

On July 14, 1960, the Security Council acted affirmatively and authorized Hammarskjold to provide the Congo "with such military assistance as may be necessary" until the Congolese government determined that its "national security forces" were able "to meet fully their tasks." The council also called upon Belgium to withdraw its troops. The original and subsequent council resolutions identified five objectives for the UN mission: (1) restore and maintain law and order, (2) prevent civil war and curb tribal conflict, (3) transform the ANC into a reliable internal security force, (4) restore and maintain territorial integrity, and (5) eliminate external interference in the Congo's internal affairs. The most specific demand was for the withdrawal of Belgian troops from Katanga and, by implication, for Katanga to end its secession.

With this broad and uncertain mandate, the UN Force was legally authorized and dispatched with the nominal consent of the Leopoldville government, but Hammarskjold made it clear the force would be withdrawn only by the Security Council. As it turned out, the security mission was terminated four years and $411 million later by the General Assembly for political-financial reasons.[9] The United States, which had more influence on the UN mission than any other state, saw the UN Force primarily as a temporary replacement for the Congo's internal security forces,[10] but the Soviet Union and the militant African states viewed it as an instrument for punishing Belgium, destroying Tshombe, and frustrating the "neo-colonial machinations" of Washington and the West.[11]

In August Hammarskjold rejected Lumumba's repeated demands that he overthrow Katanga by employing UN troops. Lumumba further demanded that UN troops at all airfields be replaced by Congolese soldiers and police, that all non-African UN troops be replaced by Congolese or other Africans, that UN aircraft be placed at his disposal to attack Katanga, and that the UN Force seize all arms in Katanga and turn them over to him. Hammarskjold's prompt rejection of these demands led to a virtual break between the two men.

The UN Force inevitably became involved in Congolese internal poli-

9. For a discussion of legal and financial aspects of the UN Force, see *ibid.*, pp. 3–25, 43–73, and 199–206.
10. *Ibid.*, pp. 75–94.
11. *Ibid.*, pp. 95–109 and 157–71.

tics in spite of a categorical injunction that it not be "a party to or in any way intervene in" or be "used to influence the outcome of any internal conflict, constitutional or otherwise."[12] The most famous case of its alleged interference occurred in early September 1960. Andrew W. Cordier, the UN representative in the Congo, closed the Leopoldville radio station and the country's principal airports during the constitutional crisis in which Kasavubu succeeded in ousting Lumumba.[13] Cordier maintains that he acted under his law-and-order mandate; nonetheless, the political effect was to advance the cause of Kasavubu and the moderates and to frustrate Lumumba and his militant supporters at home and abroad. Closing the airports prevented Soviet IL-14 planes then in the Congo from transporting pro-Lumumba ANC troops, and closing the radio station was a far greater deprivation for Lumumba, an effective rabble-rouser, than for Kasavubu who, unlike his rival, had full access to the radio in Brazzaville.

The Mobutu ANC

Though the term Congolese National Army (ANC) is frequently used in describing events in the Congo, it had little or no coherent meaning before General Joseph Mobutu took over the government in November 1965. Until then it was a national army in name only. There was a defense headquarters with some Belgian advisers, and there were quickly appointed Congolese officers, such as Mobutu himself. But there was no effective army because there were fewer than a dozen effective officers. Without responsible leadership, the troops of the former Force Publique were as sheep without shepherds. The former unity of command was fragmented beyond recognition. Various ANC units engaged in banditry or served provincial or local military or political leaders. The Leopoldville headquarters had very little control beyond the capital city.

But there quickly developed what may be called the Mobutu ANC—a small "army," at first consisting of the headquarters staff and of units at Camp Leopold II loyal to Mobutu as chief of staff. As time passed, Mobutu strengthened the forces who were reasonably loyal to him by employing Belgian advisers and training officers and by securing Belgian, U.S., and other foreign military assistance. The visible symbol of

12. Resolution S/4426, Aug. 9, 1960.
13. This incident and other United Nations–host state questions are discussed in Lefever, *Uncertain Mandate*, pp. 43–73.

the Mobutu ANC was a battalion, later two, of Israeli-trained para-troopers who served as his elite bodyguard. From the beginning Mobutu was determined to neutralize, eliminate, or control all armed units in the Congo—to transform the Mobutu ANC into a genuine National Congolese Army. With the departure of the UN Force in 1964, the support of bilateral military assistance, and the elimination of various tribal and rebel challenges with the use of white mercenaries, Mobutu—first as chief of staff, then as ANC commander, and finally as president—has gone a long way in accomplishing this objective.

By early 1961 the internal security of the Congo was incredibly complicated by the criminal and bandit-like operations of numerous small ANC units and the presence of five different and competing "armies" in the Congo—four Congolese and one foreign. Their approximate number and affiliation were:

(1) Mobutu ANC, about 7,000 troops in the Leopoldville-Thysville area.

(2) Stanleyville ANC, about 5,500 troops supporting the Lumumba-Gizenga claim to be the legitimate government.

(3) South Kasai ANC, about 3,000 troops supporting Albert Kalonji's secessionist attempt.

(4) Katanga's Gendarmerie, about 6,000 men under Belgian officers supporting Tshombe's secessionist effort.

(5) UN Force, 19,000 men from 26 African, Asian, and European states. (During the four-year mission 34 different states provided military personnel.)

The 9,400 Belgian troops (3,800 stationed in the Congo and 5,600 flown in to restore order after the July mutiny), whose alleged threat to the Congo was one of the major reasons given for UN intervention, had long since departed peaceably and voluntarily. By mid-September 1960 all Belgian troops had left, except for 231 officers and NCOs who stayed on in Katanga to advise and train the gendarmerie; they were repatriated one year later.

In this confusing situation the UN Force had in effect supplanted the ANC which was hopelessly fragmented and had become a force of disorder rather than order. Mobutu had his hands full attempting to gain and keep effective control over the Defense headquarters, the Leopoldville garrison, and the armored brigade at Thysville. Though he had no known political ambitions in the summer of 1960, Mobutu certainly recognized the necessity of creating a security force in the capital city capable of upholding the central government. In this he was supported by Washington and other Western governments.

In his attempt to create a viable military force in Leopoldville, Mobutu turned to the UN Command, one of whose objectives was to help transform the ANC into a reliable army. Hammarskjold and other top UN officials used the euphemism "training and reorganizing" the ANC, but they never fully understood that the fundamental need was to fill important posts with qualified foreigners and begin training Congolese to assume responsibility as soon as possible. The few UN training efforts failed, primarily because the training officers brought in from Afro-Asian states were not acceptable to Mobutu who preferred officers of his own choice.

General Ben Hammou Kettani of Morocco, deputy UN commander in 1960–61, was given special military training responsibilities. Though he never accomplished much in the way of training, he did have a constructive influence in building the Mobutu ANC. On August 23, 1960, Lumumba agreed to have him serve as an adviser to the ANC headquarters staff. He got on well with Mobutu and they lived next door to one another in Camp Leopold II (renamed Camp Kokolo). Among Kettani's suggestions was the creation of the ceremonial-bodyguard paratroop unit. Kettani's close association with Mobutu has led to speculation that he advised Mobutu to undertake the September coup which without violence installed the council of commissioners. U.S. officials, including several CIA agents, have also been credited with a hand in the coup. Francis Monheim, a Belgian journalist and close friend of Mobutu, suggests that Mobutu acted on his own initiative.[14] In any event, Washington and other interested Western governments promptly recognized the council and were relieved that Lumumba was out of the picture.

Mobutu's relations with UN authorities were generally cool and correct, but sometimes strained. Serious tensions were caused by the abortive attempts of General H. T. Alexander and one or two other UN contingent commanders to disarm ANC units in July and August 1960. While the complete disarmament of all Congolese troops might have been the best thing that could have happened, the UN Force was not an

14. Francis Monheim, *Mobutu, l'homme seul* (Brussels: Editions Actuelles, 1962), pp. 132 ff.

occupying army and its command had no such authority. Under Secretary Ralph J. Bunche emphasized this legal point in criticizing Alexander's effort, though Alexander maintains that Bunche backed him "completely in my attempt to persuade the Congolese soldiers to hand in their weapons."[15] In spite of Bunche's forthright statement, the nagging fear that UN officials might change their minds and attempt to disarm troops was a persistent source of tension between Congolese and UN officials and was partially responsible for several "brutal assaults" by ANC soldiers against UN military and civilian personnel.[16] Another point of irritation was the behavior of Rajeshwar Dayal of India, the UN officer in charge, who was regarded by most Congolese leaders as arrogant, condescending, and pro-Lumumba during the council period. He once referred to the ANC as "armed rabble," which hurt Mobutu because it was largely true, though too sweeping. Dayal did not get along well with Western diplomats in Leopoldville, and after considerable pressure Hammarskjold recalled him in a "deal" that also involved the transfer of the U.S. and British ambassadors.[17]

Kasavubu named Mobutu as commander of the ANC two days before the September coup. In this position, he had several advantages over his predecessor, General Lundula. As a journalist, an associate of Kasavubu, and a resident of Leopoldville, Mobutu was well connected politically. As chief of staff he had been able to gain the confidence of older men in the ANC and his seven years in the Force Publique had earned him many friends among the men who were NCOs in 1960 and 1961. Using these contacts to good effect, Mobutu placed loyal officers in the Leopoldville and Thysville garrisons. He also gained control of the military police. He was the only military member of the small and influential "Binza group" that included Security Chief Victor Nendaka, Foreign Minister Bomboko, National Bank President Albert Ndele, and the permanent secretary of the interior ministry, Damien Kandolo. This informal consulting group derived its name from a suburb of Leopoldville and its influence from the key positions held by its members. As

15. See H. T. Alexander, *African Tightrope: My Two Years as Nkrumah's Chief of Staff* (Praeger, 1966), p. 38. Bunche's statement is found in UN, *SCOR*, Supplement for July, August, September, 1960, S/4451 (Aug. 21, 1960), pp. 113–15.

16. *New York Times*, Feb. 28, 1961.

17. This conclusion was confirmed by U.S. officials in author interviews. See also Hoskyns, *Congo Since Independence*, p. 365. O'Brien also discusses U.S. efforts to oust Dayal in his book: Conor Cruise O'Brien, *To Katanga and Back* (Simon and Schuster, 1962), pp. 63–64.

ANC commander, Mobutu alone had the capacity to make a show of force in Leopoldville, an enormous political asset in the confused power vacuum that prevailed there and in the Congo as a whole.

The technical efficiency and reliability of the Mobutu ANC owed a great deal to the advice and assistance of seven to twenty trusted Belgian officers whom Mobutu refused to dismiss despite Hammarskjold's repeated insistence on the "elimination of the Belgian factor," a demand supported by the Soviet Union and the militant Afro-Asian states. Hammarskjold found equally objectionable the employment of Belgians by Tshombe, whom the Security Council opposed, and by the central government, which the council supported. Mobutu condemned this "over-simplified and completely utopian" policy of "simply ejecting the Belgian military personnel."[18] Perhaps the most important of the Belgian officers was Colonel Louis Marlière who served as a principal adviser from July 1960 to December 1964, with a one-year break in Brussels. The U.S. Embassy and other Western observers also favored the retention of the Belgian officers. Though nominally advisers, these officers actually served on the ANC general staff and in the Defense Ministry and their salaries were paid by the Foreign Ministry in Brussels.

Concentrating on building strength at the center and with little control beyond the Leopoldville area, Mobutu could do nothing about maintaining law and order in the outlying provinces. Much less was he able to take on any one of the three hostile Congolese "armies"—in Stanleyville, Katanga, or South Kasai—each challenging the authority of the central government by pretension or secession.

Adoula Regime: 1961–64

The three regimes in one year were replaced by one regime that lasted three years. During the tenure of Prime Minister Cyrille Adoula, which began on August 2, 1961, the Congo continued as an arena of suppressed conflict. All efforts at "national reconciliation" fell far short of the mark in spite of Western diplomatic support and the UN mission. The territorial integrity of the Congo was preserved, but political unity remained an elusive goal.

18. UN, *SCOR*, Supplement for January, February, March, 1961, S/4752, Add. 3 (March 6, 1961), pp. 119–201.

Adoula was moderate in domestic and foreign affairs. He had the consistent backing of Mobutu and the Binza group. On November 27, 1961, he resumed diplomatic ties with Belgium, broken by Lumumba on July 13, 1960, and later bilateral military assistance programs were negotiated with Washington and Brussels. On December 2, 1961, Adoula restored diplomatic ties with the Soviet Union, severed by Mobutu in September 1960. Because of compromising activity by Soviet diplomats, Adoula in November 1963 expelled the Russians a second time.

The UN Force, Katanga, and Stanleyville

Secessionist Katanga and rebellious Stanleyville were the two principal political challenges of the Adoula years. Katanga was the most celebrated threat, but not as serious as the complex and ever-changing Stanleyville problem which did not come to a head until the latter half of 1964.

With an implicit mandate to end Katanga's secession, but without an explicit mandate on permissible means, the secretary-general moved cautiously. A protracted debate among the chief supporters of the UN mission on how to deal with the problem was finally resolved in a clash between UN and Katanga troops in late December 1962, which forced Elisabethville (now Lubumbashi) to submit to the central government. Two earlier clashes, in September and December 1961, had been inconclusive. In all three, the UN Force killed about 350 Katanga soldiers and civilians and lost about 42 men, a ratio of about eight to one.[19]

Neither Mobutu's nor any other ANC unit played a role in the Katanga fighting. It was a pure UN effort, and it is doubtful that Mobutu was even informed of the UN plans for the final and conclusive round that followed on the heels of an eight-man U.S. military mission to the Congo, headed by Lieutenant General Louis Truman, that arrived in Leopoldville on December 21, 1962. The Truman mission signified Washington's political and material support of UN military force against Tshombe because all noncoercive efforts had failed. General Truman prepared a list of needed supplies, including a temporary bridge, trucks, armored personnel carriers, mine-clearing gear, and

19. See Ernest W. Lefever, *Crisis in the Congo: A U.N. Force in Action* (Brookings Institution, 1965), pp. 72–121.

transport and tanker planes for immediate delivery to Elisabethville by air, but before anything had arrived, the UN plan to extend "freedom of movement" throughout Katanga was triggered into action ahead of schedule by the harassment of UN troops by Katanga gendarmes, several weeks before the agreed date.

The end of secession was widely applauded. Moscow and Washington were pleased. Leopoldville was delighted. In Brussels and London, both of which had with utmost reluctance acquiesced to the use of force, there was a sigh of relief. A U.S. official said coercion was justified by success: "There are no uninvited foreign troops, no Communist enclaves, no 'army of liberation,' no reason for a single American soldier to die there, no excuse for a Soviet soldier to live there."[20]

Stanleyville was quite a different story. The city was first the capital of a rebel regime headed by Gizenga and supported briefly by Moscow, Peking, Egypt, Algeria, Mali, Guinea, and Ghana in early 1961. Even after the Soviet Union recognized the Adoula regime and withdrew its diplomatic mission from Stanleyville, it continued subversive activities against the central government. Though intensively involved in Katanga, the UN Force pursued a hands-off policy toward the Stanleyville rebels, with one notable exception. In January 1962, after a small clash between Gizenga's militia and a Stanleyville ANC unit (whose affiliation was not clear), Gizenga was arrested and taken to Leopoldville with the help of the UN Force. The rebel leader was placed under custody by Adoula. This unusual UN intervention was justified under the law-and-order mandate.

During the latter part of 1962 and most of 1963, Stanleyville was relatively quiet. Then it again became a center of discontent and tribal ferment that was exploited by militant governments seeking to overthrow the Adoula government. Stanleyville was the chief but not the only center of rebel activity that by mid-1964 controlled or harassed one-third of the country.

By early 1964 the subversive involvement of Red Chinese agents in the Congo had become a serious danger. Operating out of Peking's embassies in Burundi and Brazzaville, Red agents provided Congolese rebel groups with political and technical advice, money, equipment, and weapons, though the Chinese never succeeded in controlling the dis-

20. Address by Harlan Cleveland, U.S. Department of State Press Release No. 34 (Jan. 17, 1963), p. 2.

parate rebel elements. In June 1964, Peking's *Jenmin Jih Pao* welcomed the "excellent revolutionary situation" in the Congo.[21]

Through the Adoula years Washington continued to view communist penetration, even during the quiescent periods, as the most serious external threat to the Congo, but Russian membership in the Security Council prevented that body from acknowledging this danger while the council repeatedly condemned the virtually nonexistent "threat" from Brussels symbolized by Katangan secession.

The departure of the UN Force on June 30, 1964, coincided with the end of the Adoula regime, each of which had demonstrated its incapacity to deal with the deteriorating security situation. The four-year UN mission had an ambiguous impact upon the Congo. Its very existence depended upon the active cooperation of a voluntary coalition of states and it could not have been authorized or sustained without U.S. diplomatic, financial, and logistical support. Washington paid about 42 percent, or $170 million, of the total cost and transported 118,091 troops and 18,569 tons of cargo into or out of the Congo and airlifted 1,991 troops and 3,642 tons of cargo within the Congo in support of the effort. Though the United States led the peacekeeping coalition, it did not dominate it.

Necessarily hobbled politically, legally, and militarily, the UN Force was a marginal actor in the fundamental Congo drama. It helped to maintain a semblance of order and ended Tshombe's secession, but it failed to stem the rising rebel tide in late 1963 and early 1964. It was legally competent to move against the rebels and, according to an American military observer, prompt and energetic UN action in the early days probably would have stopped the movements.[22] In the absence of Soviet and Afro-Asian political support for moving against the insurgents and because of the phase-out of the Force, the UN Command took no action against the most serious danger to the integrity of the Congo in its first five years—a striking contrast to its sustained and dynamic effort to eliminate the far lesser danger in Katanga. It must be said, however, that the UN mission struck a significant blow for unity when Cordier closed the airports in September 1960 to prevent Soviet planes from assisting the ousted Lumumba.

21. *New York Times*, June 25, 1964.
22. Col. Knut H. Raudstein, USA Ret., former chief U.S. defense attaché in Leopoldville, 1962–65, in communication to author, April 15, 1968.

UN authorities were unable to make a contribution to the development of reliable "national security forces" for the Congo, the absence of which was the primary reason for UN intervention. In fact, Hammarskjold's anti-Belgian policies had the effect of delaying desperately needed bilateral security aid. In retrospect, it should have been clear at the outset that a multistate coalition, whose participating governments often had conflicting interests, was singularly ill-equipped politically and psychologically to help a weak government to deal with the highly sensitive problem of restoring leadership to a shattered army. No multistate agency can embody the minimum requisites of confidentiality and responsibility that one government expects of another friendly government providing security assistance.

At best the UN Force served as a stopgap while efforts could be launched to build a basic structure of central authority and internal security. At worst the UN mission postponed effective assistance from Western states and delayed the resolution of major internal conflicts by internationalizing and complicating a largely local crisis that presented no self-evident threat to international peace. At the mission's end Thant soberly acknowledged the organization's limited state-building and nation-building capacity: "The United Nations cannot permanently protect the Congo, or any other country, from the internal tensions and disturbances created by its own organic growth toward unity and nationhood."[23]

The net political effect of UN intervention was to lend support to internal and external forces working for a strong central government and against those seeking a loose confederation. With occasional exceptions, the UN effort also supported the political moderates over the militants. As a whole it tended to further the objectives of the United States and the West, and to frustrate the objectives of the Soviet Union, Red China, and the militant Afro-Asian states. This is not to say that stability and political moderation might not have been better served, and at less political cost, by traditional assistance to the Congo from friendly states.[24]

23. The secretary-general's last Congo report, S/5784, June 29, 1964, p. 42.
24. In January 1964 Tanganyika had a barracks mutiny very similar to that in the Congo in July 1960. In Dar es Salaam the problem was quickly brought under control with requested British assistance. For a brief cost comparison of the two crises, see Ernest W. Lefever, "The Limits of U. N. Intervention in the Third World," *Review of Politics* (January 1968), pp. 3–18.

The Mobutu ANC and Bilateral Military Aid

During the Adoula regime Mobutu continued his efforts to strengthen the center of the ANC and extend his control beyond the Leopoldville area. Indiscipline persisted, even near the capital, and on at least two occasions army personnel attempted to arrest and assassinate Mobutu himself. In a single four-month period in 1963 there were sixty unlawful incidents "traceable to the instability of Congolese security forces," according to an unpublished U.S. tabulation. This list did not include "ordinary" crimes committed by individual soldiers.

Mobutu's formal integration of the Stanleyville ANC into the Leopoldville ANC in November 1961 helped to precipitate Gizenga's fall. This shaky unification was effected when units of both engaged in an abortive joint military action against Katanga. As turbulence increased in late 1963, the Stanleyville area again passed beyond Mobutu's control.

The integration of Katanga's forces into the Mobutu ANC after the end of secession in January 1963 was difficult because the two establishments were suspicious of each other. Of the 12,000 or more Katangan gendarmerie, only 2,000 to 3,000 were absorbed by the ANC. As many as 10,000 soldiers, along with their weapons, disappeared into the bush, some returning to their villages and others resorting to banditry. Command of the South Katanga area was given to Colonel (later Major General) Louis Bobozo, an older man who had Mobutu's trust and who, like Mobutu, believed in close cooperation with the Belgians.[25]

While formal UN training efforts got nowhere, incidental training was provided for about 700 Congolese when the Thirteenth ANC Battalion was attached to the UN Force at the Kamina Base from September 1962 until February 1964. Some observers believe the unit was "integrated" to symbolize better UN Force-ANC relations and perhaps to keep the Congolese troops out of trouble. The battalion was never involved in UN operations.

Recognizing the UN Command had been no help to Mobutu in building a reliable army, Washington in July 1962 sent a military advisory team to the Congo to examine the problem. The resulting Greene Plan

25. Author interview with Major General Bobozo in Elisabethville, Feb. 12, 1965.

—named for Colonel Michael J. L. Greene, USA, who led the team—called for a series of bilateral military aid programs to help modernize and train officers for the ANC and included measures to eliminate unnecessary and unreliable elements from the 35,000-man army. The bilateral programs were to be coordinated by the United Nations in accordance with the Security Council prohibition against military aid outside of UN channels.

Six governments—the United States, Belgium, Canada, Italy, Norway, and Israel—indicated their interest in the plan. On February 26, 1963, after Thant had said it was "advisable and desirable" to increase "bilateral aid" to the Congo, Adoula informed UN authorities that he had requested the six states "for assistance in modernizing the ANC."[26] When the plan was condemned by the Soviet Union and some of the more militant Afro-Asian states as a scheme to impose neocolonial shackles upon the Congo, Thant backed down and informed Adoula on April 29 that he could not support it.

Adoula had no alternative but to press ahead with bilateral aid. In the absence of Thant's approval, Norway and Canada bowed out. By mid-1964 Israel had trained 220 paratroopers (including Mobutu himself), and Italy had begun training 12 cadet pilots. The First Paracommando Battalion, serving primarily as an elite bodyguard for Mobutu, was considered the army's best unit.

By far the most significant training was provided by Brussels and by mid-1964 some 75 Belgian officers and advisers were in the Congo and more than 300 Congolese had gone to Belgium for military training.

Even before Thant killed the Greene Plan, Washington had quietly embarked upon a bilateral aid effort in October 1962, and concluded on July 19, 1963, a formal agreement for a military mission in Leopoldville.[27] The program provided mainly vehicles and communications equipment along with U.S. teams to train Congolese in their use. The effort received a boost in March 1964, when Under Secretary of State W. Averell Harriman, after a six-day mission to the Congo, recommended more ground vehicles, transport aircraft, and communications

26. UN, SCOR, Supplement for January, February, March, 1963, S/5240 (Feb. 4, 1963), p. 101; and S/5240, Add. 2 (May 21, 1963), p. 2. The official UN version of this question is summarized in the Annual Report of the Secretary-General on the Work of the Organization: June 16, 1962–June 15, 1963, A/5501, pp. 14–15.

27. See Appendix B for the complete text of this agreement.

gear to buttress the ANC effort against the rebels. By June 1964 Washington had contributed $6.1 million in bilateral assistance compared to $170 million in military aid to the UN Force.[28] Total U.S. military and economic assistance to the Congo by July 1964 amounted to more than $400 million.[29]

With this help Mobutu was gradually developing a national army but as of mid-1964 the ANC was not a united or effective fighting force. With only a handful of able senior officers and few well-disciplined troops, ANC units were usually no match for the ill-trained and sometimes fanatical rebels, though in several cases ANC garrisons held out against the insurgents. The army's weakness was made manifest during the Kwilu uprising only 200 miles from Leopoldville. Without explicitly acknowledging the failure of the UN mission to strengthen the ANC, Thant accurately summarized the problem:

> . . . the ANC is still insufficiently trained and officered to cope with any major crisis. Most of the Congolese troops still show, in emergency situations, inadequate discipline and devotion to duty or country. Good officers, who are competent and earnest, would seem to be the exception rather than the rule. The result is that there is little authority at the top and little soldierly spirit in the ranks. The lack of adequate leadership and of an organic chain of command is perhaps the main cause for the present ineffectiveness of the ANC.[30]

Like other African states, the Congo suffered from a generation gap in its fledgling officer corps, made all the more serious because of the wholesale sacking of the Belgian officers by Lumumba. The newly trained young officers returned from Belgium and had to serve under little-educated men who in 1960 had been promoted from NCO positions to top command posts. Tension and misunderstanding were the inevitable result.

In spite of, or perhaps because of, the political turbulence in the Congo, Mobutu has made an effort to build a professional and nonpolitical army. Posters prohibiting "political discussions or activity" have been displayed in ANC buildings since 1960.[31]

28. *New York Times*, June 22, 1964, and *Washington Post*, June 17, 1964.
29. G. Mennen Williams, "U.S. Objectives in the Congo, 1960–65," *Africa Report* (August 1965), pp. 12–20.
30. UN, *SCOR*, S/5784 (mimeographed, June 29, 1964), p. 30.
31. Young, *Politics in the Congo*, p. 461.

Tshombe's Second Coming: 1964–65

The nightmarish quality of the Congo's political life reached its dizzy height during the turbulent Tshombe regime which survived almost a year and a half. His precarious premiership was filled with bizarre contradictions, the chief one being Tshombe himself. This engaging, persuasive, and adaptable man, the archsecessionist, was asked by President Kasavubu to return from self-imposed exile in Spain to form a transitional government of "national unity" on July 5, 1964.

Politically underwritten by Mobutu and the Binza group, Tshombe was a moderate nationalist by any common sense definition, but in communist and other militant circles he was branded a white man's puppet or the tool of European economic interests. Though he did enjoy a degree of acceptance, even respect, in Western capitals, he was not the simple instrument of Union Minière, the giant copper corporation, or any other external interest. As Katanga's president he had used European "interests" as much or more than they used him. As a shrewd politician, Tshombe was as willing to lead a nominally united Congo as he had been to lead a secessionist Katanga.[32] Washington supported Tshombe as it had all previous regimes and continued its economic and military aid. Moscow, Peking, and the militant African states opposed the central government and supported the rising rebel movements politically, materially, or both.

The Rebels and Dragon Rouge

The end of the UN security mission marked the beginning of the Congo as a normal state in at least one important respect—it was now free to deal with its security problem in its own way. Its sovereignty in this crucial area was restored and Tshombe could freely seek external military assistance from any source. Confronted with rampaging rebels, he and Mobutu promptly requested increased bilateral aid under the programs initiated by Adoula and openly recruited white mercenaries to spearhead the antirebel campaign.

32. See "Tshombe: A 1964 Profile," *The Observer* (London), July 12, 1964. Reprinted in Helen Kitchen (ed.), *Footnotes to the Congo Story* (Walker and Company, 1967), pp. 125–28.

Feeding on anarchy, weakness at the center, and disaffection in the countryside, rebel leadership, according to Young, fell into three categories: the Stanleyville plotters, the rural organizers, and the local conspirators.[33] The most significant were the plotters who had been associated with Gizenga in 1960–61 and had fled to Brazzaville where they formed in October 1963 a national liberation committee with Christophe Gbenye as its head.[34] Attempting to topple the Leopoldville government by classic coup d'etat tactics, the conspirators kidnapped Mobutu and Nendaka briefly in November 1963. In April 1964 they tried to assassinate Kasavubu and Adoula. The three principal insurgents were Pierre Mulele,[35] who had had some training in Red China; Gaston Soumialot, a long-time Lumumba supporter; and "General" Nicholas Olenga, who led the rebel army. Mulele had virtually no connection with the other two men. Local conspirators, motivated by tribal animosities and political ambition, joined the rebels to suit their convenience.

External support, including weapons and money, came from Moscow and Peking, though the volume of aid was not great. The Chinese regarded the rebellion as a "war of national liberation," and provided active direction and leadership through their agents in Brazzaville and Burundi, but they were not able to control it. Peking's great interest was expressed in Mao's dictum: "If we can take the Congo, we can hold the whole of Africa."[36] Soviet aid was provided indirectly through the Sudan, Algeria, the UAR, and Tanzania. The communist arms included Czech rifles, heavy machine guns, and Chinese antitank rockets. On October 31, 1964, for example, a Soviet-built IL-18 landed at Arua, Uganda, with supplies that were immediately carried on three trucks across the border into the rebel-held area of the northeast Congo. On November 15, 1964, the first arms from Red China were found in the Congo.

The Congo rebellion reached its high-water mark shortly after the rebel capture of Stanleyville on August 4, 1964. By mid-September the

33. M. Crawford Young, "The Congo Rebellion," *Africa Report* (April 1965), pp. 6–11. This is an excellent summary.

34. Gbenye visited the United States in September 1962 as the guest of the African-American Institute. *Africa Report* (October 1962), p. 40.

35. On Oct. 9, 1968, Mulele was executed by firing squad in Kinshasa by the Mobutu government for insurrection. *New York Times*, Oct. 10, 1968.

36. Quoted in *Africa Review* (London, February 1966), p. 6.

tide had turned because of the growing effectiveness of Mobutu's troops, reinforced by Katanga gendarmes, and spearheaded in most cases by foreign mercenaries recruited and paid by the central government. This was two months before the American-Belgian rescue mission discussed below. The early months of 1965 saw a gradual decline in the northeastern rebellion. On February 4, Mama Onema, the chief rebel witch doctor, was captured and announced that the insurgents were running out of magic. By March 29, with the liberation of Watsa, all major towns and key rebel supply routes from the Sudan and Uganda came under government control. The leaders fled to neighboring states and continued their feuding. The movement was finally crushed; three factors brought on its end—its own internal contradictions, the more effective mercenary-led ANC, and a modest amount of U.S. and Belgian logistical support.

Never united, the rebel leaders were their own worst enemy. They failed to offer a positive social or political program and had no coherent military strategy. Rebel *simba* (Swahili for "lion") warriors turned the population against their self-styled "liberators" by capricious and brutal executions and other acts of terrorism; there are estimated to have been "at least 20,000" executions of so-called "intellectuals," "counter-revolutionaries," or "American agents" by the *simbas*.[37] Many of the victims were killed with extreme cruelty and usually in public. The torture included disembowelment of living persons and the eating of their hearts, livers, and genitals while still warm in accordance with the requirements of ritual cannibalism.

Witchcraft and sorcery played an important part in the rebel movement. The *simbas* were subjected to ritual mutilation, wore amulets, and were persuaded that enemy bullets would turn into water when they struck. Some of them believed they would be resurrected in three days if killed.[38] These superstitions led to rebel fanaticism that often frightened ANC troops who demanded equally potent magic protection.

37. M. Crawford Young, "The Congo Rebellion," p. 11.

38. See "Witchcraft, Sorcery, Magic, and Other Psychological Phenomena and Their Implications on Military and Paramilitary Operations in the Congo" (memorandum prepared by James R. Price and Paul Jureidini, Special Operations Research Office, American University, Aug. 8, 1964). See also Charles W. Anderson, Fred R. von der Mehden, and Crawford Young, *Issues of Political Development* (Prentice-Hall, 1967), pp. 127–34.

Both sides committed atrocities characteristic of tribal warfare in Africa, but those of ANC units were probably less frequent and less brutal. In the first two weeks of December 1964, just after Stanleyville was reoccupied by government forces, more than 500 suspected rebels were executed without trial or publicity.[39] The white mercenaries, who occasionally used excessive violence, maintained a higher level of civility than the ANC or the *simbas*. Most observers estimate that at least 50,000 Congolese were killed by Congolese in 1964, though Lloyd Garrison of the *New York Times* estimated twice that many died.

With the fall of Stanleyville to the rebels on August 4, 1964, a tragic drama unfolded, not only for the hapless Congolese in rebel-held territory, but also for some 3,000 innocent foreign residents from nineteen countries who were being held hostage by the rebels in violation of all accepted norms. Among the hostages were a small number of American missionaries and the U.S. consulate staff in Stanleyville. Washington, Brussels, and other governments had sought to secure the release of all foreigners through the International Red Cross and the Organization of African Unity (OAU). These efforts failed because rebel spokesmen demanded that the United States force Leopoldville to cease its offensive against the rebels before they would permit evacuation of the hostages. Washington refused to capitulate to this preposterous demand.

During September and October the picture grew darker as the rebel leaders lost their tenuous control over the *simbas* and when a number of foreigners were slaughtered and rebel plans for mass "executions" became known. The crisis was intensified by rebel reverses culminating in an ANC march, led by white mercenaries, toward Stanleyville. The rebels demanded that the column be stopped. It continued. With each passing day the lives of the hostages came under increasing jeopardy. A mass slaughter by the rebels was feared when the government forces reached Stanleyville. Experienced observers assumed that the mercenary-led ANC would have had little difficulty in taking the city.

All during the negotiations, held chiefly in Nairobi between U.S. Ambassador William Attwood and President Jomo Kenyatta of Kenya, chairman of the OAU Congo committee, Washington and Brussels in consultation with Leopoldville had been developing contingency plans for an airborne mission to rescue the hostages. Finally on November 24,

39. *New York Times*, Jan. 10, 1965.

1964, after all efforts had failed, Dragon Rouge, the code name for the mission, was launched, with the full consent of Leopoldville.[40]

In a period of five days Dragon Rouge, using a dozen U.S. C-130E planes and 545 Belgian paratroopers, saved more than 2,000 innocent foreigners of 19 nationalities in the Stanleyville and Paulis areas, though about 1,000 in remote areas were not rescued. The mission was "carried out with restraint, courage, discipline, and dispatch," according to Ambassador Adlai E. Stevenson, but it evoked one of the most fanatical, derogatory, and coordinated outbursts of invective against the United States in recent decades—primarily from communist and militant spokesmen. Washington and Brussels were accused of cynically supporting "imperialist Tshombe" against the "liberation fighters" under the cloak of a humanitarian mission. Charges of "wanton aggression," "deliberate genocide," and "massive cannibalism" were underscored by government-led or permitted demonstrations, including violence against U.S. buildings in Moscow, Sofia, Prague, Cairo, Nairobi, and Djakarta, and anti-American demonstrations in Peking.

Washington had sought to avoid the rescue mission, but humanitarian considerations had eventually overridden the anticipated political cost (which turned out to be ephemeral). Dragon Rouge had the inescapable side effect of helping Leopoldville's offensive against the rebels. With very little loss of life, and in a matter of hours, Belgian paratroopers took Stanleyville and shortly thereafter the city was occupied by government troops.

The paradrop at Stanleyville was not quick enough to save all the 298 white hostages, including about 100 women and children, held in the Victoria Hotel. Minutes after the paratroopers began to land, Radio Stanleyville screamed: "Take your machetes and kill the white people!" This was the signal for the *simbas*, armed with spears and automatic rifles, to indulge in a last-minute orgy. They herded about 250 hostages into the streets and started shooting and throwing spears at random, killing 25 Belgians and 2 Americans, one of whom was Dr. Paul Carlson, a medical missionary previously accused falsely by Gbenye of being a spy. The *simbas* responsible for the massacre escaped before the Belgian paratroopers arrived.

40. For popularly written but accurate accounts of Dragon Rouge, see: David Reed, *111 Days in Stanleyville* (Harper & Row, 1965), and William Attwood, *The Reds and the Blacks* (Harper & Row, 1967), especially pp. 191–236.

The ANC and the Mercenaries

The recruitment of white mercenaries to quell the insurrection was highly controversial from the start, but both Tshombe and Mobutu regarded it as militarily necessary in the absence of any viable alternative. The ANC could not do the job and no African or European government was willing to make troops available to Leopoldville. Washington and Brussels provided logistical support, but not fighting men.

During Tshombe's tenure the number of mercenaries in his service fluctuated between 300 and 800, all individually recruited from a half dozen countries. The peak was probably reached in January 1965. Among the mercenary groups were a unit of 300 to 400 French-speaking Europeans recruited largely in Paris and an English-speaking commando unit of about 250 men. The European group came to the Congo in August 1964 on a six-month contract and fought well. The English unit, led by Major Mike Hoare, later made a lieutenant colonel by Mobutu, was widely respected for its discipline and civility.[41] Virtually all observers agree that Congolese soldiers respected white officers, whatever their nationality, over Congolese officers whatever their tribe. As one Belgian put it, the Congolese soldier says, "If the white man stays, we can stay. We need not run." He added that often a "white face" was enough to stop a company of rebels.[42]

The quality and discipline of the ANC improved little during the turbulent period when the bulk of serious fighting was borne by mercenaries. Lack of leadership remained the basic problem. A Congolese officer or NCO could not "issue an order and expect to get immediate and absolute compliance"; often he got an argument, and usually "the will of the subordinate prevails."[43] The following account of ANC cowardice and insubordination in the field is typical:

> Early in the rebellion, the rebels were fighting only with spears, machetes, and arrows. Against such opposition, one army column with rifles turned and ran so fast it left its commander to be killed while trying to catch the last truck.

41. Author interviews with Colonel Knut Raudstein, in Leopoldville, Feb. 4–9, 1965, and with John Latz, a British stringer for Associated Press in Elisabethville, Feb. 10, 1965. See also Mike Hoare, *Congo Mercenary* (London: Robert Hale, 1967), a remarkably honest and convincing account.

42. Author interview with Colonel Louis Marlière, Brussels, June 29, 1965.

43. Author interview with Colonel Raudstein, Leopoldville, Feb. 5, 1965.

Towns have fallen as the result of a single telephone call. The rebels simply phoned ahead and said they were coming. The defending government troops fled or got out of their uniforms and joined the welcomers.

On a few occasions, the army has stood and fought well, but these were the exceptions. Generally, their appetite for battle hovers near zero. Whole companies are still known to mutiny when they don't like an order.[44]

The Belgian training which was beginning to have a small effect was interrupted by the 1964 rebellion. As of February 1965 there were 150 Belgian training officers and NCOs serving in the ANC, and under pressure from Washington, Brussels agreed to increase this number to 300.[45] The Belgians also provided military advisers. A Lieutenant Colonel Jacques Noel, for example, served as chief of staff to Colonel Leonard Mulamba in Stanleyville, who in 1965 also headed the civil administration for the entire northeastern Congo.

At the Kitona Base where 1,650 Congolese were in ANC training there were 64 Belgian officers and NCOs.[46] There was also a Belgian Air Force detachment of 150 men servicing the planes that provided logistical support for the ANC. Though the Belgian officers wore their regular uniforms and insignia, they could be disciplined by Mobutu. Technically, they were advisers, but many of them wrote the orders for their Congolese superiors to sign and some filled command positions.[47]

By September 1964, a total of 664 ANC officers and NCOs had been trained in Belgium. In 1965 approximately 300 Congolese were in regular cadet training there, along with 250 in accelerated specialist courses.

United States military support to Leopoldville was a continuation of the equipment and logistical aid begun under Adoula. (The Stanleyville rescue mission in November 1964 was not a part of the American or Belgian military aid efforts. All the planes and men came and left within five days.) On August 12, 1964, Washington sent four C-130 transport planes, with maintenance and guard personnel, to assist the ANC in its drive against the rebels. A year later the last two of them were withdrawn from the Congo.

As of August 1964 anti-Castro Cuban exiles were flying the T-28 and B-26 Congo Air Force planes. There was a kind of poetic justice in this since a small number of Castro Cubans based in Burundi and Tanzania

44. Saul Pett, *Washington Post*, Dec. 27, 1964.
45. *New York Times*, April 8, 1965.
46. Author interviews with Belgian officers at Kitona, Feb. 8 and 9, 1965.
47. Author interview with a Belgian colonel, Leopoldville, Feb. 8, 1965.

fought with the Congolese rebels in the eastern Congo. According to the *New York Times*, the CIA provided the pilots through an agency-sponsored corporation, the Western International Ground Maintenance Organization, located in Liechtenstein.[48]

General Mobutu was the chief beneficiary of the significant military and political developments during Tshombe's turbulent year and a half. The rebel movement was broken and the stature and morale of the Mobutu ANC, which came to approximate a nationwide establishment, was somewhat enhanced, though it still had a long way to go. Mobutu was given more credit than the controversial Tshombe for the improved security situation. As the insurgent tide subsided, the tension between Kasavubu and Tshombe swelled. Each wanted to be top man. On October 13, 1965, Kasavubu dismissed Tshombe just as he had dismissed Lumumba five years before. The ouster of Tshombe seemed to propitiate most of the militant African leaders and they withdrew their support of the rebels. A complicated drama of intrigue and behind-the-scenes maneuvering followed, and Mobutu moved into the confused political vacuum for a second time.

Mobutu's Military Regime: 1965–70

At dawn on November 25, 1965, Radio Leopoldville announced that Lieutenant General Joseph Mobutu had dismissed President Kasavubu and would serve as president for five years. Mobutu said he acted "to save the nation, to put an end to chaos and anarchy." The bloodless coup was accepted without visible opposition and accomplished with only a token show of force. Mobutu asked Colonel (later Brigadier General) Mulamba to form a new government. Mulamba's cabinet, confirmed unanimously by Parliament on November 28, included Justin Bomboko as foreign minister and Victor Nendaka as minister of transport and communications.[49]

48. Henry Tanner, "U.S. Influence in the Congo," *New York Times*, Aug. 3, 1967. See also "How the C.I.A. Put An 'Instant Air Force' Into Congo," *New York Times*, April 20, 1966, pp. 1 and 30.

49. The three chief members of the Binza group—Mobutu, Bomboko, and Nendaka—remained at the helm until August 1969 when Mobutu made a sweeping cabinet reshuffle and dismissed nine ministers including Bomboko and Nendaka. Bomboko was sent to Washington as ambassador and former Prime Minister Adoula was made foreign minister. Nendaka was named ambassador to Bonn. In June 1970 Nendaka and Bomboko were recalled to the Congo to face an uncertain future. *Washington Post*, July 1, 1970.

Washington welcomed the new regime and recognized it on December 7, 1965. A fortnight later a new U.S. loan of $1 million was announced. By then the Mobutu government had been recognized by more than thirty states, including Belgium, France, Britain, and fourteen African states, half of which border on the Congo.

Facing the same chaos and fragmentation as his predecessors, Mobutu sought to mitigate the centrifugal forces of tribalism, regionalism, and multiple political parties by centralizing authority in the presidential office. His effort to mobilize support was pragmatic and occasionally contradictory. He immediately released the militant Gizenga who was subsequently given asylum in Guinea. He attempted to gain support from the domestic and foreign militants by invoking the legend of his archenemy Lumumba. On September 12, 1967, he unveiled a monument to Lumumba before presidents, premiers, and senior ministers from 36 African states attending the OAU meeting in Kinshasa (Leopoldville)[50] and called him "our national hero." In February 1968 he scored a victory when Lumumba's wife returned to the Congo to live after seven years of self-imposed exile in Cairo. Former Kwilu rebel leader Pierre Mulele, accompanied by Bomboko, returned on September 29, 1968, in response to Mobutu's amnesty policy, but he was executed as a traitor ten days later after a one-day trial.

Mobutu's increasingly militant rhetoric and gestures, designed to win the left, never approximated the militancy of President Nkrumah. Even less did he emulate Nkrumah's dependence upon communist states. Mobutu did consult left-leaning intellectuals at Lovanium University, largely to Africanize the Congo's image and thus win wider acceptance in tropical Africa. He continued his contacts with a broad group of Congolese and foreigners. In 1966 he "nationalized" Union Minière but continued European management and marketing. In September 1969 an agreement was announced between Kinshasa and the giant firm providing for compensation over the following fifteen years.[51]

On December 12, 1965, Mobutu asserted that government corruption since independence day had cost the Congo $43 million, warning that civil servants would be prosecuted if they accepted bribes. His regime has probably been stronger and less corrupt than any of its predecessors.

50. On July 1, 1966, the names of major cities in the Congo were Africanized as a gesture of national identity. Elisabethville became Lubumbashi, Stanleyville became Kisangani, etc.

51. *New York Times*, Sept. 26, 1969.

Mobutu had little use for independent legislative bodies and like virtually all other African politicians, he distrusted competitive politics. On March 7, 1966, he issued an ordinance that endowed the president with legislative powers and two weeks later he assumed these powers without actually dissolving the Chamber of Deputies or the Senate.

The new constitution promulgated on March 22, 1967, reflected Mobutu's views as well as the de facto situation in the Congo. It called for a presidential system, a unicameral parliament, "no more than two" political parties, and provincial governors who represented the central government.[52] It also provided for an independent judiciary and compulsory military service. As the draft constitution was being made public, Mobutu hastily established his Mouvement Populaire de la Revolution, the sole political organization in the country, whose declared aim was to pursue "a middle road between capitalism and communism" at home and "positive neutralism" abroad.

Mobutu created a one-party state and ruled by decree. Important political opponents or rivals were usually dismissed from high office or exiled to ambassadorial posts abroad. On June 2, 1966, however, Mobutu publicly hanged Evariste Kimba, who had served briefly as prime minister after Tshombe, along with three other "plotters."

As events unfolded Mobutu became increasingly estranged from left-wing elements at Lovanium University who in June 1969 precipitated a confrontation with the regime. Capitalizing on financial and other grievances, the radical students organized a demonstration designed to escalate into a general uprising against Mobutu. Twelve to twenty demonstrators were killed in the army's prompt and successful effort to stop the protesters. The university was closed and about ten student activists were tried, sentenced, and eventually pardoned by Mobutu. The government also took measures to alleviate specific problems.

Mobutu did not replace an old political structure with a new one, for there was little to replace. Instant decolonization had degenerated into anarchy. The democratic institutions envisaged in the Congo's first constitution had been formally established but had never functioned, though much of the Belgian administrative structure, if not the substance, had remained. Mobutu headed what was in effect an executive council of his own creation, consisting largely of civilians and resting

52. See *Bulletin of the International Commission of Jurists*, No. 31 (Geneva, Switzerland, September 1967), pp. 12–23.

ultimately upon the support of the army.[53] All his cabinet members and provincial governors have been civilians. Both his new government and his Council of Commissioners which ruled for five months in 1960–61 sought to neutralize competitive politics, but there was one big difference. After the 1965 coup Mobutu personally embodied the fusion of political authority and military power—he was head of the army, head of state, and head of the government all in one, though he did not formally assume the prime ministership until December 17, 1966.

Allowing for profound differences in the colonial tradition between Ghana and the Congo, and Mobutu's more "political" style, his regime resembled Ghana's National Liberation Council more than it did any other tropical African regime.

Foreign Policy Orientation

In spite of his more militant rhetoric, especially during 1966, Mobutu has remained fundamentally a moderate pragmatist in domestic and foreign affairs. Even when tensions were high, Washington and Brussels continued to be his closest allies and strongest supporters.

Anticipating U.S. support of Mobutu, Assistant Secretary G. Mennen Williams emphasized Washington's constancy toward the Congo: "The United States has faithfully and consistently supported the central government of the Congo since June 1960" under "President Kasavubu and his Prime Ministers Lumumba, Ileo, Adoula, and Tshombe."[54] Washington has been an equally steady supporter of the moderate Mobutu as ANC chief, as head of the Council of Commissioners, and as president. In October 1969 the Apollo 11 astronauts included the Congo in their round-the-world goodwill mission and Mobutu decorated them with the Order of the Leopard, Kinshasa's highest decoration.

Brussels has continued to provide the bulk of economic, technical, and military assistance to the Congo though relations between the two countries have frequently been strained, primarily because of Mobutu's occasional fiscal demands that Belgium has found unreasonable and the incapacity of the ANC or police to protect Belgian nationals during

53. See M. Crawford Young, "Congo-Kinshasa: Situation Report," *Africa Report* (October 1967), pp. 13–18, and Jean-Claude Willame, "Military Intervention in the Congo," *Africa Report* (November 1966), pp. 41–45.

54. G. Mennen Williams, "U.S. Objectives in the Congo, 1960–65," *Africa Report* (August 1965), p. 14.

periodic disturbances. The size of the Belgian population in the Congo (consisting largely of technicians, advisers, businessmen, teachers, and missionaries) is a barometer of the changing relationship. Before independence there were about 100,000 Belgians; the number dropped to about 15,000 during the 1960–61 crisis; it has since tended to fluctuate between 20,000 and 60,000. The considerable volume of Belgian aid was threatened during the periods of greatest tension. In 1967, for example, Brussels provided $70 million in economic aid (including 60 Belgian judges and 2,300 teachers and other specialists) and $3.5 million in military aid.[55] In June 1968 Mobutu was the private weekend guest of King Baudouin in Brussels, and six Belgian businessmen in the Congo received the Order of the Leopard. In November 1969 Mobutu made a state visit to Belgium, the first of any Congolese president.

Mobutu's distrust of communist states persisted, and it was not until June 1968 that he finally reestablished diplomatic relations with Moscow, broken in 1960 and again in 1963 on his insistence. Though formal relations with Kinshasa were normalized, Moscow continued its indirect subversive support of the remaining Congolese rebels who by 1967 operated mainly outside the country. Mobutu refused to establish ties with Red China and Chairman Mao continued to regard the Congo as ripe for "national liberation." Two years after Mobutu took over, Mao asserted that "the Congolese people will certainly triumph, and U.S. imperialism will certainly be defeated."[56]

Within Africa Mobutu succeeded in establishing ties with the more militant states without alienating the moderate ones that had supported the central government all along. His relations with Congo (Brazzaville) remained strained and in December 1969, Brazzaville proclaimed itself Africa's first "people's republic," climaxing a gradual shift toward the communist world since 1965. (In 1970 Brazzaville announced that Red China was erecting a shipbuilding yard on the Congo.)[57] Mobutu was the first head of state to visit Lagos after Nigeria had successfully crushed Biafran secession in early 1970 and Kinshasa contributed $600,000 to Nigerian relief.

55. For a strong U.S. tribute to Belgian aid, see *ibid.*, p. 20.
56. Mao Tse-Tung's statement was broadcast over Radio Peking's International Service in English, Nov. 28, 1967, commemorating the third anniversary of "U.S. aggression" against the Congo, that is, the Stanleyville rescue mission.
57. *Washington Post*, June 4, 1970.

ANC and Internal Security

In 1966–67 the ANC was nominally a national army, but its leadership was still very weak and its troops lacked discipline, frequently engaging in banditry and other crimes. Virtually no ANC unit had ever won a battle without the leadership of white mercenaries and fewer than a dozen ranking officers could point with pride to their record.

Weak and demoralized, the ANC confronted three major security challenges in the first two Mobutu years—mopping up remaining pockets of rebel activity in the northeast, a mutiny in Kisangani in mid-1966, and the capture of Kisangani and Bukavu by former mercenaries in mid-1967. Each challenge was complicated by the fact or allegation of complicity by foreign regimes seeking to overthrow Mobutu.

During 1966 rebel activity gradually subsided under pressure from ANC units that were sometimes led by mercenaries whom Mobutu retained in his service after he became president. The chief rebel leaders sought refuge or support in Uganda, Tanzania, Kenya, the Sudan, and the UAR, Algiers, and Cairo. Havana continued to provide some training assistance. By the end of the year the remaining vestiges of the rebellion that had started in late 1963 were virtually wiped out. In December Mobutu proudly announced that 800 *simbas* had joined the ANC.

The second challenge was the mutiny and capture of Kisangani on July 23, 1966, by 600 to 800 former Katanga gendarmes, who had been previously integrated into the ANC. After protracted negotiations involving Prime Minister Mulamba,[58] the city was liberated on September 25 by ANC units led by 100 mercenaries under Lieutenant Colonel Bob Denard.

The third and most dramatic challenge came from a group of former mercenaries of a half dozen nationalities who had served Mobutu well, but who were now expendable largely for political reasons, including Mobutu's effort to satisfy the militants in the Organization of African Unity. Their expendability was an important factor in the mini-rebellion launched by Major Jean Schramme, a Belgian mercenary who had served Tshombe and Mobutu. On July 5, 1967, some 150 mercenaries led by Schramme and supported by about 900 Katangan troops

58. Mulamba was dismissed by Mobutu on Oct. 26, 1966, and named ambassador to New Delhi.

captured Kisangani and Bukavu. Schramme soon abandoned Kisangani but kept control of Bukavu and the surrounding area. Not supported by any government, he acted more like a soldier of fortune than a man with any clear political objective. He appeared sympathetic to Tshombe who four days earlier had been kidnapped and held in Algeria after his plane had been hijacked over the Mediterranean, but no connection between Tshombe's ambitions or fate and Schramme's activities has been established.[59]

The Schramme operation was a great embarrassment to Mobutu whose 32,000-man ANC was powerless to dislodge the 150 mercenaries and the 900 Katanga troops, though almost half the army was assigned to the task. Mobutu's prestige was at stake and the United States for the third time provided logistical support to the central government to meet an internal crisis. (The first was in 1961–63 to support the UN Force against Katanga, the second in 1964–65 to help suppress the rebellion.) This time Washington dispatched three Air Force C-130 transports which arrived on July 10, five days after the capture of Kisangani. Ethiopia sent four F-86 jet fighters, which for technical reasons were not involved in operations, and Ghana provided several pilots. The Congo had eighteen transport planes of its own.

The dispatch of the C-130s with 150 supporting American airmen aroused an unexpected furor in the U.S. Senate. The operation was denounced as "immoral intervention" that would pave the way for "another Vietnam." Senator Richard B. Russell said it was "unjustified intervention in a local disturbance."[60] The planes moved several ANC units and rescued some civilians. The first plane was withdrawn from the Congo on July 23, the second on August 4, and the last on December 10.

By the time of the Kinshasa OAU meeting, September 11–14, 1967, ANC military action against the mercenaries, supported logistically by U.S. planes and politically by international pressures, brought

59. Tshombe was imprisoned by Algerian authorities until his sudden death on June 29, 1969, which according to an autopsy report signed by eleven doctors was caused by natural heart failure. *Washington Post*, July 1, 1969.

60. *New York Times*, July 11, 1967, and *Washington Post*, July 10, 1967. See also John W. Finney, *New York Times*, Dec. 17, 1967, who maintains that the sending of the three C-130 transports precipitated "what may prove to be the most significant foreign policy action" of the 1967 Congress, namely the Senate resolution stating that the President should not commit U.S. armed forces to conflicts on foreign territory without "affirmative action" by the Congress.

Schramme to the point where his chief aim was safe conduct out of the Congo. On November 4, under an arrangement facilitated by the International Red Cross, the 120 remaining mercenaries with 900 Katanga troops and their 1,500 dependents were safely evacuated from Bukavu into nearby Rwanda. Many of the Katangans have returned to the Congo under an amnesty arrangement. The mercenaries were repatriated to Europe in two Dutch DC-6s on April 24, 1968, after Mobutu withdrew his demand that they be extradited to the Congo.

ANC: Command, Discipline, and Training

The fact that the Congo after mid-1967 ceased to rely on foreign mercenaries to lead its military operations does not mean that the ANC had become an effective army. As of 1970 it was far from that. Still suffering from the traumatic loss of its Belgian officer corps in 1960, the "internationalization" of the Congo crisis, the four-year occupation of the UN Force, and the insurrectionary activity of 1963–66, the tattered remnants of the old Force Publique had not been rebuilt into a unified and effective statewide military instrument in spite of the best efforts of Mobutu. In terms of command and control, discipline, morale, and combat performance, the ANC as a whole ranged from poor to fair on a scale that would rate the Ghana Army as good. The exceptions, when particular units under Congolese command fought well against rebels, were very rare. The low but gradually improving state of the ANC was largely influenced by circumstances beyond its control.

To the extent that the army had any cohesion or unity, it was largely through the efforts of its indefatigable commander. Mobutu hires, fires, and reassigns officers to meet the security and political requirements of his regime, much in the manner of Emperor Haile Selassie, but perhaps with less skill. The chain of command remains weak and unpredictable, and the response of a given ANC unit in a combat situation is still problematical.

The officer corps has been slowly strengthened by the influx of young second lieutenants and NCOs trained in Belgium. The older, politically appointed officers have tended to resent the young newcomers. Within a year after Mobutu assumed power the number of general officers was increased from 3 to 13, colonels from 14 to 56, and majors from 55 to 93—a reasonable officer corps for an army of 32,000. The NCO ranks were significantly reduced in the same period. Slightly less than 2 percent of ANC personnel were officers, slightly more than 3 percent NCOs, and 95 percent were in the lower enlisted grades. Apparently the ANC still had no privates second class, perhaps out of a perverse memory for Lumumba.

The ANC is organized into six territorial brigades with a normal complement of supporting units. Mobility and communication remain serious problems in the vast expanse of the Congo which is almost the size of Western Europe.

The foregoing statistics are considerably less important for understanding the ANC than the quality of discipline among its officers and men. While there has been some improvement, the incidence of crime and corruption was still high compared to other tropical African armies. The crimes committed by ANC personnel, sometimes involving officers, include illegal "tax" collections, extortion, bribery, and frequent roadblock shakedowns at gun point in which travelers are robbed and occasionally killed. These shakedowns have even occurred in the Kinshasa area. ANC soldiers have robbed civilians, including some Europeans, in broad daylight. As late as January 1968 some ANC soldiers sold weapons to *simba* rebels. Some observers believe that ANC soldiers are the chief perpetrators of extortion, violence, and brutality in the Congo. More often than not these flagrant cases of indiscipline are overlooked by the responsible officers. Military punishment is neither swift nor sure, though there have been rare exceptions. Mobutu has established a judge advocate unit under a Belgian colonel in the ANC headquarters, but it has been able to do little to correct the situation.

The long-range answer to indiscipline is more and better training, a period of political stability in the Congo, and a determination at the top to enforce the military code. External assistance has focused on improving training facilities in the country and making available training opportunities abroad. During the Mobutu regime Belgium and the United States have continued to provide most of the military aid as well as public safety assistance. France has provided some light machine gun carriers and Italy some trainer planes and jet fighters. The Congo also has two DC4s, ten DC3 transports, and six Alouette helicopters.

Mobutu's objective of establishing a full-fledged military academy has not been achieved, but the Kitona Base has become a major army training center, commanded by a Congolese officer and operated by about 75 Belgian officers and NCOs with the assistance of about 400

Congolese. The former Belgian base was turned over to the Congolese in January 1965 after the UN Force relinquished it, and by the end of the following year it had given basic training to 5,435 recruits. Though most of these young men came from the western Congo, strong efforts have been made to establish regional balance among the new recruits. Kitona offers specialized training in such areas as engineering, transportation, and communications, as well as courses for NCOs and junior officers. In-service training for promotion is also available.

In addition to Kitona there are a number of special military training facilities, largely in the Kinshasa area, including a paratroop instruction center at the Ndjili airport, a commando training center at Kotakoli, a transportation school at Kinshasa, and a pilot training school at Ndolo. A one-month paratroop course at Ndjili started in mid-1964 with about 15 Israeli instructors. Several thousand Congolese, including at least 115 women, have become parachutists.[61] An 18-month course for training paratroop instructors is also given. The commando center was started in 1965 and is operated by a Belgian officer. The transportation school is perhaps the only training facility that has functioned continuously since 1960.

The Congolese Air Force is barely off the ground, though the first 12 cadet pilots were sent to Italy in October 1963. As of 1969 a handful of Congolese were qualified to fly small propeller aircraft and a nucleus of staff officers for the air force had been created. Instruction and technical advice at the Ndolo flight school was provided by about 50 Italian Air Force personnel. The Congolese Air Force was also assisted by a team of Belgian officers and technicians.

Serious training in the Congo became possible only after the situation was stabilized in 1967. Since then Belgium has provided officer and NCO training for Congolese at the Royal Cadet School in Laeken, the Royal Military School, the Infantry School at Arlon, and other schools. As of early 1969 approximately 1,000 Congolese had been trained in Belgium, an average of about 120 a year since 1960.

Military assistance from the United States has consisted largely of equipment—aircraft, ground vehicles, and communications gear—and on three occasions, temporary logistical air support for specific operations. United States equipment training teams and other military ad-

61. *New York Times*, June 10, 1969.

visers have served in the Congo. About 100 Congolese military personnel were trained in the United States from 1960 through 1969. From
fiscal 1960 through 1968, U.S. military assistance to the Congo totaled
$198.5 million, or an average of slightly over $24.3 million a year. This
included $170.7 million given to the UN Force and $27.8 million provided bilaterally. This heavy investment, compared to what Washington provided elsewhere in central Africa, is a manifestation of the U.S.
interest in maintaining stability in the area. The expenditure has sometimes been criticized as excessive by those who hold that Washington
has overestimated the dangers of communist penetration.

The statewide Mobutu ANC of mid-1970 has not been battle tested.
It is preoccupied with strengthening its command structure and improving its discipline by training at home and abroad, the real effects of
which are just beginning to show. Its main security function in the
immediate future is to safeguard the frontier and to be ready to control
civil disturbances the police cannot handle. Barring unforeseen developments, the ANC will not be compelled to deal with invasion by an African or extra-African state. Under these circumstances, some observers
have argued for a somewhat smaller and more efficient and disciplined
ANC. The need for greater efficiency and discipline is undeniable, but
the size of the force must be related to the size of the country, the state
of internal security, and the efficacy of the police. If Mobutu's 25,000-
man National Police Service, established in 1966, has developed the
capability to deal with normal law-and-order problems, there would
appear to be little action left for the ANC other than border patrol and
intervention in major disorders. But who knows how large the next
challenge to central authority is going to be? Further, in tropical Africa
the military have a substantially greater symbolic and ceremonial role
than in most industrialized states, and size and visibility are important.
Ghana's large army is a case in point.

By shrewd manipulation, tender care, and genuine interest, Mobutu
has built an army reasonably loyal to him and his regime. But since
loyalty is often an ephemeral quality, Mobutu has taken extraordinary measures to insure political reliability at the center, especially in
the defense headquarters, in the Kinshasa garrison, and in his own two
paratroop battalions which together form the living nucleus of the
Mobutu ANC.

Evaluation of the Regime

For almost five years the Congo has been a one-party state under the firm leadership of General Mobutu, who rules by decree and is backed by the army he commands. It is essentially an executive regime with a largely civilian administration, though there is an independent judiciary that includes a number of Belgian judges. Mobutu's two chief objectives have been internal stability and normal diplomatic and economic ties with his African neighbors and the great powers. A moderate at home and abroad, he has stabilized the Congo and put it on a steadier course. Measured against certain criteria of political development— movement toward competitive politics, a separation of powers, and broad participation in the political process—the Congo has not moved very far. But under Mobutu it has gained its first chance to move since independence day. His regime has created the necessary but not the sufficient conditions for constructive political development and economic growth and, as such, represents an advance over its predecessors. Mobutu's most difficult task is to prepare for a peaceful transition to a constitutional regime. When he took over he said he would rule for five years—until November 24, 1970—but the date of the transition is less important than the circumstances under which it takes place.

The Congolese Police Service

For the first half of its history the Force Publique, all of whose officers were Belgian, served as an army and police force throughout the Congo. From 1926, when a small police corps was established in a handful of urban centers, until 1960 the Force continued to play a major if not dominant role in preserving internal law and order. In 1948 the urban police were absorbed into the new and more comprehensive Territorial Police Service, which was designed to provide protection in the territorial subdivisions of the provinces. In 1958 the gendarmerie was created, formalizing a functional division of the Force Publique in which certain units were placed at the disposal of the territorial and provincial authorities to perform essentially police duties. In addition, there were the local all-African police accountable to the traditional chiefs.

The Police before Independence

Like the regular military units, the gendarmerie was more fully detribalized than the Territorial Police. All gendarmerie officers were Belgian. Armed with the same rifle used by the Force Publique, they also constituted a reserve for the Force. (In 1960 both the gendarmerie units and the regular Force units were placed under the Ministry of Defense and integrated into the ANC. There has been little distinction in equipment, training, or function between an ANC gendarmerie battalion and a regular ANC infantry battalion.)

The mission of the Territorial Police was not always clearly distinguished from that of the gendarmerie, though it performed less of a constabulary role and more of a classic police function. Locally recruited, the Territorial Police were ethnically identified with the population they served. Africanization of officer positions proceeded slowly and by 1960 there were two or three dozen Congolese officers at the local level, none in the higher command structure. Functions of the Territorial Police included the enforcement of Belgian laws (as opposed to tribal mores), the protection of public buildings, and the operation of state prisons. The police were normally unarmed but in emergencies were issued rifles; some officers and NCOs had sidearms. They were not as well trained as the gendarmes, but better trained than the Tribal Police. Each province had a police school; in 1957 a more advanced school was established in Leopoldville. There were over 9,000 Territorial Police in the entire Congo in 1960.

The Tribal or Chief's Police, responsible to the chief of a rural district, were recruited by voluntary enlistment in the district they served on a ratio of one policeman to 1,200 inhabitants. This all-African force maintained order, assisted in native courts, operated local prisons, and performed other services for the chief. The men had no firearms but usually carried rubber sticks and handcuffs. The character and functions of the Chief's Police were almost identical to those of the Native Authority Police in Ghana.

Each of these categories of police was apolitical. They played no political role before independence or in the army mutiny during the first month of independence. In general they served their Belgian officers loyally. In terms of status and morale, the gendarmerie ranked above the Territorial Police, and the Territorial Police ranked far above the Chief's Police.

Territorial Police: 1960–66

The fragmentation within the Congo in mid-1960 involved the police as well as the army, and for essentially the same reasons. When Lumumba dismissed the Belgian officers and NCOs of the Force Publique virtually all the Belgian officers of the Territorial Police left as well. In Katanga a small number of Belgian military officers stayed on for about a year; several dozen Belgian police officers remained also and are still there. In both the army and the police instant Africanization meant instant anarchy. Most police vehicles, radios, and other equipment were stolen or destroyed. The police forces in most cities deteriorated badly, while in the rural areas police ranks grew to several times their previous size mainly for political reasons. The Leopoldville force of 1,500 men became ineffective and patrolling and traffic control practically ceased.

Since the Congo had no national police service, the disintegration of the Territorial Police was all the more serious. Locally recruited and administered and without adequate leadership, the police structure was fragmented and many policemen found it convenient to serve the whims of the newly promoted Congolese police officers or provincial politicians. Quality and discipline were further diluted by the loss of many experienced police to the army where the pay was higher and more reliable, and by the vast influx of raw recruits who swelled the ranks to 25,000 according to some estimates.[62]

When the UN Force arrived in the Congo in 1960 it acted as an emergency substitute for both the army and the police. Regular UN troops performed many civil police functions in urban areas, particularly in Leopoldville and Stanleyville. Both Nigeria and Ghana provided special police units which simultaneously substituted for and trained Congolese police. Although the UN mission was more effective in working with the Congolese police than with the ANC, it made little progress in creating a reliable police service or in providing a competent officer corps for it. All the pre-independence police training schools, except the one in Elisabethville, were unable to sustain themselves and all had closed operations by 1962.

The situation was further aggravated when on January 1, 1963, the country's six provinces were split into twenty-one, each with an autono-

62. M. Crawford Young, "The Congo Begins to Stir," *Africa Report* (October 1963), pp. 9–11.

mous and expanded police force. The scarcity of competent officers became an even greater problem and local political influence on the police
increased. Discipline and operations continued to suffer.

The United States and Belgium were greatly concerned about the
deplorable state of the police service. In September 1963, nine months
before the UN Force left, the Agency for International Development
initiated a modest public safety program. When the first American
police officer arrived in the Congo

> ... there had been no [Congolese] policemen in Leopoldville for five
> months. The force had gone on strike because it was not paid. The Govern-
> ment had responded by discharging it.
>
> The provincial forces were barely functioning, often amounting to little
> more than the personal gangs of the provincial governors. The police
> academy [at Leopoldville], built by the Belgians before independence, was
> a shambles.[63]

By late 1965, after two years of Belgian, American, and other public
safety assistance, the police school system had been rebuilt with training facilities located in several of the larger cities. By then U.S. aid had
totaled about $2 million, including equipment, the provision of several
advisers, and the sending of six Congolese police officers to Washington
for a short course in civil disturbance control at the International Police
Academy.

Consistent with the general objective of the U.S. public safety program—to help the participating state to develop a reliable police service
—the aim in the Congo has been modest: "We are not trying to turn out
criminologists, or give them polygraphs, or laboratories, or fingerprint
files. We are just trying to get a functioning police force."[64]

The Tribal or Chief's Police continued to function after 1960, but
since their jurisdiction was limited primarily to enforcing local tribal
mores, they were in no position to fill the law-and-order vacuum left by
the army and the Territorial Police.

The National Police: 1966–70

To improve nationwide internal security, President Mobutu in
November 1965 ordered the establishment of a National Police Service.
His basic aim was to enhance the effectiveness of the police by centraliz-

---

63. *New York Times*, April 18, 1965.
64. A U.S. public safety adviser quoted in *ibid*.

ing control, minimizing the influence of local politicians, and reducing the swollen ranks to manageable levels by imposing uniform recruiting and training standards. On July 20, 1966, the National Police Service was established under the Ministry of the Interior and charged with the traditional responsibilities of law enforcement in urban and rural areas throughout the country.

An effort to detribalize and deregionalize the police by assigning men to serve outside of their home provinces has resulted in the transfer of about 10 percent of the force. As of mid-1968 some 1,500 officers had been relocated for this reason. (In some local areas the Tribal Police continued to operate, but with gradually diminishing functions. They are not a part of the National Police.)

As of late 1970 the strength of the National Police was about 20,800 and efforts were under way to reduce it to the authorized level of 20,000 by enforcing recruitment, training, and promotion standards. By statute, new recruits are supposed to have six years of elementary school and officer candidates four years of secondary education. In practice, however, many of the police are only semiliterate. In-service training is provided for men seeking promotion.

Two national police academies, one for 250 in Kinshasa and the other for 200 in Lubumbashi, by 1968 had trained over 1,000 recruits, 120 NCOs, and 278 commissioned officers. There are plans for developing regional school facilities (at Bukavu, Luluabourg, Mbandaka, and Kisangani) with a combined capacity of about 300. The academy curriculum tends to overemphasize legal questions and the liberal arts to the neglect of some of the more practical aspects of police work. To correct this bias, communications and other courses have been added and special training is given in vehicle driving and maintenance.

The Congolese Police Service is still heavily dependent upon foreign advice and assistance. Brussels has provided the great bulk of police aid since 1960, most of it in the form of advisers, technicians, and instructors, the number varying with circumstances. In early 1967, for example, there were some fifty Belgian police specialists in the country—ten serving as police school instructors and the rest in various advisory capacities at police headquarters throughout the country.

Nigeria provided an instructor program for Congolese officers from 1964 through 1966 and has also trained several groups of Congolese commissioners in Nigeria.

Since the U.S. public safety program began in 1963, Washington has contributed approximately $500,000 a year, the major portion allocated for equipment. To meet the serious transportation need, 264 motor vehicles and 3,200 bicycles, together with spare parts and tools, have been provided. U.S.-financed garage, storage, and maintenance facilities have been constructed at Kinshasa. Communications gear, training equipment, textbooks, office and sports equipment, and 16,000 police uniforms have been furnished. Police schools have been rebuilt and expanded and in late 1970 a new police headquarters, including communication and transportation facilities, is to be opened.

A small number of American public safety advisers have been assigned to the Congo and 82 Congolese police officers have had training in the United States, half of them at the International Police Academy. The first U.S. training adviser was sent to Kinshasa in 1963 and by late 1969 there were 6 advisers dealing with general administration, communications, logistics, municipal problems, and training.

Any evaluation of the National Police must necessarily be tentative because of the newness of the service. The organization and objectives are sound, but as of 1970 an effective and professional national force was more a dream than a reality. Though significant improvements had been made, administration and management were weak at all levels, and corruption and nepotism were not uncommon. There have been instances of armed robbery, extortion, and rape by police officers, though the frequency of such crimes is considerably lower among police than among ANC troops.

The statutes against crime and corruption have not been consistently or evenly enforced. In April 1968 a rare exception occurred when 8 police officers found guilty of bribery were literally drummed out of the service in full view of 2,000 police in uniform and their families. The ceremony was televised in Kinshasa. The offenders were publicly stripped of their insignia, belts, and shoes and forced to leave in disgrace with only their shorts and shirts. As far as is known, the Superior Disciplinary Council, a quasi-judicial committee presided over by the minister of the interior or his deputy, has never been called upon to deal with police indiscipline or crime.

Other problems that have confronted the Congolese police include the lack of adequate budget support, prejudice against Belgian advisers on the part of a few second-level Congolese officials, and Mobutu's reluctance to provide sufficient arms in numbers and types. The arms deficiency was partially resolved during the Schramme revolt in 1967 when Mobutu reluctantly "lent" the police several thousand ANC weapons. Most observers believe Mobutu fears that a strong and well-armed police force might threaten his military regime. This is one reason why he continues to assign essentially police functions to the ANC, a practice that confuses the jurisdictional lines of the police and the army.

As far as can be ascertained, officers of the National Police have generally been loyal to the Mobutu regime and have not become improperly involved in politics. While the police have had Mobutu's support, there has been some improper intrusion of lesser politicians into police matters to the detriment of the service.

In most tropical African states the threat to security is primarily internal, and it is impossible to make a tidy distinction between police and military functions. This is particularly true in the turbulent Congo where neither force has been conspicuously effective in maintaining order. Normally the police are responsible for internal order, except in serious civil disturbances when the army is brought in. Thus some U.S. public safety experts have argued that there should always have been more emphasis on rebuilding the police and correspondingly less emphasis on the ANC. Now that the major security challenges have been largely overcome, increased attention to strengthening the National Police seems warranted so that less reliance for maintaining internal law and order will have to be placed on the ANC.

ETHIOPIA

International boundary
Province boundary
National capital
Province capital
Railroad

0   100   200
                          miles

SAUDI ARABIA

RED SEA

YEMEN

KHARTOUM

Nile

Kassala

ERITREA

Massawa

Asmara

Blue
Nile

TEGRE

Makale

White
Nile

BAGEMDER

Gondar

LAKE
TANA

WALLO

Assab

SO. YEMEN

F.T.A.I.

DJIBOUTI

GULF OF ADEN

GOJAM

Dase

Berbera

Debra-
Markos

SHOA

Diredawa

Tug Wajale

SOMALIA

WALAGA

Nakamet

ADDIS ABABA

Harar

Hargeisa

Holeta
Debra Zeit

Jijiga

HAUD

Gore

Jima

Asala

HARAR

ILUBABOR

ARUSSI

OGADEN

KEFA

Goba

Arba Minch

Yirga
Alem

BALE

GAMO-
GOFA

Administrative line

SUDAN

SIDAMO

SOMALIA

LAKE
RUDOLF

UGANDA

KENYA

MOGADISCIO

INDIAN
OCEAN

CHAPTER FOUR

Ethiopia

The soldier's work is to follow orders, not to engage in politics.
MOTTO OF THE IMPERIAL BODYGUARD

THE CONTRADICTIONS of contemporary Ethiopia and its
continuity with the past are personified in Emperor Haile Selassie I who,
more than any other man, has shaped the destiny of this ancient land
during the last half century. Since 1917 when he emerged as regent after
a prolonged power struggle, his chief political aim has been to unify this
weak, poor, and diverse land by establishing full imperial authority over
all its peoples. In his persistent pursuit of unity and prestige for his
country, his methods have been benevolently paternalistic, authoritarian, and sometimes harsh.

Since ascending the throne in 1930, the Emperor has been a remarkably effective leader. Even while exiled in London during the five-year
Italian occupation (1936–41), Haile Selassie was the proud symbol of
his tormented homeland. Both before and after the occupation he
sought to consolidate his control over the semi-autonomous feudal lords
through a skillfully manipulated system of rewards and punishments
and by building a statewide military service able to crush any provincial
challenge.

A gradually modernizing monarch, Haile Selassie believes "tradition
cannot be abandoned at once, but we shirk our responsibilities . . . unless we begin working for the future."[1] Claiming the lineage of King
Solomon and the Queen of Sheba, he has been stoutly supported by the
old nobility, the landed aristocracy, the traditional military leaders, and
the conservative clergy of the Ethiopian Orthodox Church of which he
is the patron and defender. He has used the power drawn from these

1. Quoted by Alphonse A. Castagno, "Ethiopia: Reshaping an Autocracy,"
Africa Report (October 1963), p. 3.

133

traditional sources, not to sanctify the past, but to move his country cautiously into the twentieth century. Through the more Westernized elites—business, professional, and military men who have lived or been educated in Europe or the United States—he has introduced significant reforms into the church, the government, and the armed forces. He has demonstrated an unusual capacity to meet the minimal demands of both the traditional and more modern interests. Ethiopia, as a sympathetic observer noted, is attempting to "begin modernization under a traditional despotic authority."[2]

Ethiopia is a loosely knit and ethnically heterogeneous land that has been under "virtually unbroken Amhara rule for at least seven centuries."[3] Other tribes have both feared and respected Amhara authority which, reinforced by the influential Ethiopian Church, is the most powerful force for national cohesion in the country. Some critics brand it as "feudal oppression" and "Amhara imperialism."[4] Though Haile Selassie has appointed some non-Amharas to high-ranking civilian and military posts, the leaders of the other principal ethnic groups are not satisfied. He has shown most confidence in the Tigre people who share the Christian faith and who, together with the Amhara, constitute the traditional Abyssinian culture.

The Emperor's critics and admirers alike have great respect for his consummate political skills. His greatest ally is the authoritarian ethos of the Abyssinian tradition which disposes the majority of Ethiopians, particularly the Amharas and Tigreans, to accept imperial decrees and lesser decisions with little or no question. His paternalistic posture and his autocratic hand evoke respect—almost reverence—among the masses, though the Westernized elite prefer a more modern and democratic style. He skillfully employs rewards (including outright gifts) and retribution and the threat of retribution (imprisonment, exile, death) as instruments of political control. He balances one group or interest off against another. In the deft use of these means, buttressed by an effective system of informers, he has often been compared to a successful Byzantine emperor. He can at once be ruthless and forgiving, arbitrary

2. Donald N. Levine, *Wax and Gold: Tradition and Innovation in Ethiopian Culture* (University of Chicago Press, 1965), p. 189.

3. *Ibid.*, p. 3.

4. See, for example, a critical review of Levine, *Wax and Gold*, by Hagos Gabre Yesus, *Challenge*, Journal of the Ethiopian Students Association in North America (August 1966), pp. 62–73. The writer is a Tigrean who formerly lived in the United States.

and reasonable in dealing with opponents, all of whom he tends to regard as personally disloyal to him.

Haile Selassie is emperor in fact as well as in name. He dominates all agencies of government and media of communication.[5] Though the external forms of his administration have been modernized and a limited popular franchise instituted, Ethiopia does not have a genuinely independent judiciary; Parliament, which includes the "elected" Chamber of Deputies and a Senate appointed by the Emperor, is largely an instrument of the imperial will. The Emperor retains supreme authority and combines the powers and duties of the chief of state and head of government. The 1955 constitution asserts: "By virtue of His Imperial Blood, as well as by the anointing He has received, the person of the Emperor is saved, His dignity is inviolable and His power indisputable."

The Emperor has introduced administrative reforms and attempted to broaden the base of his political power, but Ethiopia remains fundamentally a one-man, "no-party" state.

> The educated elite is still very narrowly recruited. The use, primarily, of ascriptive criteria of selection preserves existing class lines and assures, if not complete loyalty to the Emperor, at least loyalty to the existing class structure. The absence of political organization has meant the lack of a ready-made communications network among the members of this elite, thus reducing its ability to take concerted political or economic action. The interests favoring change are therefore highly fragmented. . . . Untouched by new political organizations, politically informed only by the government's communications monopoly and by the traditional local autocracy, it [the vast majority of the population] is beyond the reach of political appeals from the new elites.[6]

People, Land, and Economy

Situated in the exposed horn of Africa, Ethiopia has had to fight for its existence against a variety of external foes for a thousand years. That it has preserved its independent status is a tribute to the toughness

5. The Ethiopian press in 1966 and 1967 was characterized as having a "high degree" of government control by the *Freedom of Information Center Report* (May 1968), University of Missouri School of Journalism. This places it in the same category as the Soviet press.

6. Robert L. Hess and Gerhard Loewenberg, "The Ethiopian No-Party State: A Note on the Functions of Political Parties in Developing States," *American Political Science Review*, Vol. 58, No. 4 (December 1964), p. 950.

of its warrior-leaders. Ironically, however, the very absence of a recent European colonial past, except for the Italian occupation, has denied Ethiopia certain educational, economic, and political influences that every other tropical African state has profited from. In Ghana under the British, for example, literacy rose from zero to 25 percent, the per capita income reached $200, and a small professional and middle class came into being. Tribalism was eroded and a nascent sense of national identity emerged. A constitution, law, courts, and an efficient and representative statewide system of government was created, supported by reliable military and police services. Because of different historical and geographical circumstances, the Belgian political contribution to the Congo was not as great.

In contrast, Ethiopia gained little of the cultural, economic, and political heritage of Western Europe, except for what the Italians transmitted to Eritrea, a former colony, which became an Ethiopian province in 1962. This is a major reason Ethiopia is one of the least developed African states. Recognizing this, the Emperor since 1941 has actively sought economic, political, and military advice and assistance from Europe, the United States, and other developed states.

With the addition of Eritrea, the area of Ethiopia increased to 457,000 square miles—five times larger than Ghana and less than half the size of the Congo. This mountainous country borders on the Red Sea in the north, on the Sudan in the west, on Kenya in the south, and on the Somali Republic and the French Territory of the Afars and the Issas (formerly French Somaliland) in the east. A broad central plateau, deeply etched by the Blue Nile and other rivers, forms the heartland of Ethiopia, including the bulk of the population, the capital Addis Ababa, and the other principal urban centers. There are two ports on the Red Sea—Assab and Massawa.

The Ethiopian population, estimated at 23.5 million, represents more than forty different tribes, the most important being the Amhara, Tigre, and Galla. The Galla people are the most numerous. Christians comprise almost half the population, while 35 percent are Moslems and the rest largely animist. Reflecting the dominance of the ruling group, Amharic is the official language. It is the native tongue of about 20–25 percent of the people and is used as the tongue of instruction through the sixth grade. Acknowledging the need for a language adequate for modern life, the Emperor shortly after the Italian occupation ordered that English be the sole vehicle of instruction in all government secondary schools. Consequently, the entire younger generation of the educated elite speaks English. About 30,000 Europeans and about 6,500 Americans live or are on temporary duty in the country.

The educational level is low even by African standards, and the Emperor has placed heavy emphasis on improving the situation. About 5 percent of the adults are literate and only 1.4 percent of the population is in primary and secondary school, in sharp contrast to 13.3 percent in Ghana and 11.5 percent in the Congo. Approximately 3,500 attend teacher training institutions or Haile Selassie I University in Addis Ababa.

About 70 percent of the economy is based on agriculture, with coffee supplying more than 60 percent of the country's foreign exchange. In spite of land reform efforts, ancient practices and a system of tenant farming present formidable obstacles to substantial improvement in agricultural productivity. Manufacturing, the fastest growing sector of the economy, has not yet had a significant impact. The gross national product of Ethiopia is about $1.5 billion and the per capita income approximately $64. While the official growth rate is put at 2.5 percent, some observers claim that it is actually closer to 1 percent.[7]

The United States Interest

Since 1903 Washington has had formal and friendly relations with Ethiopia. In the late 1940s, as decolonization in Africa approached, the United States saw in Ethiopia a stabilizing force in a strategic area of rapid change and potential conflict. Located close to the Suez Canal, the Persian Gulf, and the Indian Ocean, Ethiopia stood between the Arab world and the emerging black states. Its strategic value was further enhanced because it was by far the more influential of the two independent tropical states (the other being Liberia), and its Emperor was a widely respected and effective moderate in domestic and foreign affairs.

When Britain phased out its military aid to Ethiopia in 1951, a decade after the country had been liberated, Washington became the chief

7. Claire Sterling, "The Aging Lion of Judah," *The Reporter* (Feb. 9, 1967), p. 29.

source of arms and military training. Between 1953 and 1969, U.S. military aid to Ethiopia totaled $147 million, compared to about $40 million for thirteen other tropical African states. The American program has been larger than that of all other donor governments combined. The principal reasons for this substantial commitment are the political-strategic importance of Ethiopia, and the willingness of the Emperor to continue the U.S. Army communications facility, Kagnew Station, located at Asmara in Eritrea, which in embryonic form dates back to 1942. The agreement to regularize the existence of Kagnew was signed in Washington on May 22, 1953. A mutual defense assistance agreement was signed the same day, making clear the relationship between the station and U.S. aid.[8]

The parallel interests of Ethiopia and the United States are also illustrated by the sizable U.S. economic aid program which amounted to $195.1 million in the 1950–69 period. Because of his interest in collective security, and with Washington's encouragement, Haile Selassie provided several Imperial Bodyguard battalions for the United Nations' operations in Korea and the Congo. Washington has also encouraged the Emperor's leadership in the mediation of disputes between African states.

Though the Emperor leans toward the West, particularly Washington, he remains formally nonaligned and regards himself as a leader of the neutralist world. He has normal diplomatic and trade relations with the Soviet Union and has received both economic and military assistance from Moscow. For the most part, Soviet behavior has been much more circumspect in Ethiopia than in the Congo, Ghana, and several other African states,[9] but on March 13, 1969, three Russian and three Czech officials were expelled for allegedly instigating student disorders in Addis Ababa. In 1959 Moscow extended $100 million in credit which has been gradually drawn upon for various technical aid projects. (In April 1967, for example, a Soviet-built oil refinery began operation at the seaport of Assab.) At the same time the Emperor has taken a dim view of Moscow's substantial military aid to Somalia. Addis Ababa does not have diplomatic relations with Cuba or Red China.

8. The text of the defense assistance agreement appears in Appendix B.
9. See Sergius Yakobson, "The Soviet Union and Ethiopia: A Case of Traditional Behavior," *Review of Politics* (July 1963), pp. 329–42.

The Imperial Armed Forces until 1960

Throughout Ethiopian history the successful warrior and the warrior class have played a crucial political role because military power and political authority are virtually identical in Abyssinian culture.

> The political involvement of the military is not a phenomenon that needs to be explained; on the contrary, a distinction between the two realms is difficult to make. . . . Military virtues have ranked among the highest in the Abyssinian value system; military titles have been among the most prestigious in their social hierarchy; military symbolism has provided a medium for important national traditions and a focus for a good deal of national sentiment; military statuses and procedures have influenced patterns of social organization in many ways.[10]

In all states there is a close connection between the man who prevails with the spear and the man who presides with the scepter, but in Ethiopia he is likely to be the same man. Long before Mao's famous dictum, Haile Selassie knew that political power grew out of the point of a spear. He has always given first priority to military strength and has sought with considerable success to personify martial power along with political and ecclesiastical authority. For this reason, the Ethiopian Army has always played a significant political role.

The contemporary Ethiopian Army is the product of the gradual consolidation of military power in the hands of successive Ethiopian emperors and of invited foreign assistance. The Imperial Army traditionally coexisted along with regional armies until the middle 1940s when Haile Selassie developed a single national army whose mandate was coterminous with the state. Until the reign of Emperor Theodore (1855–68), Ethiopian armies were raised ad hoc to meet particular threats or to engage in campaigns of conquest. Ephemeral and inefficient, these unprofessional armies relied on the valor and ruthlessness of the individual warrior and the great esteem accorded him. "The Abyssinian military ethic took the form of a cult of the hero. Personal bravery—not discipline, training, honor, or self-sacrificing loyalty—was the paramount virtue in Abyssinian warfare."[11]

---

10. Donald N. Levine, "The Military in Ethiopian Politics: Capabilities and Constraints," in Henry Bienen (ed.), *The Military Intervenes: Case Studies in Political Development* (Russell Sage Foundation, 1968), p. 6.
11. Levine, *Wax and Gold*, p. 272.

In 1855 Emperor Theodore sought to consolidate his political power by establishing an imperial army equipped with modern weapons and loyal only to him. Emperor Yohannes (1872–89) also tried to modernize the army by importing firearms from Europe and by attempting, unsuccessfully, to instill discipline through the employment of a British training sergeant. Menelik II, who became emperor in 1889, continued to import European weapons and hired French training officers. His superior army prevailed over his provincial adversaries and he conquered much of what is now Ethiopia.[12]

After Haile Selassie became regent in 1917, he undertook more serious efforts to modernize and unify the Ethiopian Army. Several Ethiopian officers were sent to St. Cyr Military Academy in France in the 1920s, and in 1929 a Belgian military mission arrived in Ethiopia to train the Imperial Bodyguard and organize training centers. In 1934 a military academy was established at Holeta under Swedish management.

In 1935 when the Italians struck, the Emperor's modernization efforts had barely made a dent on the largely tribal, ill-trained, and regionally commanded forces. Virtually all of the 25,000 troops were still traditional warriors armed with spears and antique rifles. There were few professional officers. The military organization remained largely fragmented and individualistic. Until 1942 "there were no collective provisions for the supply of troops. Each man was left to fend for himself, drawing upon the supply of grain he brought along and whatever booty he could acquire on the warpath; the preparation of his food was left to the wife or servant who accompanied him to battle."[13] After the Ethiopian troops were defeated in 1937, many of the warriors continued to harass the Italians by guerrilla tactics and thus helped to prepare the way for the British liberation in 1941. The British command embraced various African elements, including the 24th Gold Coast Brigade and the First South African Division, the latter along with the South African Air Force playing a major role in the Abyssinian campaign.

Immediately after the Italian occupation, Haile Selassie launched three major reforms designed to reduce the power of the old provincial nobility and establish his authority over the entire country: (1) tax collection was centralized under the Finance Ministry, (2) the provinces

12. Richard Greenfield, *Ethiopia: A New Political History* (Praeger, 1965), pp. 122–24.
13. Levine, *Wax and Gold*, p. 262.

were placed under the Interior Ministry, and (3) provincial armies were abolished in favor of a standing statewide army. Highest priority was given to the establishment of the Imperial Ethiopian Armed Forces. In the fiscal year 1943–44 the Emperor allocated 38 percent of the state budget for military reconstruction and training. From then until 1960 military expenditures averaged almost 25 percent of the rising state budget. Essential training was provided by the British military mission from 1942 until 1951 when Washington became the principal external source of training and equipment.

Before the task of military reconstruction could move ahead it was necessary to deal with a serious internal security problem, the lawlessness of the traditional warriors who patriotically had engaged in guerrilla war during the Italian occupation. Lacking this constructive outlet for their valor, many of them turned to banditry and ravaged the countryside. To absorb, disarm, and control these men, the Emperor formed a loosely organized Territorial Army with a vaguely defined military reserve function. By 1960 many of the active territorials had been taken into the regular army or the national police, though some are still on active duty in the more remote areas of the country.

Haile Selassie gave special attention to reconstituting and revitalizing the Imperial Bodyguard as an elite military force whose primary functions were to protect the Emperor, the Imperial Palace, and the capital city, and to serve on state ceremonial occasions. In some respects the Bodyguard was similar to the President's Own Guard Regiment (POGR) of Nkrumah and Mobutu's paratroop battalions. The Bodyguard was developed not only as a prestige security force loyal to Haile Selassie, but as a standard of quality and efficiency for the regular army troops to emulate.

Though formally under army command, the Bodyguard was personally controlled and directed by the Emperor, and most of its officers were drawn from men who had attended the Holeta Academy before the Italian conquest. It became the best trained Ethiopian military force of the 1950s, and in 1951 it provided the Kagnew battalions that had a distinguished record in Korea. By 1960 the Bodyguard numbered about 6,000 men who were organized into nine infantry battalions equipped with light armored vehicles.

Haile Selassie, like Nkrumah, clearly favored his Bodyguard over the regular army. He provided his elite troops with superior military equipment and amenities and accorded them higher status. The Bodyguard had its own newspaper and for a while even its own radio station for entertainment. Its officers had their own plush club which was a center for cultural, social, and sports activities. This privileged position gave the officers and men a sense of solidarity and high morale.

The Imperial Army, including the 6,000-man Bodyguard, had grown to over 26,000 men by 1960. Organized into 23 infantry and 4 artillery battalions, the regular army also had an armored squadron, and an airborne rifle company. Army expenditures for fiscal 1959–60 were almost 9 million U.S. dollars[14] and the total military allocation was about 17 percent of the state budget, the largest single item. The army was still underdeveloped by middle-range Western standards, however. Much of its British and Swedish equipment was obsolete, and American replacements had not been widely distributed. The equipment breakdown rate was high because of carelessness, neglect, and the lack of trained mechanics, all reflecting the absence of a tradition of maintenance.

During this period, one of the Emperor's devices for consolidating his power was to force a differentiation of functions among the elite in the capital and the provinces. He attempted to separate political, military, and ecclesiastical authority, and within the military to divide the functions and responsibilities into modern categories—army, air force, and navy. This functional differentiation weakened any possible opposition in the military establishment and simultaneously gave Haile Selassie more effective control over the separate services.

An independent air force, organized in 1947 with the aid of Swedish advisers, by 1960 numbered over 1,000 men and consisted of a transport squadron of DC-3s and DC-7s, two squadrons of light bombers, a squadron of F-86 jet fighters, and eighteen training craft. The embryonic Ethiopian Navy was begun in 1955 with Norwegian assistance. Based at Massawa, the principal Eritrean port, the navy by 1961 consisted of two Yugoslav motor torpedo boats, five American coastal patrol boats, and a reconditioned U.S. seaplane tender.

Performance, Morale, and Discipline

Considerable military progress was made between 1941 and 1960, but the armed forces still were far from meeting the Emperor's goals for

14. All cost figures in this chapter, as elsewhere in the book, are in U.S. dollars. The Ethiopian dollar is officially worth 40 U.S. cents.

centralized and professional military services. The army and the air force were clearly capable of maintaining internal security and countering an attack by any immediate neighbor, but they were no match for the United Arab Republic's army or any other modern military force.

Despite the arbitrary and often harsh penalties meted out by officers to enlisted men, morale among the ranks was quite high. Promotion in the enlisted ranks was fairly rapid. This boosted morale because military service was regarded as a lifetime commitment and noncommissioned officer status was eagerly sought and highly respected. Officer morale was generally good, but it was affected adversely by the fact that the salary, especially for young officers, was considerably below that of comparable positions in civil government. The regular army officers understandably envied the Bodyguard officers, whose high morale and esprit reflected their superior training and equipment, their distinctive uniforms, and other privileges.

The generation gap within the army officer corps—the younger and better trained officers were wedded to modern equipment and techniques and the older were distrustful of new ideas—was hardly present among air force officers, most of whom had been trained in the United States.

Recruiting, Training, and Benefits

The Ethiopian respect for warriors and the fact that military life was a certain route to social advancement and economic security assured an ample flow of voluntary recruits into the armed forces.

After 1941, noncommissioned officers came mainly from the patriot warriors who had fought the Italians in the underground, dissatisfied rural youths seeking to better their status, and the urban unemployed. The army offered these predominantly illiterate young men a respected career with relatively high wages, adequate housing, and security. According to reliable estimates, approximately 35 percent of the enlisted men were Amhara, 25 percent Tigre, and 40 percent Galla and other tribes.

In 1958 the Emperor established a new military academy at Harar near Addis Ababa to supplement the Holeta Military School founded in 1934. Holeta became essentially an officer candidate school offering six- to nine-month courses on strictly military topics and conferring the rank of second lieutenant. Harar was a full-fledged military academy offering a three-year course, including many academic subjects. Its graduates also received the rank of second lieutenant, but they could earn a B.S. degree with an additional year or two at the university.

By 1960 there was an air force school at Debra Zeit and a naval cadet school at Massawa. These schools, like the Harar Military Academy, offered academic instruction. All the schools, including Holeta, stressed development of (1) a loyalty to the state transcending any particular ethnic loyalty, (2) an ethic of professional competence in place of the traditional "martial enthusiasm and wanton bravery,"[15] and (3) a code of professional duty to replace the ancient custom of using military service as a vehicle of personal political ambition.

The postwar officer corps formed a significant slice of the new elite, representing 10–12 percent of all Ethiopians who had been educated beyond the secondary level. Officer candidates, including those for the Bodyguard, were drawn largely from the top graduates of secondary schools and sent to the Harar Military Academy. Slightly over half of the active officers were Amhara from middle-class, land-holding families. About one-quarter were Tigreans of the same social background, and the remaining quarter came from the Galla and other tribes.

The high income of the senior officers was augmented by free housing, a free car, and servants. Since there were no substantial retirement benefits for regular officers, they tended to remain in the service until death, thus blocking the promotion of younger officers. This was another source of resentment.

Identity and Political Orientation

Acutely aware of the uncomfortably close historic tie between military power and political ambition, Haile Selassie sought assiduously to develop in the military services a recognition of their instrumental role and the habit of unquestioned obedience to the crown. He emphasized the professional character of the military forces which precluded their involvement in the political realm. His efforts to create a nonpolitical army strongly supported by the United States and other governments providing military aid were largely successful, except for the abortive coup of December 1960. Before and since the coup attempt, the armed forces have played a supportive role, not actively intervening in politi-

15. Levine, "The Military in Ethiopian Politics," p. 15.

cal matters, but upholding and almost identifying themselves with the authority and person of the Emperor.

There were some political differences among military officers, largely reflecting the generation gap rather than traditional ethnic divisions. The enlisted men, primarily because of their low educational and social level, showed little interest in political matters. Among the officers, however, there was a growing political and social consciousness during the 1950s, especially among the younger ones, some of whom came from poor families, and most of whom had Western military training. Having been exposed to the larger world by their training or active duty in Korea, some of them began to question the traditional Ethiopian "pattern in which a privileged few live at the expense of a relatively impoverished many."[16] Most of the officers regarded the army as a valuable modernizing and nationalizing force in Ethiopian life, but a few felt that the government should move more energetically in political and economic reform.

The older officers, particularly those who had been in exile with the Emperor in Britain and had maintained close ties with him, tended to accept the backward conditions with equanimity and were indifferent or hostile to proposals for substantial reform. A large uncommitted group of officers was prepared to cast its lot with the prevailing trend. No significant group believed that Ethiopia had an expansionist mission beyond its borders, and all officers were proud that the Ethiopian Army was represented in Korea.

The Imperial Bodyguard officer corps, by the mid-1950s the most cosmopolitan and professional unit in the armed forces, was more strongly influenced by the advocates of change than any other military group. A number of them became interested in the internal problems of Ethiopia, and in the late 1950s a small group had begun to discuss specific reforms.[17]

The Abortive 1960 Coup

During the night of December 13, 1960, while the Emperor was in Brazil, a coup was launched by Brigadier General Mengistu Neway, commander of the Imperial Bodyguard, and his brother, Girmame

16. Levine, "The Military in Ethiopian Politics," p. 22.
17. Greenfield, *Ethiopia: A New Political History*, pp. 361–62.

Neway, an American-trained intellectual and governor of Jijiga, apparently with the expectation that the regular army and air force would make common cause. The brothers Neway were joined by Lieutenant Colonel Workneh Gebeyehu, head of the Internal Security Service and a former Bodyguard officer, and the chief of police, Tsigue Dibou. All four plotters were Amharas.

Their declared goal was to install a progressive regime, but the weight of evidence suggests that this was more an attempt to seize power than to effect basic political and social reforms. It appears that the ideology of reform played a significant role in the thinking of only one of the chief plotters, Girmame. The immediate strategic objective of the plotters was to take all key points in Addis Ababa and win over or imprison principal political and military leaders. The insurgents lured principal Internal Security and military officials, advisers of Haile Selassie, and other figures to the Palace by falsely announcing that the Empress was on the verge of death. On arrival they were arrested. Bodyguard troops seized control of communications centers and stationed themselves at key points in and around the capital city.

At noon on December 14 when it appeared that the rebels were in control of Addis Ababa, Crown Prince Asfa Wossen in a radio broadcast proclaimed the installation of a new "revolutionary" government and the end of "three thousand years" of oppression, poverty, and ignorance. Noting that Ethiopia was "lagging behind" the newly emerging African states, he said the new regime would pursue the goal of economic and political modernization. He also announced military pay raises for all ranks, with a starting salary in all ranks between private and sergeant of $16 a month, and an increase in the salaries of officers up to major of some $20.[18]

All evidence indicates that the crown prince was a tool of the insurgents and acted under duress. His assertion that he made the broadcast with a gun at his head was true, at least figuratively.

The coup was not well planned or executed and the plotters miscalculated the response of the army and air force and the mood of the people.[19] Two principal figures marked for arrest and detention, Major

18. Quoted in *ibid.*, p. 417. All the financial figures are quoted in U.S. dollars, not Ethiopian dollars.
19. For a brief and balanced view of the coup, see Christopher Clapham, "The December 1960 Ethiopian Coup d'Etat," *Journal of African Affairs* (December 1968), pp. 495–507.

General Merid Mengesha, army chief of staff, and Brigadier General Assefa Ayena, deputy chief of the air force staff, eluded capture and established a command center at the First Army Division headquarters for the forces loyal to the Emperor. On December 15 and 16 army units, inspired in part by the patriotism and bravery of Territorial troops in the area, moved in against the rebels. The air force joined the loyalist cause, dropping leaflets carrying a statement by Patriarch Basilios threatening the rebels with excommunication, which helped rally the population to the Emperor's side. Air force F-86 fighters attacked the Palace, shot up the top floor of the Imperial Bodyguard headquarters, and strafed the Bodyguard club and motor pool.

In spite of the disturbed situation, some U.S. military advisers continued to report for duty to their Ethiopian Army or Air Force units where they gave advice on how to deal with the rebels. No American engaged in combat operations and none fired a shot or piloted a plane.

On December 16, after the air action and 24 hours of fierce ground fighting, the rebels were all but finished. More than 2,000 soldiers and civilians had been killed. The fleeing Neway brothers were quickly captured—Girmame was shot dead and Mengistu lived to stand trial. Police Chief Tsigue Dibou was killed in the fighting and Security Chief Workneh Gebeyehu committed suicide to avoid being captured and shot.

Immediately upon his arrival in Addis Ababa on December 17, the Emperor announced that the three-day revolt had been "quickly crushed by the Ethiopian Army and people." The regular army and air force had earned Haile Selassie's gratitude, won public acclaim, and diminished the prestige of their resented rival, the Imperial Bodyguard. All this added up to an enhanced political position for the two regular services.

Why did the top officers of the Emperor's elite Bodyguard in which he had invested so much interest and prestige turn against him? The answer lies ironically in the very quality and cohesion he deliberately sought in the Bodyguard, and to a considerable extent achieved. The exalted position of its officers, reinforced by their continuing Western contacts, gave them leverage for influence and latitude for discontent. Though they employed the rhetoric of modernization, their attempt to seize power was largely motivated by other factors, including sheer political ambition and the desire to square old grudges. They also resented what they regarded as the excessive and evil influence of Palace advisers or cronies of the Emperor.

To avoid a repetition of this traumatic experience, Haile Selassie reorganized the Bodyguard and took measures to tighten security throughout the armed forces. He completely replaced the Bodyguard's officer corps with loyal regular army officers. On January 12, 1961, he pardoned all the Bodyguard soldiers involved in the coup.[20] The ringleaders were placed on trial. General Mengistu Neway and a half dozen others were hanged. Earlier, 3,100 suspected rebels had been arrested. Of these, 400 were freed, 2,000 released on bail, and 700 detained.[21]

The regular army and the air force were quick to seize upon their newly won status by publicly demanding better pay. In a wholly unprecedented action a large delegation of army officers and men marched on the Imperial Palace on March 20, 1961, to demand a salary increase. When they reminded the Emperor that they had saved his throne, he had little choice and granted all enlisted men an increase in pay and allowances of $6.50 a month, which brought them more in line with civilian government employees of comparable status. Shortly thereafter the air force struck for higher pay. Haile Selassie responded by assigning the strikers to manual labor. In protest some of them dug ditches across the runway at Dire Dawa airport and again he felt compelled to meet the demands. These salary concessions, won through public demonstration, symbolized the Emperor's heavier reliance on the army and air force and made it clear that they were major forces to be reckoned with. These successful efforts were followed by continuing and insistent requests for more modern equipment and more foreign training that would result in greater efficiency and enhanced prestige for the armed services. The military demands never encroached upon the political sphere or implied the need for any basic change in the economic or political system.

In political terms the Emperor responded to the abortive coup by punishing the principal rebels, forgiving lesser offenders, and rewarding his loyal officials. He also made some modest reforms as a concession to the demands of the insurgents. He appointed some younger men to high posts and in May 1961 announced the establishment of a

20. *Africa Report* (February 1961), p. 11.
21. Greenfield, *Ethiopia: A New Political History*, p. 432.

professional civil service and a pension program for government employees.

The involuntary involvement of the crown prince in the abortive coup cast a shadow over his relationship with the Emperor, though the Emperor has taken no action to prevent the prince from succeeding him to the throne. In the latter 1960s observers noted a growing confidence of Haile Selassie toward his son.

Since 1960 there have been plots and rumors of plots in this society where scheming and intrigue have been salient if disquieting features, but all were "discovered" and defused at an early stage. In August 1961 several persons were executed for conspiratorial activity earlier that year. Perhaps the most noteworthy event was the arrest of Brigadier General Tadesse Birru, deputy chief of staff of the Territorial Army, and eight others on November 1, 1966, for allegedly plotting against the government with the support of certain Galla leaders. On August 2, 1968, Tadesse Birru and one of the other conspirators, former Army Lieutenant Mammo Mezemir, were sentenced to death by the High Court in Addis Ababa.

Ethiopian Forces Serve Abroad

At the time of the 1960 coup some 2,500 Ethiopian Bodyguard troops were serving with the UN Force in the Congo, but the Emperor made no move to bring them home. As if to demonstrate that he had the situation fully under control, he kept this substantial number of troops in the Congo until the UN Force left in June 1964. During the four-year operation, the Ethiopian contingent averaged 2,500 men, almost 10 percent of the entire army. Battalions were rotated every twelve months. Addis Ababa contributed a total of 120,000 man-months to the Congo effort, second only to India which provided 142,000 man-months.[22] India, however, sent only 1 percent of its army. On the African scene, Nigeria sent 26 percent of its army and Ghana 32 percent, but neither had its contingents there for the entire 48 months as did Ethiopia. With an average of three officers at the UN headquarters in Leopoldville, Ethiopia had three times the representation of any other African state

22. Ernest W. Lefever, *Uncertain Mandate: Politics of the U.N. Congo Operation* (Johns Hopkins Press, 1967), pp. 158, 178, and 228.

with troops in the Congo. Ethiopia also provided a competent UN commander, Lieutenant General Kebede Gebre, who served longer and with greater distinction than any of the other four UN commanders.

A decade before as a colonel, Kebede Gebre commanded the first of several battalions sent to Korea. From 1951 until 1954, some 5,000 officers and men from the Imperial Bodyguard served as a part of the U.S. Seventh Division in Korea where their tough and effective fighting earned the respect of American officers. In the Congo the Ethiopians also did a solid job, but their performance was somewhat less distinguished primarily because of the unique character of the Congo mission, including the unusual constraints on the use of force and the absence of specific guidelines. The excessive use of force by a handful of Ethiopian troops in Katanga in December 1961 can be attributed to the fact that the newly arrived battalion, without adequate briefing, became engaged in unfamiliar city combat involving civilians. Further, the Ethiopian troops in the Congo were not operating under a command as disciplined and orderly as that in Korea.

In the fall of 1961 the Emperor provided five air force jet fighters to support the UN effort in Katanga. Six years later, in August 1967, in response to a request from President Joseph Mobutu, Haile Selassie sent four F-86 jet fighters to the Congo to support the effort to dislodge Major Schramme's mercenaries from Bukavu.[23] Though the planes never were involved in operations because they lacked sufficient range, the fact they were sent was a political boost to the Mobutu regime.

In July 1964 the Emperor sent a six-man air force team to Dar es Salaam in two transport aircraft and six T-28s to assist in training personnel for the Tanganyika Air Force.

This remarkable record of voluntary military assistance abroad in conflicts far removed from Ethiopia's immediate interests demonstrates the Emperor's sustained interest in supporting the United Nations and his desire to assert leadership in Africa and the larger world. For example, as head of the Organization of African Unity's consultative committee for Nigeria, he spearheaded negotiations to end the Nigerian civil war. After the Korean experience he recognized that his troop contribution had earned him international prestige and that his officers and men had received valuable free training and experience. His military

23. See Chap. 3, pp. 119–21.

statesmanship also enhanced his bargaining power when seeking military aid from Washington and other potential donors.

Eritrean Separatism

The sending of Ethiopian troops abroad is all the more remarkable in view of the two major security problems that have persisted through the 1960s—Eritrean separatism and Somali irredentism. In the latter 1960s a number of other security problems arose, including sporadic student revolts at Haile Selassie I University, student demonstrations that intermittently closed schools in the provinces, antitax agitation in Gojam Province that briefly flared into violence during 1968, and continuing dissidence among the Arussi Gallas of Bale and Sidamo provinces.

Since 1960 an Arab-supported guerrilla movement, the Eritrean Liberation Front (ELF), has sought to wrest the coastal province of Eritrea from the Ethiopian empire. A rugged mountainous area of 48,000 square miles, this former Italian colony borders on the Red Sea and has a population of about two million—approximately 40 percent Moslem, 40 percent Christian, and the remainder animist. Eritrea, colonized by the Italians in the late nineteenth century, was occupied by the British from 1941 until September 16, 1952, when it was federated with Ethiopia as a semi-autonomous, self-governing territory under a UN resolution. Ten years later, on November 16, 1962, it was incorporated into Ethiopia as a province against the wishes of a determined minority of its inhabitants.

Economically, politically, and culturally, Eritrea is the most advanced province of the country, and an articulate minority of its residents resent being united with "backward" Ethiopia. Many Eritreans have a sense of pride rooted in their own history and identity, reinforced by their decade of self-government. The Moslem fear of being swallowed up by Christian Ethiopia is deliberately exploited by the dissidents. For these reasons, says a resident observer, "the virus of separatism affects the whole body politic."[24]

The sporadic violence against pro-Ethiopian officials in Eritrea during

24. Author interview with a Western observer, Asmara, Eritrea, Aug. 23, 1967.

the federation period has evolved into a small but reasonably well-organized insurgency operation under the ELF which demands the expulsion of the "Ethiopian occupation forces" who "are continuing to implement the criminal plan for annihilating the Arab people."[25] The front seeks an independent Eritrea with close ties to the militant Arab states. An early chairman of the ELF, Tedla Bairu, a Christian Eritrean who had formerly advocated union with Ethiopia, has been replaced by Idris Muhammad Adum. The ELF headquarters in Syria, employing revolutionary rhetoric common to communist-influenced "liberation" movements, declared in 1967 that since its establishment in 1961 the ELF had secured "its control over the western countryside" adjacent to the Sudan,[26] an obvious overstatement.

Recognizing Eritrean insurgency as a major threat to imperial unity, the Emperor has undertaken a substantial pacification program, including military and police operations as well as propaganda efforts to convince the people that union with Ethiopia is to their advantage. He has insisted that the insurgency is the work of a "foreign hand" which is "endangering the whole of Ethiopia."[27]

In 1967 the ELF numbered about 1,000 well-armed men who enjoyed easy sanctuary across the soft Sudan border where the front had an operations base located at Kassala. Approximately 200 to 400 "freedom fighters" have gone through the ELF training center in Damascus. The ELF relies largely on communist-made arms, though these weapons are procured almost exclusively from sympathetic third countries, such as Syria, Egypt, and Iraq, which have also assisted with advisers and training facilities. In March 1967 Addis Ababa announced that Cuba and perhaps China had agreed to provide ELF training, and in June 1969 two shiploads of Chinese arms reportedly reached the Eritrean insurgents.[28]

In 1967 the ELF force was divided into five commands, each with about 200 men operating in 40-man formations and supported by rudimentary communications and a "fairly sophisticated intelligence system" to monitor government troops. The front, armed with weapons

25. ELF statement broadcast by Radio Damascus, March 23, 1967.
26. Radio Damascus, Sept. 1, 1967.
27. Imperial address, Radio Addis Ababa, Jan. 6, 1967. He also said he had warned of the "foreign hand" as early as 1954, eight years before Eritrea was incorporated.
28. *New York Times*, March 3, 1967, and *Washington Post*, June 22, 1969.

from pistols to machine guns, used classic guerrilla tactics—terrorizing the population and attempting to assassinate village leaders and other officials who were regarded as unsympathetic. Kagnew Station, which is located in Eritrea, has not been a terrorist target, but several Americans have been apprehended by the ELF and subsequently released. In July 1965 two American servicemen with the U.S. Air Force Mapping Mission were kidnapped by the front and released unharmed two weeks later, but only after the kidnappers were subjected to the pressure of a combined military-police operation.[29]

Early in 1967 there was an increase in ELF terrorist activity in the western sector; civilians were attacked and several policemen, an army colonel, and a high-ranking Interior Ministry official were murdered. On the night of July 11–12 the ELF ambushed and killed eighteen policemen without sustaining a casualty. The Ethiopian Second Army Division intensified its pacification effort, which had been less than effective and marked by vacillation between brutal retaliation and amnesty offers. One army action killed twenty ELF and at least a hundred civilians.

On September 28, 1968, Radio Damascus, on the occasion of the ELF's eighth anniversary, declared that 5,000 "occupation" troops had been killed in Eritrea since 1960. This figure was refuted by Ethiopian authorities who asserted that offensive government action involving planes and commando police had broken the back of the ELF and reduced the guerrilla forces to fewer than 1,000 near the Sudan border. During most of 1967 and 1968, insurgency efforts slackened because of Arab preoccupation with Israel, the closing of the Suez Canal in 1967, which temporarily cut off almost all outside aid, and a border agreement in February 1967 between Addis Ababa and Khartoum. Earlier, the Sudan had provided sanctuary to ELF fighters and to as many as 20,000 Eritrean refugees, thus exacerbating traditional border tensions, and Ethiopia had admitted an estimated 12,000 Sudanese refugees. The Khartoum agreement to end political sanctuary in both countries, though difficult to enforce, has eased the tension considerably. The ELF suffered a serious setback when they were defeated by government forces during a pitched battle at Hal Hal in September 1968.

Following the arrival of two shiploads of Red Chinese arms in June

29. *Washington Post*, April 30, 1967.

1969, there was an upsurge of ELF terrorist activity. Two Ethiopian air-liners were hijacked over Ethiopian territory; one was forced to land in Aden and the other in Khartoum. The ELF also claimed credit for dam-aging a plane on the ground in Karachi, Pakistan, and another in Frank-furt, Germany.[30] In December 1969 two front members attempting to hijack an Ethiopian airliner were slain in mid-air by plainclothes guards, one using a knife. The front also sabotaged power and water installa-tions at Asmara on April 4, 1969. On September 9, 1969, the U.S. con-sul general in Asmara was abducted by ELF agents in western Eritrea and lectured on the front's objectives. He was forced to sign a document stating he had been treated well and was released after two hours. This incident, according to observers, indicated a new audacity but not new strength for the ELF.[31]

The pacification program in Eritrea is likely to be a protracted effort. With the province's wealth and strategic position on the Red Sea and the Kagnew Station near Asmara within its borders, the Emperor will neither surrender to the guerrillas nor launch a massive campaign against them that would involve disproportionate civilian casualties.

Somali Irredentism

In contrast to Eritrea where the insurgents seek political indepen-dence, Ethiopia is threatened in the east by the Somali Republic's claim to a large area inhabited by Somali-speaking tribesmen. Of the nearly 1 million external Somalis whom the republic seeks to integrate, about 500,000 are in the Ogaden and Haud regions of Ethiopia and another 200,000 in the North-Eastern Region of Kenya. The territorial claim, to be pursued peacefully according to the Somali constitution, has been exploited by unauthorized but tacitly supported Somali guerrilla action on both sides of the border. This has led to serious clashes be-tween the regular military forces of both sides. The seriousness of the problem, exacerbated by the nomadic character of the Somali tribesmen, banditry in the border area, and third-power military assistance to Ethiopia and Somalia, is evidenced by the mutual defense pact signed

30. *New York Times*, Sept. 14, 1969.
31. *New York Times*, Feb. 13, 1970.

by Ethiopia and Kenya on November 22, 1963, providing for joint military planning against border violations of either state.

Addis Ababa has appeared willing to renegotiate disputed border areas on the basis of old treaties and maps, but Mogadiscio has not accepted this approach which at best could yield only minor frontier adjustments far short of her irredentist claims. Somalia would be delighted with a plebiscite in the Somali-speaking areas, but obviously Ethiopia and Kenya reject this approach to territory lying within their widely accepted frontiers.

Since Somalia became independent on July 1, 1960, border clashes between Somali nomads and Ethiopian police and military units have been frequent, often precipitated by camel-raiding, cattle-rustling Somali bandits who attack Ethiopian police posts, shoot up villages, and return to their home villages as heroes. The situation became more grave in 1963 when an Ogaden Liberation Front was formed under the leadership of Muktal Dahir, a Somali who was bitterly anti-Ethiopian. It appointed a shadow government which at one point seemed on the verge of declaring an independent Ogaden free to merge with Somalia. Dahir also established and led an irregular Ogaden Liberation Army which received indirect support from Mogadiscio and for about six months in late 1963 was able to exercise de facto control over most of the Ogaden countryside. Dahir's guerrilla operation ambushed army and police outposts, mined roads, and kept units of the Third Army Division holed up in isolated garrisons.

In early 1964 the frequency of the clashes increased along the 900-mile Ogaden frontier and they eventually led to a two-day war. On February 7 a Somali attack on an Ethiopian post at Tug Wajale led to retaliatory raids by Ethiopian F-86 and Saab aircraft against Somali posts and border villages.[32] The Defense Ministry in Addis Ababa reported that 30 Ethiopians had been killed and 50 wounded, while the Somalis had sustained 400 dead and 750 wounded. The Somalis reported that 350 Ethiopians had been killed compared to 307 Somalis. The escalating conflict led to a clash between regular military units on both sides on February 27–29. The Ethiopians seized the initiative and at one point bombed a locust control camp just two miles from the Somali city of Hargesia. Fortunately, both armies ran out of fuel and

32. Keesings Contemporary Archives (1963–64), July 11–18, 1964, p. 20176.

were forced to stop fighting. The Organization of African Unity had called for a cease-fire on February 14 which provided a face-saving out for both sides; sporadic fighting between elements of the Third Division and Somali irregular forces did continue throughout March.

The two-day war apparently broke out without careful planning by either side. Though Ethiopia had the upper hand, the Third Army forces suffered from logistical and communications problems. While this weakness could be construed as a reflection on the quality of U.S. military advice, it would be more correct to assume that American advisers sought to end the fire fight and dampen the conflict. To avoid U.S. involvement, the three-man military advisory team with the Third Army Division was not permitted to visit field units in the Ogaden for about a year when the tension was highest.

At a mediation conference in Khartoum March 25–30, 1964, the two disputing parties agreed to pull back their troops from a demilitarized border zone. After things quieted down, the Emperor launched a pacification program in the Ogaden, including plans to dig wells and build schoolrooms and dispensaries. Since 1965 the Ogaden has been relatively calm, but has remained under special military control. The demilitarized zone was patrolled by the police until late 1968. The Ogaden Liberation Front has not been a serious threat, but small clashes have occasionally been set off by bandit activity.

The Ethiopian-Somali problem is complicated, but not necessarily exacerbated, by the fact that both states receive external military assistance, Ethiopia from Washington and Somalia, since its independence, from the Soviet Union. Somalia also receives technical assistance from Communist China as well as economic aid from the United States and other Western states. In November 1963 the Russians offered a $32 million program to equip, train, and enlarge the 6,000-man Somali Army. Simultaneously, a plan for $15 million in military aid for Somalia was proposed by the United States, Italy, and West Germany in an effort, as Haile Selassie was informed, to preempt Soviet influence. Mogadiscio rejected the Western package in favor of the economically more attractive Soviet program. To ease tensions, Washington and Moscow made it clear in 1964 that they did not want to stimulate an arms race between Ethiopia and Somalia and urged them to end the fighting.

By 1968 the Somali armed forces had grown to about 8,500 men. Soviet equipment and arms were supplemented by Russian military advisers, training officers, and construction supervisors. Even with improvements in size and efficiency, the Somali military establishment of 10,000 men in 1970 was vastly inferior to that of Ethiopia.

The Ethiopian-Somali confrontation eased considerably after July 1967 when Mohammed Ibrahim Egal became prime minister of the republic, ending a succession of leaders who had indirectly supported the Ogaden Liberation Front. Egal, convinced that guerrilla activity was not yielding the desired results and that the Somalis were being hurt more than helped, reached an agreement with Kenya to normalize relations in October 1967 and with Ethiopia the following September. Kenya and Ethiopia lifted the state of emergency in the border areas and road and air traffic has become normal.

A military-police coup in Somalia on October 21, 1969, eliminated the two foremost advocates of détente from the political scene. President Abdirashid Ali Shermarke was the victim of an assassination just before the coup and Prime Minister Egal was replaced by a revolutionary council that renamed the country the Somali Democratic Republic. Thus far the change of regime has had no visible effect on relations with Ethiopia and Kenya.

Military Aid and Training

Tested involuntarily at home and voluntarily abroad, the Ethiopian armed forces have performed well by tropical African standards, but the Emperor recognizes they still have a long way to go; hence his unflagging interest in continued training and foreign military aid. Maintaining his formal neutral stance, Haile Selassie accepts economic aid from East and West, but he clearly has more political confidence in the West, particularly the United States.

As the primary supplier of military hardware and training, Washington transmitted $118 million in aid between 1953 and 1968, compared to a total of $34.8 million for 13 other tropical African states.[33] Approximately 15 percent of the aid to Africa and to Ethiopia was for training military personnel; the remaining 85 percent was for equipment. All but 4 of the 182 Ethiopians receiving U.S. military training in fiscal 1967

33. In addition to regular military aid, Ethiopia has received $19.6 million in excess stocks and $5.9 million in other grant aid.

went to the United States. During the same year 18 Ghanaians and 9 Congolese received training in America.

American military aid is provided under the 1953 agreement that established a Military Assistance Advisory Group (MAAG) mission in Ethiopia. This aid is in part a payment for Kagnew Station, whose present lease expires in 1978, but Ethiopia would doubtless have been offered military and economic aid, though at a substantially lower level, on the strength of its military and political significance alone.

Kagnew Station is a $70 million U.S. Army communication facility, spread over 3,500 acres in and around Asmara. One of the largest high-frequency centers in the world, it is a "vital link between stations in Maryland and the Philippines, part of the globe-girdling chain that includes installations in Hawaii and California."[34] In 1969 there were about 3,000 U.S. military personnel and their dependents at Kagnew. The total number of Americans in Ethiopia was about 7,500, including missionaries, teachers, and Peace Corps volunteers.

The living quarters, shopping area, and recreational facilities of Kagnew are similar to those of any U.S. Army post of comparable size. This American island has its own schools, church, post exchange, and newspaper—the four-page, semimonthly *Kagnew Gazelle.* The sensitive electronic equipment is guarded, just as it would be in the United States, but the forest of glittering antennas stands wholly unprotected on farmland plowed up to the guy wires. Kagnew is not a military *base;* the only arms there are those required for protecting the equipment and personnel. It has no role in missile tracking or guidance.

The station is relatively serene and secure. The Emperor and many other Ethiopians visit it frequently and the U.S. Army operates a quiet but active community service program in and around Asmara. There is intermittent negotiation over land questions, but there has been no significant government pressure to terminate the lease, or even to modify the agreement, though a number of younger government officials and many university students in Addis Ababa are opposed to Kagnew.

The major goal of U.S. assistance has been to enhance Ethiopia's capacity to maintain internal security and defend itself against external threat. The primary MAAG mission has been to teach basic tactics and organization in the army and air force. In 1964–65, for example, U.S.

34. Donald H. Louchheim, "Costly U.S. Station Strains Ties With Ethiopia," *Washington Post,* May 1, 1967.

teams went out and taught tactics at the battalion level of the army. Washington has provided a small amount of counterinsurgency training in recent years.

Operating for 17 years, the military aid program has had a significant effect on all aspects of the Ethiopian armed forces. American equipment has gone a long way in modernizing the regular army and Imperial Bodyguard and in creating an air force from the ground up. Washington has supplied the air force with 12 F-86 jet fighters, 5 T-33 jet trainers, and 12 supersonic F-5s—a total of 29 jet aircraft—as well as a transport squadron of C-47 and C-54 planes. The navy has received five 95-foot U.S. coastal patrol boats, four 40-foot patrol craft, four landing craft, and a reconverted 18,000-ton American seaplane tender that serves as a training vessel and the naval flagship. Washington has provided the army with antitank and antiaircraft weapons, 54 medium tanks (M-41), and 39 armored personnel carriers.[35] The air force has American-equipped workshops capable of maintaining and overhauling jet engines. Non-American equipment includes about a dozen Swedish Saab trainer planes, two 60-ton Yugoslav torpedo boats built in 1951, and 6 Canberra B-2 light bombers from Britain.

The transfer of American equipment has been accompanied by a comprehensive training program for Ethiopian officers and NCOs. Between 1953 and 1968 this effort brought 2,523 Ethiopians to the United States where they were trained, along with Americans, in a variety of facilities from jet pilot bases to staff and command schools. In the same period 114 Ethiopians were trained in U.S. facilities in Germany. Approximately half of the entire officer corps has received some American instruction.

Through its MAAG mission in Addis Ababa (numbering 107 men in 1970, though it has been as large as 304), Washington has provided advice and assistance to the military services and to the Infantry School at Holeta, the Air Force Training Center at Debra Zeit, the Naval Academy at Massawa, and the Haile Selassie I Military Academy at Harar. U.S. Air Force officers have been particularly active at the Air Force Training Center which has an officer candidate school and offers instruction in flying, aircraft technology, electronics, weather observation, and administration. A four-year Air Force Academy was opened at

---

35. *Washington Post*, May 3, 1967.

Debra Zeit in late 1968 with plans to enroll 15 cadets a year. The air force follows the American pattern in military doctrine, training, and performance standards and is the most modern, professional, and efficient of the military services. Washington has provided army instructors, including the staffing of the Army Parachute Training Center at Debra Zeit.

Sweden, Norway, France, India, Britain, and Israel have also provided a modest amount of training and advisory assistance. Communist countries have not provided military aid, but there has been nonmilitary assistance from some of them.[36]

American military assistance and advice of all kinds, reinforced by the aid of the smaller states, have clearly enhanced the professional competence and efficiency of the armed services from the top command to vehicle maintenance, influencing military doctrine, command structure, training practices, and recruitment standards. Given the extremely disorganized situation in 1950, the slow movement toward greater efficiency in the army has been significant and in the air force remarkable.

The Armed Forces in 1970

In 1970 Ethiopia had the largest military establishment, including the most modern air force, between the Sahara and the Zambezi. In 1969 Addis Ababa spent about $37 million for military defense, 13 percent of the state budget of $284 million, or 2.4 percent of the gross national product of $1.5 billion.

Ancient military habits and traditions were gradually giving way to more Western influences. The gulf between officer and enlisted man was still great, and the reflex of absolute obedience to the Emperor was virtually unchanged. Officers and men alike were proud of their profession and the population looked upon them with esteem. The rivalry between the Imperial Bodyguard and the regular services had been largely dissipated by the 1960 coup attempt, and there was a mood of growing unity in the military establishment. This is not to say there was no tension beneath the surface or competition between the services for a bigger slice of the defense budget.

36. A short summary of Soviet bloc aid to Ethiopia is found in Marshall I. Goldman, *Soviet Foreign Aid* (Praeger, 1967), pp. 178–80.

Size, Character, and Deployment

The Emperor remains commander-in-chief of the armed forces which are administered by the defense minister. The highest military officer is the chief of staff of the armed forces. The army, air force, and navy commanders constitute a council of commanders. In this largely Western-style military organization the Emperor continues to play an unusually active and direct role in the selection, transfer, and retirement of all officers of colonel rank and above, as a means of maintaining his political control.

In 1969 the armed forces numbered about 41,200 men as follows: army, 38,000 (including the Bodyguard of 7,000); air force, 2,200; and navy 1,000. In addition, there was the Territorial Army of about 7,000 whose "value as a reserve force is doubtful, since it is poorly equipped" and trained.[37] The Territorial Army, like the police, is under the Interior Ministry. Counting only the standing armed forces, there are 573 inhabitants per serviceman in Ethiopia, compared to 500 in Ghana, and 470 in the Congo.

The army is organized into four divisions: the First Division (Bodyguard) is located in Addis Ababa. The Fourth Division is headquartered in the capital, but most of its units serve in the southwestern provinces. The Second Division is located in Eritrea and the Third Division serves in the Ogaden and Harar. There are about thirty-five infantry battalions, approximately nine in each division, and five artillery battalions, one in each division. There is also an airborne battalion and an armored battalion. Elements of the air force have seen action briefly in the Ogaden, and air force planes have been sent to the Congo on two occasions. The navy is actually a small coast guard whose chief function is to control smuggling.

Discipline, Morale, and Efficiency

In efficiency the air force, said to be on a par with that of Japan or Turkey, ranks far above the army, though the Bodyguard battalions rank with the best in tropical Africa. Recruitment, training, and promo-

---

37. David Wood, *The Armed Forces of the African States* (London: Institute for Strategic Studies, 1966), p. 21.

tion standards are higher in the air force than the army. Entrance into the air force requires at least a tenth-grade education; this is not true of the army where many men are still illiterate or semiliterate.

The army continues to suffer from lack of mobility and inadequate communication facilities, and maintenance remains a serious problem. The Ethiopians have traditionally depended upon the Italians, Greeks, and other Europeans to do everything mechanical for them. Vehicles, radios, and other equipment are frequently rendered inoperative by misuse and lack of care, such as the common failure to change oil in a truck. Some progress has been made by training mechanics, other technicians, and drivers. Again, the air force has made the greatest advances. In the workshops at Debra Zeit, jet engines are repaired and overhauled and maintenance equals that in the Moroccan and Greek air forces.

Among the enlisted men morale is generally good. Compared to village life or unskilled urban labor, the material and educational rewards of military life are attractive. There has been no dearth of recruits for the army, though in late 1969 the Emperor said he was studying a proposal for compulsory military service.[38] The development of discipline and followthrough in army ranks tends to be an uphill battle because the men are culturally conditioned not to act until an emergency and then to overreact. There are still far too many poorly trained, traditional "spear chuckers" in the army, said one observer. In recent years recruitment standards have risen somewhat and lifetime service has been replaced by a seven-year term that enables the army to screen out the less desirable men. A three-year period of service designed to tighten standards is under consideration.

Virtually all officers are respected members of the "new nobility," recipients of many material and social advantages. Morale is occasionally eroded by the arbitrary intervention of Haile Selassie in the selection, promotion, or transfer of officers. There is growing discipline in the officer corps, but in spite of considerable Western training, there persists a strong reluctance to exercise authority and take initiative, even at the higher levels. A friendly military observer once remarked that the Emperor was the only man in the country prepared to make a tough decision. The situation is improving, particularly in the air force.

38. *Washington Post*, Nov. 3, 1969.

Identity and Political Orientation

In important respects Ethiopia is more like Thailand and Iran than the newly independent states of tropical Africa, all of which are struggling for a cohesive political identity. The dominant Amhara-Tigre culture is proud and confident. As Haile Selassie has moved toward modernization he has not been confronted with the problem of Africanizing the civilian and military elite, but rather of Westernizing it. The Emperor's heavy dependence on foreign assistance since 1941 has been a kind of voluntary and selective embracing of Western tutelage similar to that in Iran and Thailand. Ironically, in all three countries the United States has because of circumstance taken the lead in providing assistance without domination.

Ethiopia has not been spared the problem, common to all tropical African states except Somalia, of detribalizing its officer corps. As of 1970 the Amhara and Tigre continued to dominate the officer corps, holding at least 75 percent of the positions, including virtually all the highest-ranking posts. This is not likely to change significantly in the near future because the Amhara-Tigre elite dominates the leadership in all sectors of Ethiopian life. It is not an insurmountable problem as long as the Galla and other tribes are prepared to accept the situation. Perhaps more important than quantitative tribal balancing is the Westernization of the elite to the point where competence, rather than kinship, becomes the basis for responsibility and leadership.

The increasing impact of Western training has not produced a homogeneous officer corps among the three services. Ethnic consciousness and identification play a significant role in informal relations. It is not accidental that all the chief plotters in 1960 were Amhara. The growing dedication to professionalism has increased efficiency but has not led to uniformity in political outlook. "Like the new nobility, the military officers do not form a cohesive group in common interests and ambitions,"[39] though they are probably more cohesive and uniform in their outlook than any of the civilian Westernized elites because their vocation is the security of the state and the political checks on them can be more effectively exercised. The air force officer corps is considerably more tightly knit than that of the army, because air officers are younger and better trained.

39. Levine, *Wax and Gold*, p. 190.

Available evidence suggests that the officers of the armed services are far more patriotic than conspiratorial. Most observers believe that the plot of a dozen high officers in 1960 was generated by a very unusual combination of circumstances not likely to reoccur, though the passing of the Emperor will provide an opportunity for any latent discontent or hidden ambitions in the officer corps to erupt into political maneuvering and even violence. It appears, however, that the great majority of military officers are loyal to the dynasty and the Emperor and that they would be strongly inclined to play a stabilizing role in the event of efforts to prevent a constitutional transition to a successor regime under the crown prince. The dynasty is by far the most powerful unifying force in the country, and the military establishment which has gained so much support, status, and prestige from the Emperor is not likely to turn against him or his legitimate successor. During the student disorders at Haile Selassie I University in 1968 and 1969, for example, Bodyguard units were brought in to restore and maintain order. In the December 1969 riot, three students were killed as the Bodyguard and police exchanged shots with the demonstrators. The ancient identity between military power and political authority remains strong, and in subtle and not-so-subtle ways the Emperor has reinforced this traditional bond.

Effect of Military on State-Building

The armed services have made a greater contribution to state-building in Ethiopia than they have in Ghana or the Congo, primarily because of the low level of educational, economic, and political development in this ancient land. As the most modernized institution in Ethiopian society, the military has had a direct and indirect impact on the economy and the political system. Assuming that the continuation of the dynasty is essential to unity and stability and that Haile Selassie has been an effective leader, the military services have contributed to the viability of the state by upholding the authority of the Emperor. The army and air force saved the Emperor in 1960 and they have helped contain the challenges in Eritrea and the Ogaden.

The Imperial Bodyguard contribution to the UN efforts in Korea and the Congo have helped build the state and develop a sense of national cohesion by earning international prestige for Ethiopia. The armed forces have also made a substantial contribution to economic and civic development, both essential to broadening the base of political participation. Hundreds of men have acquired new skills that are desperately needed in the civilian economy. The Flight School at Debra Zeit has trained pilots for Ethiopian Airlines. The literacy program within the armed services is significant in a country where only 5 percent of the population can read.

The armed forces are a school for citizenship where the enlisted man may for the first time identify himself with Ethiopia as a whole. Tribal affiliation, though still important, is downgraded in a conscious attempt to develop a sense of responsibility to the nation.

Prompted by American advisers, the air force has initiated a number of civic action projects which, if multiplied, could have a modernizing impact. By mid-1963, air force, army, and civilian volunteers had constructed 15 classrooms for 600 pupils.[40] In 1961 air force personnel and the agricultural experiment station at Debra Zeit undertook a community development project to "improve the standard of living" of the local population. They built four schools, established a craft and recreational center, and drilled six wells. Addis Ababa was provided $167,000 in U.S. military aid for civic action in 1964, $6,000 in 1965, and $5,000 in 1966.[41] The net impact of the armed forces, seen most clearly in the air force, has been toward political stability and gradual modernization.

The Ethiopian Police

Maintenance of law and order in a country with an ancient tradition of banditry and lawlessness is unusually difficult. The great majority of Ethiopians still live in small, remote villages or isolated patches of land devoted to grazing or primitive farming. The symbols of political authority and the instruments for enforcing order have seemed far away, except during times of conflict and violence. Tribal and regional rivalries have been a persistent source of turbulence. Civil police were not a part of traditional Abyssinian society and the problem of internal

40. Anthony J. Auletta, "Ten-Nation Progress Report," *Army* (July 1963), p. 56.
41. *Foreign Assistance Act of 1966*, Hearings before the House Committee on Foreign Relations, 89 Cong. 2 sess. (1966), p. 1040.

security was left to the provincial armies. For this reason plus the close bond between spear and scepter, the army has continued to exercise the primary role in maintaining order even since the statewide police were established.

The earliest police function was performed by the civilian municipal guard formed in 1916 by Emperor Eyasu to maintain law and order in Addis Ababa.[42] By 1935 the municipal guard was operating in the four other largest urban areas. Trained along modern lines by Europeans, the guardsmen were essentially local police accountable only to provincial leaders. Their duties included collecting taxes, escorting distinguished foreign visitors, and serving as bodyguards for local officials.

In 1942 following the Italian occupation, Haile Selassie established the Imperial Ethiopian Police within the Interior Ministry and designated a British officer as its chief commissioner. It was a statewide service organized into fifteen provincial commands, which in turn were divided into districts. Each district and provincial commander was responsible for the security of his area. The provincial police commissioner was accountable to the chief commissioner in Addis Ababa who was nominally responsible for all officers under him. The force was small, about 2,000 men, and poorly organized and equipped. Recruiting was haphazard and the men came largely from the ranks of the unemployed and illiterate. Irregular pay encouraged bribery or outright extortion, and policemen frequently had little knowledge of the laws they were called upon to enforce. Though responsible for training the recruits, provincial commissioners could do very little.

Commissioned officers were either promoted from the ranks or enrolled for advanced training without prior service. The officer candidate was supposed to have a secondary education or its equivalent. Training of officers was begun at Camp Kolfe on the outskirts of Addis Ababa in 1942.

In 1946 the Aba Dina Police Academy was established with the assistance of a group of Swedish police officers who remained as instructors until 1956. Israeli advisers began lecturing at the academy in 1959, and by 1965 the entire faculty was Ethiopian. The curriculum at Aba Dina, which could accommodate eighty cadets, included regular police duties, criminology, interrogation techniques, psychology, and

42. James Cramer, *The World's Police* (London: Cassell & Co., 1964), p. 286.

physical education. Those who simply passed the examination follow-ing the two-year course were commissioned as second lieutenants and those who passed with distinction could enter specialized schools for six months, after which they received a higher rank.[43]

As a rule Ethiopian policemen went unarmed, though nightsticks were used as protection. There were central weapons stores in the dis-tricts and provinces, and in case of special need the use of arms would be authorized. If the provincial police were unable to deal with a local crisis, the provincial governor general was empowered to call for mili-tary support, thus emphasizing the continuing reliance on the military for internal security.

In September 1956 Brigadier General Tsigue Dibou was appointed as police commissioner, the first Ethiopian to hold that post, and the re-maining British police officers became advisers. By 1960 the police had reached a strength of 23,000 men. Eritrea, after its federation with Ethiopia in 1952, maintained a separate police force of 3,000 men.

The Ethiopian police before the attempted coup in 1960—like their counterparts in pre-independence Ghana and the Congo—were largely nonpolitical and loyal to constituted authority. But there was a signifi-cant difference. It was one thing to serve a united and cohesive political authority like Britain or Belgium; it was quite another to serve in an ancient feudal country where authority at the center was often diluted by conflicting provincial loyalties. It was not so much that provincial police officers were disloyal to the Emperor, but rather that they served the semi-autonomous governor who had much more direct control over them than did the far-away commissioner in Addis Ababa. A serious question of dual loyalty arose only when the governor was operating at political cross-purposes with the Emperor.

The principal exception to this pattern of loyalty was Police Commis-sioner Tsigue Dibou, a favorite of the Emperor, who became one of the chief conspirators in the abortive 1960 coup.

After the 1960 Coup Attempt

The Ethiopian police system has changed very little since 1942, but the number of policemen had increased to about 31,000 by 1970. Though it is a centralized, statewide organization, the degree of provin-

43. Cramer, The World's Police, p. 287.

cial authority and initiative varies widely with circumstances. In Eritrea Governor General Ras Asrate Kassa, who is very close to the Emperor, has almost complete control over the operations of the police and the army. His considerable autonomy is likely to continue as long as the Emperor believes the Eritrean Liberation Front can best be dealt with by a strong and politically reliable governor general. Though the law-and-order mandate of the police embraces measures to counter actual or potential subversion and insurgency, like that in Eritrea and the Ogaden region, both the armed forces and the police are employed in dealing with these problems.

In recruitment, training, performance, and public esteem, the police fall substantially below the army. Since literacy is not a requirement for entering the force, 40 percent of the police are illiterate and the bulk of the others are poorly educated. Foreign advisers have recommended raising recruitment and training standards which would result in a smaller but more efficient force. Addis Ababa has taken some steps in this direction but there has been opposition at the middle command level to reducing numbers, perhaps deriving from the traditional Abyssinian view that the number of men commanded is a measure of power, just as the number of cattle owned is a measure of wealth.

By April 1968 the Aba Dina Police Academy, patterned on Western lines, had trained 980 cadets and other officers. In 1965 the two-year curriculum was replaced by a three-year course developed by U.S. advisers, and entrance requirements were raised. The first three-year class of 29 cadet officers was graduated in 1968 with a diploma from Haile Selassie I University. The curriculum emphasizes academic subjects over those of more practical application. Systematic refresher training for all officers and more practical police subjects are planned.

Recruit and in-service training for noncommissioned officers below the rank of sergeant is left to the provincial police chief and is frequently sporadic, ineffective, or nonexistent. Selected NCOs have been given in-service training in subjects such as riot control at the Emergency Force Training Center at Camp Kolfe. Some 120 NCOs were graduated from a five-month riot control course in November 1965. Between 1952 and 1962, some 370 NCOs were given training at Aba Dina Academy, designed to coach and select suitable men for promotion to officer rank. To improve the quality of NCOs the establishment of an NCO training school at Camp Kolfe has been recommended by the police commissioner.

In 1961 a new building was constructed for the Aba Dina Academy, and the U.S. public safety program provided $160,000 to equip it. In September 1965, however, the Emperor made the building available to the Organization of African Unity for its headquarters. This may have earned the Emperor prestige in Africa, but it has been a source of irritation among Ethiopian police and their foreign advisers. The academy has since been relocated in a complex of buildings formerly occupied by the army on the outskirts of Addis Ababa, and plans are under way for relocating it at Debra Zeit.

By 1965 only one Aba Dina graduate had advanced to the rank of colonel. The major commands therefore continue to be staffed by officers with little academic or formal police training. A sizable group of talented Aba Dina graduates is moving up the ladder and their influence is beginning to be felt.

Despite the raising of recruitment and training standards, the general efficiency of the force has not been significantly improved. It continues to be adversely affected by the exercise of arbitrary authority by both civilian and police officials, and personal preferences still play an important role in a largely traditional society where the line of command is often not clear, the rule of law is not deeply rooted, and the judicial system is slow and complex. Because police performance has been less than efficient, the army has continued as the chief instrument for maintaining internal order, at least in emergencies.

To improve police performance, and thereby relieve the army, a paramilitary Emergency Police Force was created in 1962 with an eventual target strength of 10,000 men. As of 1969 there were about 3,000 Emergency Police. Administered as part of the regular police service, this special branch is expected to deal with the more serious challenges, including roving bandits, political insurgents, and the illegal movement of goods and people across the frontier. It can also be used to help meet the initial thrust of an external attack.

Better trained and equipped than the regular police, the Emergency Police are supported by a statewide communications net, small infantry arms, and light armored vehicles. West Germany has provided communications gear and vehicles for the force. They have been more effective in coping with organized insurgency in Eritrea than the regular police. In counterinsurgency and other paramilitary operations, the Emergency Police have entered the traditional Ethiopian military sphere, necessitating joint planning between them and the army. Because of their superior equipment and more dramatic role, some of the ancient esteem accorded the warrior has rubbed off on them.

The small U.S. public safety program in Ethiopia, begun in 1957, had through fiscal 1969 cost slightly more than $3 million, approximately half for training Ethiopian officers and providing American advisers, and half for providing police equipment. Some 120 Ethiopian police have been trained in the United States. The U.S. public safety aid has helped establish a crime laboratory and has provided radio equipment and generators for the communications center. By 1965, some 65 trucks and 5 cars had been supplied. Fifty multipurpose vehicles were provided in 1966.

With U.S. assistance, the Ethiopian police set up a literacy program for NCOs and recruits and their dependents in 1964 and in early 1967 thé program was expanded to include members of the general public.

The number of U.S. public safety advisers in Addis Ababa has declined from an average of eight in the 1962–64 period to two in 1968 and to zero in 1969. In fiscal 1970 the entire program became the victim of austerity cutbacks in spite of strong support for it in Ethiopia and among knowledgeable U.S. officials who insisted that the elimination of the U.S. aid and advice would be a blow to the regular and Emergency Police whose increasing efficiency was beginning to enable it to relieve the army of some of its duties.

West Germany and Israel extended some police assistance during the 1960s and it appears that this aid will continue. Bonn has provided approximately $8 million in equipment together with training for its use. Since 1959 Israel has furnished training instructors and advisers, and about seventy Ethiopian police officers have been trained in Israel.

The civilian police in Ethiopia are still a new institution that has not yet fully demonstrated its effectiveness in fulfilling its basic law-and-order mandate. The creation of the Emergency Police has improved the morale and performance of the civil police. To the extent that the police have been effective in maintaining stability they, along with the army, have made a contribution to state-preservation.

Far less modernized and detribalized than the army, and especially the air force, the police have had little impact on the development of a more cohesive national consciousness.

CHAPTER FIVE

Spear and Scepter: The Three States Compared

*A large and efficiently equipped army constitutes an
alternative ruling elite to the politicians, and the army is as
much interested in stable government as any political party.
If the government is threatened with collapse through
maladministration of the politicians, the army cannot be expected
to endure the ensuing chaos passively. It is ready and eager
to step in and fill the vacuum.*

CHIEF H. O. DAVIES OF NIGERIA[1]

THE MULTIPLE INTERRELATIONS between spear and scepter in Ghana, the Congo, and Ethiopia can be understood only against the backdrop of tropical Africa's unique political situation. The behavior of the army and police is deeply affected by the fundamental political task of the central African states which is significantly different from that of the new states in contemporary Asia or in nineteenth century Latin America. In Asia after World War II, legal sovereignty was transferred from the European colonial powers to Asian political leaders, like Nehru, rooted in a rich cultural heritage of their own and also deeply influenced by the culture, institutions, and language of the West. In tropical Africa, the task of state-building fell upon indigenous leaders most of whose people were not far removed from an illiterate,

1. This prophetic statement was made in 1961 by H. O. Davies, *Nigeria: The Prospects for Democracy* (London: Weidenfeld and Nicolson, 1961), p. 76. Nigeria became independent on Oct. 1, 1960. It experienced two coups in 1966 and was torn by a bloody tribal-civil war from 1967 to early 1970.

tribal, iron-age culture. The influence of the West on these men had been more recent and superficial. The present African situation is also different from that in nineteenth century Latin American where sovereignty was transferred from the metropolitan power, not to a native elite in the new world, but to European men like Bolívar.

All tropical African states, with the notable exception of Somalia, are to a greater or lesser extent fragmented by tribalism which presents formidable obstacles to the creation of a cohesive national identity. The state-building task has been further complicated by the abrupt break with the colonial power and the fact that juridical independence was granted almost without a struggle. This massive decolonization occurred in the late 1950s and early 1960s, an era when the United States and the Soviet Union were competing actively for influence in the Third World, a factor that placed the new and inexperienced political elites in a special international bargaining position.

In spite of Ethiopia's unique history, the task of building a genuine nation state there is more like that of the newly independent states than it is different because Ethiopia too is ethnically fragmented and has had only a brief experience with statewide political and military institutions.

The basic threat to the territorial and political integrity of all the tropical African states is internal, though in several instances neighboring states have assisted insurgents by providing equipment, training, or sanctuary. Insurgents have also been assisted with weapons, training, or transportation by more distant powers, including militant African and Middle Eastern states, Soviet bloc states, and Communist China. No African state since 1960 has been subjected to a military invasion by a hostile extra-African power and the prospect of such invasion in the near future appears remote.

To deal with tribal discontent, insurgency, or secession—wholly indigenous or assisted and encouraged from outside—all African governments recognize their need for reliable and effective instruments of coercion. Since the armed forces and the civil police are confronted with essentially the same basic task of maintaining internal security, some confusion has arisen over their respective spheres of responsibility. In most countries the army as an institution is better understood and more widely respected than the police. Likewise, its function is more accepted than that of the police, for during the colonial period the metropolitan powers employed military or paramilitary forces to perform essentially internal security or police functions. The creation of civilian police in the American sense tended to be a late development of the colonial era, and in the case of Ethiopia it did not get under way until 1942. In the Congo and Ethiopia the police establishment, in contrast to the army, is a fledgling institution. In Ghana the police service, with its longer history, is more developed and better understood. In all three states, though to a lesser extent in Ghana, the police establishment and the men who serve in it have a professional and identity problem that the army does not have. The problem is further complicated because the police live and work among the people and interfere more in their daily lives to enforce a broad range of civil laws not directly related to physical security.

Even the few African states that are relatively strong at the center are characterized by the dearth of statewide political and economic institutions. The military and police establishments as instruments of the central government are statewide in authority and organization. In this situation a little coercion goes a long way. Even a small army or a well-organized police force is a "heavy institution" in a light environment. In most African states the army holds the balance of political power by its capacity to support the existing regime or by siding with an opposition group seeking to overthrow it. In a country where statewide loyalties are not deeply rooted and there are no substantial countervailing groups, a handful of military officers can tip the political balance.

The direction of military influence is determined by the political orientation and identity of the officer corps and changing political circumstances. On independence day most African armies were staffed with a majority of European officers, particularly in the higher ranks. They and the few African officers were schooled in the classic Western tradition of civilian supremacy and the nonpolitical army. British, French, and Belgian military training did not produce conspiratorial officers, though a very small number of junior African officers may have been influenced by communist agents. There was among African cadets trained at Sandhurst and St. Cyr a vague distrust of politicians similar to that found among Western officers who often contrast the bumbling politician and the efficient soldier.

The colonial armies in Africa, with rare and inconsequential exceptions, loyally upheld constituted authority. With the police they preserved law and order at home, and many soldiers fought for the metropolitan power abroad. The post-colonial African armies were not insurrectionist by tradition or experience. On independence day the officers of all tropical African armies were as loyal to the new regime as they had been to the colonial power.

Against this backdrop, the three preceding chapters have examined the actual character and role of the armed forces and police in Ghana, the Congo, and Ethiopia from 1960 until early 1970 to ascertain the impact of these instruments on political development. Political development is defined in this study as any change in the structure of government or the process of gaining and exercising political authority that enhances the government's capacity to provide security for its people and to enforce the law throughout its territory. Democratic political development is defined as change toward a more just and impartial exercise of power and toward a broader base of political participation.

The present chapter summarizes and compares the spear-scepter relationship in the three states under each of the seven areas of inquiry defined in Chapter 1. The response includes factual observations and judgments about the impact of military power upon political authority, including the effects of U.S. security assistance. Some of the conclusions and judgments suggest broader hypotheses that could be further tested by subjecting them to data on the role of the armed services and external military aid in other African states or in other areas of the Third World. The role of the police is dealt with separately at the end of the chapter.

Maintaining the State

The armed forces of Ghana and Ethiopia have performed well their basic security task of defending the state. Ghana has not, however, faced any serious internal or external military challenge. Ethiopia, on the other hand, has confronted and controlled Eritrean insurgents and Somali irredentists, both of whom were externally supported. The terrorists activities of the Eritrean Liberation Front remain a serious but apparently manageable security problem as of mid-1970.

In the Congo the story has been profoundly different. After the Congolese National Army (ANC) was stripped of its Belgian officers by

Lumumba it became hopelessly fragmented, many of its units supporting lawlessness, secession, and insurrection. For four years it was in effect replaced by the United Nations Force. General Mobutu during those years started to develop the nucleus of a statewide army, building on a few battalions in the Leopoldville area loyal to him and responsive to his command. By 1967 the Mobutu ANC approximated a Congowide army. As of early 1970 the ANC had not achieved the discipline and effectiveness of the Ghanaian and Ethiopian forces, but its command was being strengthened by the influx of Belgian-trained junior officers. Given the extenuating circumstances, the gradually strengthened Mobutu ANC on balance has made a modest contribution to security and political stability.

As a vivid and tangible symbol of the state, an army also helps to secure the political order. The late President Sylvanus Olympio of Togo said, "We cannot be an independent nation without an army of some sort," and President Hamani Diori of Niger called his army "the visible sign of our political independence" in "the eyes of the world" and of "all our people."[2] In many African countries the army is the most virile symbol of the state, especially if it has successfully met challenges to central authority. Its traditional role and its continuity with the past make it a potent source of pride in an emerging state, but its symbolic value can quickly erode if it becomes identified with a discredited regime or with any unpopular cause.

The prestige of the army is enhanced if it has fought in the war of independence or if its troops have served abroad. Ghanaian and Congolese soldiers were not involved in a struggle for independence, but the former earned respect at home and abroad for effective noncombat service in the Congo under the UN flag. Ethiopia gained even more prestige because its larger contingents in Korea and the Congo saw combat and performed well.

The Ghanaian Army won acclaim when it, in cooperation with the police, overthrew the increasingly unpopular Nkrumah. In Ethiopia the army and air force gained stature when they put down the coup against the Emperor in 1960. In sum, the Ghanaian and Ethiopian armed forces since 1960 have been a major source of engendering pride in the state.

---

2. Both quotations are in M. J. V. Bell, "The Military in the New States of Africa," in Jacques Van Doorn (ed.), *Armed Forces and Society* (The Hague: Mouton, 1968), p. 267.

The Mobutu ANC also performed a pride-giving role, though in the early 1960s its influence was limited to the Leopoldville area. In those days, Mobutu's colorful paratroop units were a special focus of identity and self-esteem in the midst of political chaos and in the presence of what was regarded as an intrusive UN occupation army.[3]

The generally positive impact of the three armed services upon the security of and pride in the state suggests that the military establishment makes its primary contribution to political stability and development by defending the integrity of the state against internal and external challenges and a secondary contribution by engendering among citizens a sense of identity with and loyalty to his political community.

Building a Nation

The distinction between a citizen's identification with his state and government on the one hand and his identification with a people or nation coextensive with the state on the other is important. The development of a people with a common historical memory is a slow, organic process stretching over generations. A state can be established instantly by fiat, though it may never become a viable state. The creation of a nation—the movement from parochial loyalties to a larger identity—is the result of many forces, such as race, religion, education, literacy, contact with the larger world, and the experience of struggle and conflict. Material resources, indigenous and imported, may or may not bear positively upon the process of developing national cohesion.

Citizenship is an arbitrary fact of birth or of the transfer of sovereignty; national identity is an acquired attitude. The two rarely coincide in tropical Africa. An Eritrean Moslem, though a citizen of Ethiopia, may consider most other Ethiopians (particularly the ruling Amharas) foreigners, if not oppressors. Many residents of Katanga, and other parts of the Congo for that matter, have regarded the central government as an alien authority, though they all share Congolese citizenship.

3. At the requiem mass for President Kennedy in Leopoldville in 1963, the paratroopers dressed in powder-blue uniforms stood at attention along the central aisle of the church during the entire service. When they marched to and from the church to martial music, it seemed that the Congolese spectators were more immediately impressed by this spit-and-polish unit, and perhaps its commander, than by President Kasavubu, Prime Minister Adoula, or the Congolese flag.

In confronting tribalism—the basic barrier to national identity—the army has generally played a constructive role in Africa, though occasionally military personnel or units have had the opposite effect. The army has made a positive contribution two ways. First, as noted above, the army is a visible symbol of the whole state, transcending tribe or section. Second, the army as the most detribalized and most modernized institution in the state is a living, if imperfect, example of one nation. An ideal national army, detribalized from the top command to the lowest level, has not yet been achieved in tropical Africa because of traditional and linguistic diversity.

The extent of military detribalization is obscured by an unusual degree of pride, prejudice, and defensiveness. Evidence suggests that the Ghanaian armed forces have achieved a modest degree of detribalization which is expressed in the Westernization of the officer corps as well as tribal balance in the command structure and in the ranks. Any statistical tribal imbalance results largely from application of objective recruiting standards. In the Congo the Belgian Force Publique was effectively detribalized down to the company level. A genuine national army is a prime Mobutu objective, but this is difficult because of the Congo's vastness and the recent history of fragmentation and conflict. All new recruits for the ANC at the Kitona training center are integrated, but thus far only a small percentage have come from the eastern area. To mitigate tribal influence, Mobutu has moved officers and tribally homogeneous units to alien areas.

Of the three countries, perhaps Ethiopia has the longest way to go before achieving fully detribalized armed forces at all levels, though the Emperor, as a proud Amhara, has actively pursued ethnic policies designed to avoid the formation of tribal cliques or units that could present a disruptive political challenge. The Amhara and the ethnically related Tigre are more advanced and hold at least 75 percent of the officer positions. There is greater statistical tribal balance in the ranks, though there are large tribally homogeneous units. This had presented something of a problem in the Ogaden region where Galla troops have shown some sympathy for Somali-speaking irredentists whom they regard as "cousins."

Detribalization in the fundamental sense involves the development of a broader worldview and set of loyalties in place of the narrower, ethnocentric habits, attitudes, and thought forms. Only a tiny fraction of tropical Africans have met this standard. In the meantime, the armed forces are mitigating the more disruptive aspects of tribalism within the military establishment by statistical balance, integration of certain units, transtribal deployment, and selection and promotion based on competence rather than kinship.

In all three states the army has become a kind of super-tribe in a state that is attempting to establish supra-tribal or national identity for its pluralistic population. When men and officers leave the armed services they take with them a more developed sense of national consciousness and pride than ordinary civilians because of their experience in a state-wide community of command and obedience that strongly emphasizes the meaning of citizenship and patriotism. Because of their symbolic and educational value as an all-state, largely detribalized, and highly visible institution, the three armies have made a positive if unquantifiable contribution to national identity and loyalty.

The armed forces can make a modest contribution to strengthening the statewide economy, and to the extent that this stimulates a greater sense of national identity, the military deserve the credit. Economic factors tend to be neutral politically, but when the larger political forces are moving toward national unity, economic development reinforces this trend because it involves the unifying disciplines of communication and transportation. Economic modernization and technology are divisive if they are used by forces challenging the state government by secession or civil war. Biafra and Katanga are examples of the use of economic skills and resources to support and even enflame provincial and tribal loyalties.

In Ghana, the Congo, and Ethiopia the armed services have contributed to economic modernization by their example of what is technically possible when resources are rationally marshaled to achieve specific statewide objectives. While this technical competence and efficiency cannot be easily duplicated in the less disciplined civilian sector, the military establishment remains an organization to emulate. The larger and better equipped forces, such as those in the Congo and Ethiopia, have an extensive communications network as well as military aircraft. This sophisticated equipment requires an infrastructure that can aid the civilian economy, though it may draw away scarce resources from pressing civilian needs.

In a more direct way, the three armies have made a modest contribution to modernization through their extensive training and educational programs. The wide range of skills from flying planes to bookkeeping has enlarged the pool of skilled manpower from which the civilian economy can draw. In Ghana and Ethiopia the administrative experience of retired military officers is in great demand. Short-term enlisted men and NCOs take their new skills back to the civilian sector. Literacy and other courses for military men and their families have helped to raise the educational level.

Civic action projects by the armed forces—ranging from literacy programs and medical care to road building and well digging—can make a positive if marginal contribution to modernization and development of a national consciousness. According to the official U.S. view, civic action should be undertaken to advance economic and social development and improve relations between the army and population, and thus enhance security and forestall or blunt insurgency. Civic action can obviously have a constructive effect in areas where there is no threat of insurgency. The largely token programs in Ghana, the Congo, and Ethiopia, in the latter two cases encouraged and aided by the United States, have had some small psychological impact on modernization, and in Ethiopia the programs have improved military-community relations in a few localities.

Civic action programs present military, economic, and political problems. Since an army's basic mission is to defend the state, it should engage in no activity—military or civilian—that detracts from this task. In an era of infiltration, subversion, and insurgency, the line between military and civil responsibility is blurred and the proper jurisdiction of military, police, and civilian agencies is constantly being reassessed. Circumstances vary widely, as must ways of meeting them, but certain considerations affect every situation. On the economic side, a soldier probably costs from three to five times as much as a civilian to do the same job because of the considerable military overhead. Compare, for example, the per capita cost of a civilian laborer or engineer with that of his military counterpart. The real cost of military civilian work, of course, is somewhat reduced if it can be demonstrated that the soldiers are otherwise underemployed which is often the case in Africa where external threats are rare. In these circumstances, civic action projects can simultaneously keep idle soldiers out of trouble and accomplish socially constructive work. In many if not most cases, the best way to deal with redundant military manpower is to cut down the size of the army and utilize the resources saved to employ qualified civilians.

It can be argued and with some plausibility that in many less developed countries the only institution that can efficiently accomplish anything is the army, precisely because obedience and discipline are a part of the system. Thus the army should build bridges and roads. But there are other alternatives. The government can draft civilian manpower or create paramilitary organizations to perform essential public tasks. Again, the answer depends upon the situation.

In political terms, close relations between the army and the civilian population are not always an unmixed blessing. There are serious possible pitfalls of civic action:

> [The] dilution of the military's security role involves risks ... deep involvement by an army in such non-military matters can also lead to corruption and inefficiency. Foreign advisers who stress the importance of the military's role in nation-building may inadvertently be encouraging the army to judge its record—and its hopes—against that of a lackluster regime. Conversely, such programs may draw important resources away from the nation's security position in the face of possible threats, and thereby encourage the armed forces to take matters into their own hands.[4]

Recognizing the limits of the military as a modernizing force, the three armed services have had a small but positive impact on education and the economy, thus making a small contribution to a more viable state and a more cohesive nation.

Their accomplishments suggest that as the most modern and detribalized institution in an underdeveloped country, the armed services when performing their security function well can contribute significantly to the organic process of developing national identity and cohesion. Moreover, they can aid economic modernization by example, by transmitting valuable skills, by stimulating the growth of a communication and transportation infrastructure, and under appropriate circumstances by engaging in civic action projects, thus making a modest contribution to nation-building.

Upholding the Regime

On independence day the armies in Ghana and the Congo had every intention of upholding the new government. In Ethiopia the armed forces since the liberation in 1941 have had a tradition of loyalty to the

---

4. Fred Greene, "Toward Understanding Military Coups," *Africa Report* (February 1966), pp. 11 and 14.

Emperor that held even during the attempted coup in 1960 and has continued to the present. In all three states the principles of civilian supremacy and the instrumental role of military power have been built into the constitutional system. In 1960 each had a defense ministry with a civilian head. President Nkrumah was commander-in-chief of the armed forces. In the Congo the prime minister was also the defense minister. And in Ethiopia the Emperor was, and has remained, commander-in-chief. In each country military expenditures were subject to parliamentary approval, though the effectiveness of this formal check on executive authority varied greatly. Nkrumah and the Emperor have had an extraordinary degree of control over all aspects of the armed forces, including the budget and the appointment, transfer, and retirement of officers. Both men sometimes breached normal government and military channels of decision in order to maintain effective political control over the armed forces. They and Mobutu as president created or encouraged countervailing forces within or outside the army as a safeguard against army disaffection or disloyalty. The man who held the scepter and the man who wielded the spear always viewed each other with a measure of anxiety and suspicion, except when they were one and the same man. In several cases the spear intervened in the political arena. This confusion between spear and scepter is to be expected in states with weak governments, a fragile tradition of civilian supremacy, and the centrifugal pressures of tribal, regional, or religious diversity.

In Ghana the army supported the government for the first nine years, though with growing reservations within the officer corps. Military officers never intruded unconstitutionally into the political arena, but the ranking commanders expressed their views vigorously on military questions and informally and cautiously on related political matters. Military advice was freely given on questions such as Ghana's contingent in the Congo and Nkrumah's abortive efforts to establish an African high command in Accra. As suspicion grew between Nkrumah and the army, the president saw in the army a threat to his political ambitions and took measures to neutralize its influence—building up the President's Own Guard Regiment as a counterweight, expelling British officers, and stimulating and exploiting rivalries among the military services. Nkrumah's fear of the army may have served as a slight brake on his efforts to consolidate all elements of Ghanaian society under his arbitrary rule, but at no point was there an overt and organized military effort to intervene until the 1966 army-police coup. Both during the National Liberation Council (NLC) period and under the subsequent civilian regime of Prime Minister Busia, the armed forces have loyally supported their government, with the exception of a small, poorly planned, nonpolitical, and abortive coup against the NLC in 1967.

In the Congo, military-political relations at the top were more complex because of the turbulence dramatized by UN intervention and the succession of five different regimes before Mobutu took over in 1965. As chief of staff in 1960, Mobutu at first supported Prime Minister Lumumba, but in September Mobutu "neutralized" him and initiated the five-month Council of Commissioners, all the while upholding President Kasavubu as chief of state. Mobutu as ANC commander stoutly defended the central government within the limits of its capacities, including the regimes of Prime Ministers Ileo, Adoula, and Tshombe, until November 1965. The non-Mobutu fragments of the ANC joined with political and tribal forces seeking to secede from or replace the central government. Eventually these fragments were eliminated or incorporated into the emerging statewide ANC.

Since independence day Mobutu has been the most influential military figure in the Congo, and for most of the time a powerful political figure as well. This close connection between spear and scepter, and their nearly complete identity since 1965, was almost inevitable because of the government's overriding preoccupation with efforts to achieve unity and internal security and the serious vacuum of civilian political organization and talent in the Congo. From the outset Mobutu acted as a balancer, pacifier, and umpire; when he took over as president, he emerged with a firm and unchallenged grasp on both spear and scepter.

In contrast to the Congo, the Ethiopian story is simple. Since the abortive coup of 1960 the armed forces have been consistently loyal to the Emperor though there have been occasional unconfirmed rumors of military plotting. Because key officers of his Imperial Bodyguard had sought to dethrone him, the Emperor completely reorganized this elite force and conferred added status on the regular army and air force which had smashed the insurgents. The close historic identity between political authority and military power in Abyssinian culture seems not only to have survived the events of 1960, but actually to have been strengthened in subtle ways. The military still does not intrude into the political arena, but the Emperor constantly intervenes in military affairs to insure his nearly absolute control. In a very real sense, he too holds both spear and scepter.

As of mid-1970 the armed services of Ethiopia are loyally upholding the regime of a traditional, autocratic, but modernizing emperor; the military of Ghana are supporting a freely elected, democratic, civilian government; and the Congolese Army is loyal to the military-civilian regime of a progressive general-president. Since each of these varied regimes enjoys the consent of the politically significant segments of the population and each is encouraging political and economic development, military support constitutes a constructive contribution to state-building. This suggests that the armed services can make their most effective contribution to political stability and development by upholding a responsible regime.

Replacing the Regime

The three successful and two abortive coups discussed in this study are evaluated below in terms of the four types of coups, defined in Chapter 1. These four pure-type coups, briefly summarized here, can be categorized by the fundamental motivation of the plotters, but in the real world the extraordinary intervention of the military in the political sphere is usually the product of multiple motivation.

The security coup is undertaken to replace a regime incapable of defending the state from internal or external challenges. Its chief object is order and security.

The reform coup is prompted by the desire to change the character or policies of the existing regime. It seeks to eliminate corruption or to initiate new domestic or foreign policies.

The new elite coup is little concerned with security or policy and is motivated primarily by ambitious men who seek power.

The punitive coup is motivated by real or pretended grievances in the military establishment against the regime and is not concerned with either security or policy. It is more concerned with punishment than with power.

It is abundantly clear that the army-police intervention of February 24, 1966, in Ghana was essentially a *reform coup* with security implications. It was undertaken by men who sought to replace temporarily the corrupt and arbitrary Nkrumah regime whose domestic and foreign policies had brought bankruptcy at home and alienation from Ghana's former friends abroad. The plotters profoundly resented Nkrumah's turning to Russia and Red China for military and intelligence advisers, his efforts to neutralize the army, and his use of the police as an instrument of arbitrary political control. Though the army was suffering status deprivation, this was not a punitive coup or a simple grab for power. With one minor exception the members of the National Liberation Council did not enrich themselves personally, and they relinquished power peaceably and on schedule to a constitutional successor regime.

The abortive countercoup against the NLC on April 17, 1967, led by a disgruntled lieutenant, was more a personal, *punitive coup* than anything else. While it had little political significance, it did point up certain glaring weaknesses in the NLC's military and other security arrangements.

The Congo experienced two Mobutu coups. The first intervention on September 14, 1960, was almost a textbook example of a *security coup*. The government was paralyzed by a power struggle between Kasavubu and Lumumba, each of whom had dismissed the other, and political chaos was being exploited by the Soviet Union. In a bloodless intervention, Mobutu acted to "neutralize" the "governments" of Lumumba and of Joseph Ileo who had been appointed by Kasavubu to replace Lumumba. On the same day Mobutu expelled the Soviet and Czech embassies and created his Council of Commissioners, a temporary ruling group recognized by Kasavubu. Mobutu assumed the position of ANC commander-in-chief and became de facto head of government. He relinquished power peaceably to Ileo on February 9, 1961. In this critical period of slightly less than five months Mobutu succeeded in stabilizing the central government in the face of the rival Gizenga faction in Stanleyville which had external communist support.

Five years later, on November 25, 1965, General Mobutu intervened a second time to "save the nation" and "put an end to chaos and anarchy" resulting from the political stalemate caused by the conflict between Prime Minister Tshombe and President Kasavubu. Proclaiming himself president for five years, he assumed the defense portfolio and established an essentially civilian regime. This bloodless takeover was a combination *security-reform coup*. Mobutu was fed up with chaos and indecision and was displeased by some of Tshombe's economic and foreign policies.

The abortive effort to oust Emperor Haile Selassie in December 1960 appears to have been an essentially *new elite coup*, although it was amply adorned with the rhetoric of a reform coup. Evidence suggests that the chief plotters sought to replace Haile Selassie and his inner circle and used Prince Asfa Wossen as a reluctant puppet to legitimize their effort. They spoke of ending "three thousand years" of oppression, poverty, and ignorance and of initiating modernizing reforms, but they had no realistic alternative policies. The poorly planned coup failed because the insurgents underestimated the loyalty of the regular army and air force and the power of the clergy. Had the self-proclaimed "revolutionary" coup succeeded, it might well have unleashed forces of chaos and internal conflict that would have betrayed its high-sounding goals and weakened the state to the point where Egypt or other regional powers would have been tempted to intervene. Thus the crushing of this coup by the regular army and air force was a solid contribution to Ethiopian stability and political continuity, necessary but not sufficient prerequisites for constructive political development.

The 1966 Ghana military-police coup appears to have been the least costly way of ending political and economic deterioration, creating an interim regime capable of pursuing sound domestic and foreign policies, and paving the way for the restoration of a responsible civilian government based generally on the constitutional foundation bequeathed by the British. Even a temporary success of the 1967 countercoup would have slowed up the restoration process. In short, military intervention in Ghana in 1966, like the Mobutu coups in the Congo in 1960 and 1965, helped to correct a politically dangerous antecedent condition and to establish a minimal degree of stability essential to positive political change.

External communist involvement was a factor in both the Ghana coup and the two Mobutu coups. Soviet and Chinese military officers and advisers serving in Ghana at the request of Nkrumah were a major reason for the disaffection among army and police officers. The 1960 Kasavubu-Lumumba conflict was exacerbated by Soviet political and military support for Lumumba. In the second Mobutu coup, Kasavubu's alleged willingness to make a deal with the rebels, who enjoyed the political support and some material assistance from the Soviet bloc and Red China, and the incapacity of the central government to deal with the rebels, were primary factors in prompting Mobutu to act. Direct communist involvement was not a factor in the abortive Ethiopian coup in 1960, though the plotters may have been partly inspired by the example of President Nasser's militant reform regime in nearby Egypt. The authors of the successful coups in Ghana and the Congo and the finishers of the attempted coup in Ethiopia were all motivated to some extent by a belief that internal weakness was being or would be exploited by communist states or their militant allies.

The experience of Ghana and the Congo with military intervention has some general predictive value for tropical Africa and other areas in the Third World. The classic recipe for a security or reform coup includes four principal ingredients: a weak, floundering regime riddled by corruption; the absence of a legitimate political alternative capable of assuming power and exercising authority; increasing disaffection among significant elites with the domestic or foreign policies of the regime; and the presence of a military elite able and willing to intervene.

These and related conditions have already asserted themselves in a half dozen African states and are likely to do so for the next decade or two. The coup propensity in African states is further strengthened by the recognition in military and civilian leadership circles that political power is the one almost certain path to wealth and status, at least temporarily, and that a successful military coup is the quickest and cheapest way to achieve political power. This road to the top in a weak and relatively noncompetitive society requires little in the way of leadership or political expertise other than the capacity to connive effectively. Plotters motivated solely by personal ambition are capable of executing only a new elite coup which at best will not harm the state. The first coup in Sierra Leone was apparently one of this kind.[5]

Whether the net impact of unconstitutional military intervention on political development is positive or negative can be determined only by assessing the situation in the light of all viable alternatives for dealing with the problems the coup was designed to correct. Of the coups undertaken to deal with chaos or other real problems, some will have largely constructive results like those in Ghana and the Congo. Others will simply hold on the lid temporarily or even exacerbate the antecedent conditions.

Some writers have sought to establish a relation between military coups and such tangible factors as the size of the army, the size of the

5. See William L. Bishop, *Three West African Nations: A Comparative Study* (New York: American-African Affairs Association, 1969), pp. 14–18.

military budget, or the amount of foreign military assistance. No such relationship has been established in the African experience or elsewhere because the fundamental causes of coups are political and psychological, not technical or economic. A political vacuum or chaos invites intervention and under certain circumstances, which are not quantifiable or wholly predictable, the army is the most likely candidate to fill the void.[6]

This suggests that when an existing regime is too weak, corrupt, or arbitrary to govern and no legitimate political agency is capable of taking over, effective military intervention to arrest chaos or disintegration or to prevent external intervention can facilitate constructive political development.

Domestic Policies

If moderate domestic policies are those instructed by a pragmatic and experimental approach as opposed to an ideological approach, the net impact of the military establishments in Ghana, the Congo, and Ethiopia has been to reinforce the internal forces working toward moderate programs. This was true of the African experience because the armies contributed to internal stability, a condition that enhances the prospects for the moderates, just as instability tends to play into the hands of the more extreme elements. Both Washington and the communist governments have recognized this relationship between stability and moderation and have shaped their policies accordingly. An army that helps maintain stability in a state permitting political competition tips the scales in favor of moderate economic and political policies over militant ones.

6. Henry Bienen concludes that no correlation can be established between coup propensity in Africa and the size of the army, defense budget, or the source, character, or amount of external military aid. Henry Bienen, "Foreign Policy, the Military and Development: Military Assistance and Political Change in Africa," in Richard Butwell (ed.), *Foreign Policy and the Developing Nation* (University of Kentucky Press, 1969), pp. 91–92. The studies of Charles Wolf, Jr., lead to a similar conclusion for Latin America. He says there is no positive correlation between the character or direction of the government of a Latin American state and the size of the military budget, per capita defense spending, or the quantity of U.S. military assistance. See Wolf, *United States Policy and the Third World: Problems and Analysis* (Little, Brown, 1967), pp. 90–109. See also Joseph E. Loftus, *Latin American Defense Expenditures: 1938–1965* (RAND Corporation, 1968).

In addition to this indirect effect of its security role, the army has a direct influence on the regime's significant domestic decisions. In Ghana, the Congo, and Ethiopia the top military officers have been and are active members of the leadership elite. As spokesmen for a powerful pressure group that commands a substantial portion of the state budget, their views are taken seriously in the highest councils of government, principally on security questions, but also on nonsecurity matters. Since the military establishment competes with other programs for scarce material resources and human talent, it is fair to assume that in the confidential negotiations of any regime the military officers will emphasize the importance of the security services. Furthermore, they can insist with some persuasiveness that security is or should be the preeminent responsibility of the government and that there is a security angle to virtually every important domestic problem.

Third World armies are frequently alleged to receive a disproportionately high share of scarce state resources to the detriment of economic development. This allegation can only be sustained if it can be shown that the armed forces are larger than necessary, that they have expensive equipment they do not require, or that the officers and soldiers are receiving costly unessential material benefits. The size of the army is a political decision that takes into account the range of security threats, economic resources, and prestige factors. On all these points the officer corps presents its views. There is no evidence that in Ghana, the Congo, or Ethiopia military pressure has been the most significant, much less the decisive factor in determining the size of the armed forces.

Essentially the same interplay of forces determines the type of equipment sought for the armed forces. To maintain high morale and loyalty in the services, military men may need more psychic and material fringe benefits than civil servants. Evidence suggests that most of the pressures for a high level of material support of the armed forces in Ghana, the Congo, and Ethiopia have come from the top political leaders who recognize that a satisfied army is as essential to their continued political control as it is to state security.

Competent outside observers conclude that each of the armed forces as of early 1970 could be reduced in size without impairing security if recruitment standards and training were improved, particularly in the Congo and Ethiopia. The net result would be more efficient and ready forces, probably at slightly less cost. Whether the marginal savings would be plowed into economic development is problematic, since there is rarely a simple transfer of resources from one area in a state budget to another.

There is no evidence that Ghana's NLC or the Mobutu regime was more generous with the armed forces than a civilian regime would have been. In neither case was there a significant change in the defense budget after the coup, nor did either regime exhibit a greater disposition to acquire sophisticated "prestige" weapons and equipment than its predecessor. If anything, these partially military regimes seem to have had a more matter-of-fact and professional view of the military as an instrument of state security than did the former governments.

In confronting the economic problem, the most pressing nonsecurity issue in most African states, the regime must make a choice between two general approaches—"African socialism," to use one of Nkrumah's favorite slogans, or the more pragmatic, problem-solving approach that emphasizes the role of the market. Many African politicians trained at the London School of Economics and other institutions in Britain and France have been indoctrinated with a moderate, democratic version of Marxism that emphasizes state ownership and distrusts private investment. Some have been influenced by the undemocratic, non-market models of the Soviet Union and Red China. Many of the younger African university graduates who have been influenced by Keynesian economics have embraced the pragmatic approach. This more flexible approach is favored by all the Western states that provide economic and military assistance, just as state socialism is advocated by communist governments.

Most African politicians pursue an approach that combines socialist and pragmatic elements, the more militant ones leaning toward Karl Marx and the more moderate ones leaning toward Lord Keynes. These two perspectives bear upon the fundamental question of what kind of economy the state should have and on a series of smaller decisions about specific economic problems and projects. In debating these decisions the military officers of Ghana, the Congo, and Ethiopia have clearly supported the pragmatic approach. European and American trained officers tend to have a problem-solving approach that respects practical expertise, suspects abstract theory and political dogma, and focuses on getting the job done efficiently. Politically they are moderate, rejecting the extremes of left and right. It is not possible to measure the extent of military influence in economic decisions, because there have always been other forces pushing in the same direction, but under the inexorable pressure of economic facts, most African politicians have moved away from a vague socialist stance toward a more flexible and realistic approach.

The military emphasis on expertise, on getting the facts (intelligence), and on promoting men on the basis of training and experience—virtues found in varying degrees in different African states—may have had a moderating and constructive effect on the process of Africanization in the economy and the administration. Except for the bizarre case of Lumumba's instant Africanization of the Congo officer corps in 1960, replacements for European officers in the new states have been made gradually and largely on merit. This policy was followed in Ghana for the first four years. Elsewhere expatriate officers in advisory and command positions continued to play a significant role in the early years of independence. As of early 1967 there were "more than 550 British officers and NCOs in Africa on secondment or in training teams."[7] In 1969, for example, Zambia announced that former British officers would continue to be employed under individual contract.[8] In Ethiopia, U.S. Army and Air Force officers have played a key advisory role.

Continued employment of foreign officers by some African political leaders is not solely professionally motivated. Several heads of government have good reason to believe that a military coup against them is less likely if reliable British or French officers remain in key command or advisory posts. They know that Western Europeans are schooled in the nonpolitical tradition, but they are less sure of their own African officers. Perhaps Nkrumah would still be in power if he had not suddenly dismissed his British officers in September 1961. Be that as it may, gradual Africanization in the military has served as a constructive example for the economy and the administration which are sometimes subjected to strong political pressures, particularly from opponents of the regime, to speed up the process regardless of its effect on efficiency, productivity, or morale.

In assessing the impact of the three armies on domestic policies, it should be noted that all the civilian and military regimes have been committed to modernization and economic development. As Nkrumah

7. Bell, "The Military in the New States of Africa," p. 265.
8. *New York Times*, Jan. 19, 1969.

increasingly adopted more militant and doctrinaire policies, including the launching of large "state enterprises" and the placing of severe restrictions on basic civil and political rights, his armed forces had at most only a slightly inhibiting effect. After the 1966 coup the politically pragmatic army-police regime dismantled unproductive government enterprises, encouraged private investment, effected fiscal and monetary reforms, and restored a substantial measure of civil rights.

The little influence that the Mobutu ANC had on domestic economic and political decisions during the first years of the Congo's independence was in the moderate direction. As the key military figure, General Mobutu has been essentially a moderate in domestic and foreign matters, although during his first several years as president he employed some militant rhetoric primarily to gain the support of the more militant African leaders. More than any other man in the Congo, Mobutu opposed all extremists, notably the communist-backed rebels, with all the resources at his command. Mobutu's distinction between local grievances and militant, leftist demands in the student demonstration of June 1969 at Lovanium University illustrates his moderate orientation.

Emperor Haile Selassie has been a consistent moderate in domestic policy, highly pragmatic and nondoctrinaire. He has welcomed foreign assistance and private capital and in this he has had the full support of the armed forces. In all three states the net impact of the military has been to lend support to the moderate approach toward domestic economic and political problems. This suggests that by performing their security function well, and thus enhancing political stability, the armed services tend to strengthen those forces inside and outside the government that support moderate as opposed to militant domestic policies. Moderate tendencies are further reinforced if the military establishment is Western-oriented and has a pragmatic nonideological approach to problem solving.

Foreign Policy

The moderating influence of the armed forces of Ghana, the Congo, and Ethiopia has been even more pronounced in foreign policy. All three states are officially neutral with respect to big-power alignments and all are members of the Organization of African Unity. Their chief foreign policy goals, like those of neighboring states, are to prevent invasion, curb externally directed subversion, and secure as much material and diplomatic assistance from the industrial powers as possible consistent with their political independence. Since none is capable of countering a serious military challenge from a medium power, survival is largely a function of an external balance of forces, and foreign policy the principal instrument of national defense. When the Congo was threatened, it was protected from chaos and subversion primarily by U.S. military assistance, first through the UN expeditionary force dispatched largely in U.S. Air Force planes, and later through bilateral aid from Washington and Brussels.

The African armed forces play a multiple role in national defense and foreign policy. As an instrument of state policy, the army is a factor in the military equation of the area and thus contributes to or detracts from the larger balance of power which is the chief guarantee of each state's security. The army also has a major influence on the direction of foreign policy, primarily because of its dependence on external assistance. The army "may be the symbol and guarantor of national independence," but by "its very existence" it "increases its government's dependence on the outside world."[9]

All African armies north of the Zambezi, including those of Egypt and Algeria, are largely dependent upon the industrial states for weapons, equipment, and a continuing flow of spare parts. The tropical states are also dependent on outside officer training and advice, and most are still closely tied to the former colonial power for this assistance. Since military dependence upon one patron may imply excessive political dependence, some states have sought to reduce the risk by securing arms and associated training from one or two additional sources. Relying on multiple patrons may spread the political liability, but unless the aid is carefully planned it will also spread confusion by introducing incompatible arms and equipment, if not military doctrine and procedures.

For practical and political reasons Ghana, the Congo, and Ethiopia have all turned to several states for military aid and training. The Ghana Army is still an essentially British-type system in spite of some

9. William J. Foltz, "Military Influences," in Vernon McKay (ed.), *African Diplomacy: Studies in the Determinants of Foreign Policy* (Praeger, 1966), p. 79.

Russian aid and training in the latter Nkrumah years. When Nkrumah expelled his British officers and advisers, he turned to Canada and other Commonwealth countries for advisory aid. The growing tension between Ghana's Sandhurst-trained officer corps and a Nkrumah regime moving closer to the Russian and Chinese orbit contributed significantly to the 1966 coup.

Since shortly before the end of the UN period, the Congo has relied principally on Belgium for military training and advice and on the United States for aircraft, trucks, and communications equipment. The political objectives of these donor governments have been compatible with those of the Congolese regime and no serious differences have developed between donor and recipient or between the army and the government on foreign policy questions.

Since 1960 Emperor Haile Selassie has been primarily dependent upon Washington for military training and equipment. Sweden, Norway, France, India, and Israel also have provided a modest amount of training and advisory assistance. Aid from these varied but politically compatible sources has helped to blunt criticism, chiefly from militant states, charging that Ethiopia is a "puppet" of Washington because of the Kagnew Station agreement.

Ethiopia, the Congo, and Ghana since 1966 have each pursued a moderate and independent foreign policy, in part because of the character and source of external military and economic assistance. One major aim of U.S. aid is to help the recipient state become strong enough to defend its interests in the face of contrary threats and pressures from other states. A strong and reliable army, assisted by a friendly power that places no compromising political demands upon the recipient government, undergirds rather than subverts independent political behavior.

The professional outlook and politically moderate disposition of the officer corps in the three countries reflect their Western training and continuing contact with Europeans and Americans occasioned by the ongoing military assistance programs. Military men in Africa, as elsewhere, are generally cautious and would discourage crusades against neighboring states or subversive efforts to overthrow white regimes in Africa. Nkrumah's designs against his immediate neighbors were replaced by the live-and-let-live policy of the National Liberation Council and Busia regimes. Ghana's camps conducted by Russian and Chinese advisers to train guerrilla units for operations against certain white and black regimes in Africa were summarily closed after the 1966 coup.

Though Mobutu has not eliminated Angolan guerrillas from the border area of the eastern Congo, he has curtailed their activities more than any of his predecessors, partly because he appreciates the vulnerability of the Congo to the illegal flow of men and matériel from neighboring states in support of rebel groups.

A moderate on the larger world scene, Haile Selassie adopts a militant posture, at least rhetorically, when he supports the OAU "liberation" efforts aimed at the white regimes in southern Africa. He does not, however, permit insurgency training camps on Ethiopian soil.

It is noteworthy that none of the three states, nor any other tropical African state for that matter, has offered to provide any of its regular troops for a campaign to overthrow the regimes in the Portuguese provinces, Rhodesia, or the Republic of South Africa, which are frequent targets of vilification in African speeches at the United Nations. This fact reflects not only the military weakness of the African states, but also a political reluctance to become involved in distant crusades that do not bear on their immediate interests. For some of the same reasons no African state offered troops to Prime Minister Tshombe in 1964 when the Congo was seriously threatened by communist-supported rebels. That situation was complicated by the fact that the militant African leaders, and some of the moderate ones, were more sympathetic to the rebel cause than to the Tshombe regime. The only time since 1960 that regular tropical African troops were deployed in another African state was in the Congo under UN auspices.

As of mid-1970 all three states had diplomatic and trade relations with the United States, Western European countries, and the Soviet Union, though they all inclined toward the West and had close and multiple ties with Washington. None was receiving military aid from any communist state, and it would be safe to predict that a proposal to do so by any government would be stoutly resisted by its officer corps.

It seems reasonable to assume that since most armies tend to be more prudent and less volatile than political leaders in the underdeveloped world, the army generally will have a moderating influence on foreign policy. This influence is reinforced by increased contact with Western military advisers and increased dependence on Western aid.

Structure and Process of Politics

In most tropical African states today genuine, peaceful, competitive politics is virtually nonexistent and the base of political participation is narrow. Several countries, including the Congo, Kenya, and Tanzania, which started out with several parties, have become one-party states. Since the idea of a loyal opposition is alien to the African tradition, there is seldom an effective and legal political opposition. Ethiopia is a no-party state ruled by a nearly absolute monarch, and an election there is a symbol of political support rather than a means for selecting leadership. Throughout central Africa the politically significant public is very small, though in Ghana and a few other states with a more developed economy and a relatively high literacy level the base is broader. In the Congo, elections have had little meaning because there is no tradition of statewide political debate and decision. In most of the states without a legitimate and constitutional alternative to the regime, effective leverage upon the government is exercised primarily by influential elites and pressure groups, usually in the capital city.

The army as one of the most powerful of these elites has considerable influence on domestic and foreign policy, but while supporting the regime it has little impact on the structure or process of politics. By upholding the regimes in Ghana, the Congo, and Ethiopia, the armed forces have tended to reinforce the status quo while at the same time, in their state-building and nation-building roles, they have helped lay the foundation for further political development. By defending the state and symbolizing its unity, each army has strengthened national identity, loyalty, and pride, all essential to a broad-based political system. Through vocational training, educational programs, and civic action projects the armies have added to the pool of human talents and helped to build the infrastructure necessary for political communication, but they are only one among several institutions supporting modernization and social communication. These developments have a long way to go, especially in the Congo and Ethiopia, before traditional tribal loyalties are eroded and an effective national political participation becomes possible.

All available evidence suggests that the 1966 intervention in Ghana made a substantial and positive contribution to the structure and process of politics. The National Liberation Council, though illegal and unconstitutional, had greater respect for justice and the rule of law than the Nkrumah regime. This was expressed in the way domestic decisions were made and carried out. More important, the NLC returned the country to a freely elected government under a new constitution embracing the separation of powers, universal franchise, and other democratic institutions. The future alone will tell whether Ghana has the moral, intellectual, and political resources to sustain the new democratic political system.

In the Congo the picture is not as clear, mainly because Mobutu has had a far more difficult task. In the urgent problem of restoring internal order he has done better than any of his constitutional predecessors. He has generally exercised his extraordinary powers with restraint and moderation, has shown little disposition to act oppressively, and has not sought to impose a regressive, authoritarian political system upon the country. Mobutu has not yet confronted the trauma of transition, which according to his original statement is to take place in November 1970. What form of government will be provided for in the new constitution? Certainly a transplanted Western democratic system will have less chance to take root in the Congo than in Ghana. Whatever the form of government may be, the Mobutu regime has facilitated political development by replacing a corrupt and ineffective regime by a better one, by dramatizing some of the requirements of responsible government, and by making preliminary provisions for a peaceful transfer of power to a civilian successor.

These conclusions suggest that armed services, when performing their security function well, help create an environment of stability conducive to constructive political development, but that they have little influence on the structure or process of politics. However, when intervening in the political sphere to avert imminent disaster, the armed forces help to preserve the possibility for constructive politics. Their involvement can alter the structure of government and the process of making political decisions, during or after the interregnum. The nature of this alteration is determined not only by the intervention, but also by other circumstances.

Twelve Hypotheses

In the course of analyzing the situation in Ghana, the Congo, and Ethiopia under the seven areas of inquiry, twelve hypotheses have evolved. Their validity can be further tested and refined by subjecting them to empirical data from other developing states in Africa or elsewhere. They are stated formally below in the order they were arrived at:

1. The armed forces make their basic contribution to political stability and development by performing well their central function of defending the political and territorial integrity of the state against internal and external challenges.

2. As a vivid symbol of the state, a respected military establishment by its very existence engenders among citizens a sense of pride in and identity with their political community.

3. As the most modern and detribalized, deregionalized, defactionalized, and nonsectarian institution in an underdeveloped country, the armed services when performing their security function well can make a significant contribution to the organic process of developing national identity, cohesion, and loyalty.

4. As the most modern and technically oriented statewide institution in an underdeveloped country, the armed forces can aid economic modernization by example, by transmitting valuable skills, by stimulating the growth of a communication and transportation infrastructure, and under appropriate circumstances by engaging in civic action projects, thus making a modest contribution to nation-building.

5. As long as the central government is effective and legitimate (elastic categories that are politically defined by significant groups that give or withhold consent), the armed services make their most effective contribution to political stability and development by upholding the regime.

6. When a regime is too weak, corrupt, or arbitrary to govern and there is no legitimate political agency capable of taking over, effective military intervention to arrest chaos or disintegration or to prevent external intervention, depending on the performance of the interim regime, can facilitate constructive political development.

7. By performing their security function well, and thus enhancing

political stability, the armed services in an underdeveloped state tend to strengthen those forces inside and outside the government that support moderate as opposed to militant domestic policies.

8. If the military establishment is Western oriented and has a pragmatic and nonideological approach to problem solving, it further reinforces the moderate tendencies in an underdeveloped state.

9. Since most armies tend to be more prudent and less volatile than the political leaders in the underdeveloped world, the army generally has a moderating influence on foreign policy.

10. The moderating influence of the armed services on external policy is reinforced by increased contact with Western military advisers and increased dependence on Western assistance.

11. When performing their security function well the armed services help create an environment of stability conducive to constructive political development, but they have little influence on the structure or process of politics.

12. When intervening in the political sphere to avert disaster or effect reform, the armed forces help to preserve the possibility for constructive politics. Their involvement can alter the structure of government and the process of making political decisions. The nature of this alteration, which can occur during the interregnum or become manifest in the successor regime, is determined in part by factors other than the intervention.

Police and Political Development

In many tropical African countries the police service is the junior partner in the task of maintaining internal security. In virtually all states the armed services perform police-type, law-and-order functions, including border patrol, counterinsurgency operations, and riot control. The distinctive roles of the police and the army are more clearly defined in the former British and French territories than in the former Belgian Congo and Ethiopia. For this reason the Ghana Police Service plays a role similar to that of the police in Britain or the United States.

In the Congo and Ethiopia a statewide police service is a relatively recent and an almost embryonic institution compared with the army which is larger and stronger and enjoys a venerable tradition. That army tradition has been seriously tarnished in the Congo since independence day, but nevertheless the role of the soldier in both countries is better understood if not always more respected than that of the policeman.

A statewide police service was not created in the Congo until 1966. Before then the country was served by Territorial Police, established in 1948, who were provincially based and administered. For the most part, the Belgian Force Publique performed both police and military functions. In Ethiopia the statewide police were created in 1942; but in 1962 a special force, the Emergency Police, was established to deal with those security threats beyond the capabilities of the regular civilian police. In both countries the police are not yet well trained, though the situation is improving. In Ethiopia the discipline and performance of policemen in all ranks fall short of that of comparable members of the army or air force. In the Congo the discipline of policemen sometimes exceeds that of soldiers.

In all three states the police service is less influential and effective than the armed services in performing major missions, primarily because the armies possess more formidable instruments of coercion and a more responsive command system. The armies are better supplied and equipped, more mobile, and more tightly controlled and disciplined, and their centralized command structure is supported by modern communication facilities and a tradition of obedience. In contrast, the statewide police are weak, more lightly equipped, more decentralized, and often less well trained and disciplined. The attributes of both security services vary widely in the three states, but in each the army is a heavier institution with a more direct bearing on the regime and the administration than the police. This weight differential is expressed in their respective slices of the state budget and the volume of external aid each receives. In fiscal 1968, for example, U.S. military assistance to African states was approximately $25 million, while public safety aid to the same states amounted to about $2.5 million. For these and related reasons, the police establishment in all its manifestations has had a less consequential impact on political development than the armed forces in Ghana, the Congo, and Ethiopia, in terms of the seven areas of analysis.

Maintaining the State

In a more developed state a modern police service is the "first line of defense" against internal threats because it is competent to deal with local disorder and the early stages of more serious challenges. This capability is rooted in a reliable intelligence network, a responsive communications system, and mobility. This traditional law-and-order mission has in general been performed by the Ghana police, but in the Congo and Ethiopia it has been shared with the military services.

Since independence day the Ghana police have performed well, but during the latter Nkrumah years three disabilities eroded their performance and public esteem: First, Nkrumah deliberately hobbled the service by purging top-ranking officers, by curtailing the force (in manpower, budget, and arms), and by transferring certain functions to special security agencies accountable personally to him. Second, he intervened politically in police matters and thus compromised the chain of command. Third, he obliged officers to enforce regulations they regarded as arbitrary or unconstitutional, particularly the nominally constitutional but unpopular Preventive Detention Act. Further, some policemen became involved in Nkrumah's system of patronage and bribery. Consequently the police service lost considerable public respect but by mid-1970 it had been largely restored because of police participation in the popular coup against Nkrumah and the generally correct performance of the police since then. On balance, the Ghana police have helped to defend the state and to symbolize it by their presence at important ceremonial occasions. Under the National Liberation Council, police and military units had equal billing and exposure in guarding government buildings and in serving at important public functions.

The newly organized Congolese police have understandably made little contribution to internal security, though their performance is improving. They have not yet become widely respected instruments or symbols of state authority. Prior to the 1964 rebellion they tended to be fragmented along the divisive political and regional lines in the Congo. From time to time since 1964 they have demonstrated their capacity to deal with rebel activities, sometimes more effectively than the army. In Kivu province in 1967, for example, they performed well.

Compared to the armed forces, the Ethiopian police have made a small contribution to internal security. With a reasonably good record in Eritrea and the Ogaden, the Emergency Police have already earned a degree of public esteem.

Building a Nation

Though centrally administered, the three police services are more provincially oriented, less detribalized, and less modernized than the armed forces. Their contribution to national identity and pride has thus been minimal. Their influence in this area will always be limited because of their more localized functions, though it will tend to increase with increased detribalization, professionalization, and effectiveness. Again the Ghana police are well ahead of their counterparts in the Congo and Ethiopia.

The police of various Third World states, including Chile, the Dominican Republic, and Thailand, have engaged in various civic action projects that contribute directly to economic and political development. Emergency relief, school construction, agricultural assistance, and medical care are often carried out to counter or discourage insurgency. The police in Ghana, the Congo, and Ethiopia have not engaged in civic action though there has been some discussion about their entering this area.

Upholding the Regime

Since 1960 the state police in the three countries have upheld the existing government, except in Ghana when the police commissioner joined the military coup that ousted Nkrumah..Serving under the unpopular Nkrumah regime, the police were more vulnerable than the military, because they were closer to the people and were obligated to enforce unpalatable laws and arbitrary regulations. The Ghana police have been loyal to the National Liberation Council and Busia regimes. Since 1960 the Ethiopian regular and Emergency Police have loyally supported Haile Selassie against subversive and irredentist challenges.

Replacing the Regime

Acting against tradition and presumably against the sentiments of his junior officers, Police Chief Tsigue Dibou was a principal plotter in the abortive coup against Haile Selassie in 1960, the only significant exception to Ethiopian police loyalty in modern times. In Ghana, Police Commissioner J. W. K. Harlley was a major leader, if not coauthor, of the coup against Nkrumah. Since the political development of both countries was served by the way both events actually turned out, police participation in the Ethiopian coup attempt was ill advised, while police involvement in the Ghana coup was well advised. The Ghana police have played an important and constructive role in the leadership of the National Liberation Council. The Congolese police had no special role in the 1965 Mobutu coup or in the subsequent regime.

Domestic Policies

To the very small extent that the three police establishments have influenced domestic policy, the general direction of their effect has been similar to that of the military—toward a pragmatic rather than an ideological approach to problem solving. The police members of the NLC have had some direct impact on nonsecurity questions in Ghana, but there is no evidence that the police service as such has had a special influence on domestic policies.

Foreign Policy

By virtue of receiving equipment and technical and training aid from abroad, almost exclusively from the West, the three police services, like the three armed services, are Western-oriented. This Western connection of the police reinforces prior decisions to turn to the United States and Western Europe for security assistance and advice. The presence of a handful of U.S. public safety advisers in the Congo and Ethiopia has provided more channels of communication between Washington and the two governments.

Structure and Process of Politics

In the Congo and Ethiopia the police have supported the existing political structure and processes and have had little influence one way or the other. In Ghana the police inescapably became instruments of Nkrumah's oppressive measures, and thereby reinforced his regime, but the police have given greater and more consistent support of the NLC, which took significant steps to restore the rule of law, and to the subsequent Busia government.

Three Hypotheses

This generally positive appraisal of the police services in Ghana, the Congo, and Ethiopia suggests three hypotheses applicable to other areas:

1. In most developing states the police service is regarded as the chief instrument for maintaining law and order and the first line of defense against subversion and insurgency. The role of the police in performing the latter function is usually complicated because the army is necessarily involved in the internal security role, especially in countries facing serious insurgency problems.

2. The police services have less impact on political development than the armed services, because the police establishment has less prestige and less coercive force and is more decentralized than the army.

3. The most important contribution the police service can make to political development under an effective regime is to perform well its central law-and-order and security functions.

CHAPTER SIX

U.S. Military
and Public Safety Aid

African defense against subversion, like African development, must be borne most directly by Africans rather than by outsiders.

PRESIDENT RICHARD M. NIXON[1]

THE POLITICAL IMPACT of the armed forces and police services of Ghana, the Congo, and Ethiopia is the primary focus of this study. A secondary theme is the role of external military and public safety assistance, particularly from the West and especially from the United States. This study concludes that the army and police of these three countries have played a constructive political role. It is therefore appropriate to assess the influence of U.S. security assistance on the indigenous security instruments as well as on state-building, nation-building, and other factors in the political drama. This chapter evaluates the effect of U.S. military and public safety aid, drawing hypotheses and policy conclusions directly from the case studies as well as advancing collateral and supplementary observations drawn from the author's related studies in tropical Africa. Though these broader observations are not based directly upon the foregoing analysis, they tend to be supported by it.

Ghana, the Congo, and Ethiopia have received military and public safety aid from several external sources. Aid to the Congo and Ethiopia has come overwhelmingly from the West. The Congo has received a large volume of security aid from the United States and Belgium and

1. *United States Foreign Policy for the 1970s*, President Nixon's report to the Congress, Feb. 18, 1970.

much smaller amounts from Italy and Israel. Sweden, Norway, France, India, Britain, and Israel have provided a small amount of training and advisory assistance to Ethiopia, supplementing the far larger U.S. program of hardware, training, and advice. Neither the Congo nor Ethiopia has received security aid from communist states, but several communist governments have provided some material assistance to rebel groups seeking to overthrow the regimes in both countries. In contrast, Ghana received an estimated $10 million in security aid from communist governments during the latter Nkrumah period; Britain, Canada, and the United States have provided a modest amount of such assistance to Ghana.

U.S. Military Assistance

The volume of U.S. military aid, like economic assistance, is one barometer of Washington's interest in an area or a state. The continent of Africa received in U.S. military aid (including training) in the 1950–68 period $218 million out of a world total of $33.3 billion, a bit over 0.5 percent. Tropical Africa received $152.8 million or about 0.4 percent. The three case study countries received, in the same period, $138 million, the lion's share going to the Lion of Judah. The volume of U.S. aid received by each state for that period and for fiscal 1968 under the military assistance program (MAP) is given below along with the size of the U.S. military group in the country in 1968.[2]

	1950–68	Fiscal 1968	Personnel in military group
Ethiopia	$118,000,000	$17,400,000	162
Congo (Kinshasa)	19,900,000	3,800,000	63
Ghana	100,000	less than 50,000	0

The 1969 allocation for tropical Africa was $17,350,000, over half of it for Ethiopia; Ethiopia, the Congo, and Liberia were the only states in the area chosen to receive both equipment and training assistance.

It is not possible to identify, much less quantify, the multiple effects —intended and unintended—of U.S. military aid to Ghana, the Congo, and Ethiopia, but the case studies do suggest the general direction of its influence on security, political, and foreign policy developments. The

2. U.S. Department of Defense, International Security Affairs, *Military Assistance Facts* (May 1969), p. 17.

impact of external military aid is limited because it operates primarily through the existing military establishment whose quality and responsiveness largely determine its effects. Limited and marginal external influence, however, can be significant or even crucial in a delicately balanced situation. In a weak society where the presumption for chaos is high the incremental effectiveness and morale of the army conferred by foreign aid may be decisive in a crisis. The ill-planned but nearly successful countercoup in Ghana in 1967, for example, might have succeeded had it not been for British military equipment, training, and advice during the previous decade.

U.S. military aid not only affects the armed services to which it is directed but the regime that negotiates the bilateral agreement for such assistance. The participating state invites external aid because it believes it will serve its interests. Both sides enter into military aid arrangements cognizant of the mutual benefits. Seen in this light, such a program is a foreign policy instrument for both Washington and the recipient regime. From the initial negotiations to the completion of the program, there are multiple contacts and opportunities for mutual influence between American diplomats and military personnel on the one side and their host state counterparts on the other. These personal and professional contacts provide continuing channels of communication and understanding that supplement those of diplomatic, economic, and cultural intercourse. Their ultimate value of course depends upon the mutuality of interests and the quality of advice being transmitted.

In Ghana, where Britain has been the primary Western source of military aid, the recent and small U.S. program has had little influence. In the Congo, U.S. equipment assistance and Belgian training aid have made a significant contribution to the gradual improvement of Mobutu's army. In Ethiopia, which has received substantial American equipment, training, and in-country advice, the influence on the army and air force has been considerable. Aid-induced efficiency has clearly helped the Congolese and Ethiopian armies to deal more effectively with their security challenges.

The American emphasis on professionalism and the visible presence of modern military equipment have increased the prestige of the armed forces as a symbol of the state and fostered a greater sense of national identity. Detribalization efforts within the armed forces, encouraged by

U.S. advisers, have also strengthened the nascent national consciousness. Haile Selassie's dispatch of Imperial Bodyguard troops to Korea and the Congo, strongly supported by Washington and made possible by U.S. equipment, enhanced the international image of Ethiopia. The modernization of the armed forces with logistical and communications equipment, wholly a result of military aid, has had a direct and indirect impact on the economic infrastructure and has facilitated statewide communication and administration. The small civic action projects, made possible largely with U.S. aid, have made a token contribution to modernization. In these and other ways military aid has contributed to maintaining the state and to building a greater sense of national consciousness by increasing, slightly or substantially, the capacity of the three armed forces to perform their security mission and thus enhance the stability, integrity, and prestige of the state.

Evidence suggests that Western military aid to the armed forces in the three states has had only a marginal impact on the political behavior of their armed services, which has been determined largely by internal forces. The net impact of British training in Ghana may have been to delay the coup against Nkrumah because the concerned army and police officers were indoctrinated with British inhibitions against unconstitutional intervention, but this training neither caused nor prevented the coup. The same can be said for the abortive countercoup in Ghana.

It is equally true that U.S. military aid neither caused nor prevented the two successful Mobutu coups and the unsuccessful coup in Ethiopia. It may, however, have had a marginal effect on the immediate outcomes and long-range consequences of these events. Whether an attempted coup fails or not depends upon the operation of delicately balanced forces—military, political, and psychological. The successful outcome of Mobutu's 1960 coup was assured by various factors, including the decision of the UN representative, Andrew W. Cordier, to close all airports to Russian aircraft which were about to be placed at the disposal of the ousted Lumumba. There was no bilateral U.S. military aid in the Congo at that time. When Mobutu intervened in 1965 there was a U.S. mission of about three dozen military personnel in the Congo, but there is no evidence that these advisers influenced his ultimate decision. The success of this second coup was also due to many internal factors, especially the loyalty of key army units to Mobutu. It could be argued that this loyalty was reinforced by Belgian and American training and assistance, but it would be incorrect to conclude that such loyalty was the result of external aid. Washington's detachment from the internal struggle in Ghana and the Congo is demonstrated by the fact that the Nkrumah and the National Liberation Council (NLC) regimes, as well as the half dozen Congo regimes, were speedily accorded diplomatic recognition and at no time did the United States suspend diplomatic relations with any regime of either state.

During the 1960 coup attempt in Ethiopia there were about a hundred U.S. military advisers in the country. Many Ethiopian Army, Bodyguard, and Air Force officers had been trained in America during the preceding decade and all the military services had received a significant amount of U.S. equipment. The coup was spawned in the Bodyguard and was put down by loyal army and air force troops. American officials, civilian or military, were not involved in planning the coup, and its outcome was at most only indirectly related to U.S. military assistance. The verdict was determined by the relative strength of the plotters and the loyalists, though it is true that some U.S. officers reported to and advised their regular army and air force units during the two-day crisis.

U.S. military aid had no discernible impact one way or the other on the incidence of military intervention in the three states during the 1960s, and the outcome in each case was largely determined by the interplay of domestic factors. U.S. aid may have marginally reinforced the winning side in the second Mobutu coup or in the abortive Ethiopian coup, but this would be virtually impossible to demonstrate. U.S. military training may have had some impact on the effectiveness and perhaps on the restraint with which the prevailing forces in the Congo and Ethiopia exercised their power. Both Mobutu coups were bloodless. Were it not for American influence, the crushing of the Ethiopian insurrection might have been less restrained than it was.

The NLC intervention was a security-reform coup, and the two Mobutu interventions were essentially security coups. The Ghana and the second Mobutu coups were followed by interim reform regimes, the NLC's program being the more soundly based. Washington supported these two regimes with economic, military, and public safety assistance. For the same political reasons Washington supported the Ethiopian regime after the abortive coup. In none of these crises did the fact of

U.S. aid or the presence of military advisers entangle the United States in domestic conflict, unless aid to the government is construed as interference in internal politics.

American military aid to the Congo and Ethiopia has marginally buttressed the forces of moderation and responsibility. In domestic policy, particularly on economic issues, U.S. aid has reinforced the army's disposition to emphasize expertise, facts, rationality, and the pragmatic as opposed to the doctrinaire approach to public problems. This is not unimportant in countries where the top military officers are active participants in the ruling elite whether or not there is a military government.

The moderate foreign policy orientation of post-Nkrumah Ghana, the Congo, and Ethiopia is both a cause and effect of Western military aid. Immediately after Nkrumah's ouster, Washington initiated programs of military and economic assistance. Prime Minister Busia, President Mobutu, and Emperor Haile Selassie are all Western-oriented, so they naturally have turned to the West for assistance, the acceptance of which has further reinforced their moderate approach to issues in the larger world. Each of these nonaligned states recognizes it has parallel interests with Washington and other moderate governments in maintaining stability and warding off subversion from communist and other militant governments. During the 1960s none of the three embarked upon foreign military adventures, though Nkrumah sponsored and supported some unsuccessful subversive forays against his neighbors and trained insurgents for action against other regimes. Busia has strongly opposed interfering in the affairs of other states. Mobutu still permits Angolan guerrillas to live in and operate from the Congo, but he keeps a close eye on them. The Emperor talks about "liberating" the blacks in southern Africa, but neither he nor any other African government has made available any regular troops for this purpose.

External military aid has had little effect upon the basic structure and process of politics in the three states, but to the extent that aid has contributed to internal stability it has helped produce a climate conducive to peaceful political development. In some situations the aid-strengthened army has served as a balancer or mediator to prevent competing factions from tearing the government apart. U.S. assistance has strengthened the NLC, which surrendered power to a civilian regime, and has helped Mobutu who has taken steps to establish a constitutional successor.

Six Hypotheses

The accumulated evidence indicates that military aid has been an effective instrument for serving U.S. foreign policy objectives and the parallel goals of Ghana, the Congo, and Ethiopia. The equipment, training, and advice provided has helped to meet the basic security and political requirements of each recipient country as perceived by its leaders and has strengthened the internal forces of stability essential to peaceful political development. This generally positive appraisal suggests six hypotheses regarding U.S. military assistance in tropical Africa:

1. U.S. military aid has a limited impact upon the participating state because the aid is channeled through the existing military establishment whose quality and responsiveness largely determine the effects of external assistance. Aid can, however, be a significant influence in a delicately balanced situation.

2. Such aid usually enhances the efficiency and capability of the armed services which are thus better able to insure the stability essential to constructive political development.

3. It tends to reinforce those elements within the participating state and its armed forces committed to a moderate and pragmatic (as opposed to a militant and doctrinaire) approach to domestic and foreign policies.

4. It tends to have less effect upon the domestic political scene in the participating state than upon its foreign policy.

5. It tends to have more influence on long-range political developments within the recipient state than upon short-range developments or particular events. Such assistance has little effect on the frequency or character of military intervention in the political sphere.

6. It has little impact on the structure or process of politics of the participating state unless the aid happens to reinforce a military establishment during a period when it is exercising a significant influence in this area.

Role of U.S. Public Safety Assistance

Since its public safety program began in 1954, the United States has provided advisory, training, and equipment assistance to the police forces of almost sixty Third World states. Administered by the Agency for International Development (AID), the public safety program has compatible but not identical objectives with those of the military assistance program. The basic purpose of both is to enhance security in the recipient country and thus to contribute to stability in the area. Public safety aid is designed to do this by improving the quality and efficiency of the statewide civil police service.

In its efforts to assist the recipient state in maintaining law and order "under humane, civil concepts and control," the public safety program seeks to develop "within the civil security forces" the capability for (1) regular police operations, (2) detecting and identifying criminal and "subversive individuals and organizations and neutralizing their activities," and (3) "controlling militant activities ranging from demonstrations, disorders, or riots through small-scale guerrilla operations."[3]

Recognizing that Third World police services have a normal law-and-order mission and should be the first line of defense against insurgency, Washington has emphasized training and equipment for riot control, intelligence, and communication to counter politically significant challenges, especially those with external support. In serious crises the responsibility for dealing with insurgency must be shared by the police, the intelligence services, and the armed forces. Some statewide police services have special branches to deal with subversion and insurgency, and in some countries Washington has supported police-operated civic action projects to help extend the control and services of the central government in remote areas threatened by infiltration or guerrilla activity.

Compared to military aid, police assistance has been very small, though the proportion of public safety to military aid has been rising as the latter has declined. The figures for the two grant programs for fiscal 1969 for the world (less Vietnam and Thailand) and for Africa follow:

	World	Africa
Military assistance	$589,400,000	$21,300,000
Public safety assistance	7,590,000	1,130,000

In this year the worldwide cost of public safety was about 1.3 percent of that for military aid. In Africa the portion was 5.3 percent. The African slice of military aid was 3.6 percent of the total, while the African share of police aid was 15 percent.

3. U.S. Department of State, Agency for International Development, Office of Public Safety, *A.I.D. Assistance to Civil Security Forces* (July 12, 1967), pp. 1 and 2.

In 1968 police aid was provided to sixteen African states. Ten of these were served by resident U.S. public safety advisers: Chad, Congo (Kinshasa), Ethiopia, Ivory Coast, Kenya, Liberia, Niger, Rwanda, Somalia, and Tunisia. The Congo had six advisers and Ethiopia four. All sixteen states sent police officers to the AID-operated International Police Academy in Washington for training courses of three or four months or for specialized police training elsewhere in the United States. Of some 700 African police officers trained in the United States as of November 1969, Ethiopia provided 120, the Congo 82, and Ghana 25.

The equipment–training ratio in public safety aid stands in sharp contrast to that in military aid. Worldwide, 70 percent of police aid goes for equipment compared to 85 percent of military aid. In Africa police equipment is 56 percent of the budget. The remaining 44 percent covers the training and advisory functions. If public safety advisers abroad were paid from extra-program funds, as are military advisers who are paid from the regular U.S. Defense budget, the equipment–training ratio would shift even further in the direction of training. This ratio means that public safety aid provides for more personal association between American and African officers than an equal expenditure in military assistance. Since the primary emphasis is on the training of command and training officers, American influence has a multiplier effect that infuses the entire police service.

The effect of the small U.S. public safety aid in tropical Africa has been modest but constructive. With its solid British base, the Ghana Police Service has required relatively little external assistance. In Ethiopia and the Congo, American training, advice, and equipment are partially responsible for the slowly growing effectiveness of their services. Ethiopia has had the largest U.S. program in tropical Africa. Before it was terminated in mid-1969, Washington had trained 120 officers, provided $160,000 in equipment to the Aba Dina Academy, and helped to expand and upgrade the curriculum. It had also assisted in training noncommissioned officers, established a crime laboratory, and strengthened the police radio network. With U.S. encouragement and aid, the Ethiopian police started a special internal literacy program in 1964 and later opened it to the public.

The preceding analysis supports a general hypothesis:

U.S. public safety assistance enhances the efficiency and capability of the recipient police service and tends to reinforce existing elements committed to just and humane methods of law enforcement. This, in turn, has the effect of enhancing stability and undergirding the moderate and pragmatic approach to domestic problems.

Future of U.S. Security Aid

This comparative study of the impact of spear upon scepter in Ghana, the Congo, and Ethiopia, including the effects of U.S. security assistance, suggests a number of collateral observations about the future of American military and public safety aid to tropical Africa that may prove pertinent to other countries in Africa, Asia, and Latin America.

The first observation is predictive. It is likely that a small volume of U.S. security assistance will continue in tropical Africa for the indefinite future. The modest American military and police aid of the past decade (including sales) has served the interests of both parties, and each regards such aid as a low-cost and low-risk instrument of foreign policy. The low-risk attribute is demonstrated by the record of U.S. involvement and noninvolvement in Africa. In 1960 Washington became involved militarily though indirectly in civil strife in the Congo, a country that had received no previous security aid. The reverse occurred in Nigeria, where the United States remained militarily aloof from the civil war, though it had previously provided some military assistance to Lagos. U.S. combat involvement, as President Nixon pointed out in his 1969 Guam statement, is determined by America's vital interests, not by its military assistance program.

For these reasons, a modest military aid and military sales program in tropical Africa should be continued and should operate, with certain exceptions, generally along existing policy guidelines. To acknowledge that tropical Africa ranks below the African Mediterranean states and southern Africa, in terms of U.S. political, strategic, and economic interests, is not to say that stability and political development in this area are of no concern or that efforts toward these ends should be abandoned in the face of more pressing strategic responsibilities in Europe, Asia, or Latin America. The maintenance of local stability tends to contribute to areawide stability, which helps keep tropical Africa in the low-interest category commensurate with its geopolitical position in the world. Stability (not to be confused with stagnation) also permits the effective use of scarce resources and enables the African states to place more emphasis on economic and political development.

The 1968 limit of $40 million for military grants and sales to Africa appears fair in view of the diminishing aid funds available, the political demands on Washington elsewhere, and other ways to supplement grant aid. One of these ways is to persuade European and other friendly states to make available additional security assistance. Another is to supplement regular MAP aid with special military grants and "excess stocks." MAP assistance in Ethiopia was augmented by more than $25 million in this way during the 1950–67 period:[4]

MAP funds	$118,200,000
Value of excess stocks	19,600,000
Other military assistance grants	5,900,000
Total	$143,700,000

Washington also provided Addis Ababa with $222,300,000 in economic assistance during the same period, increasing the total resources of Ethiopia by $366 million. This added wealth has made it easier for the government to shift its internal resources from one purpose to another. Consequently, an amount larger or smaller than the total volume of aid labeled as military may have gone for military purposes. If the recipient decides to shift its resources, there is "relatively little the United States can do to control this process of substitution,"[5] but presumably American advice on this matter is not lightly dismissed. In 1959 the Draper Committee warned that economic and military aid to underdeveloped countries were "neither alternatives nor competitors. Both are means of achieving related aspects of our total foreign policy objectives, and they are mutually complementary."[6]

Military sales are a means of supplementing military grant aid of all kinds. Two recent studies of military assistance support the U.S. move from grants to sales when it is economically feasible in Africa and elsewhere. One recommends that the Defense Department focus on "simple, unsophisticated equipment" for sub-Sahara Africa and "emphasize purchase of replacement equipment and spare parts from U.S.

4. U.S. Department of State, AID, *U.S. Overseas Loans and Grants and Assistance for International Organizations*, prepared for the House Foreign Affairs Committee (March 29, 1968), p. 86.

5. Andrew F. Westwood, *Foreign Aid in a Foreign Policy Framework* (Brookings Institution, 1966), Brookings Staff Paper, p. 5.

6. U.S. President's Committee to Study the United States Military Assistance Program, *Composite Report*, Vol. 1 (Aug. 17, 1959), p. 59.

commercial sources."[7] The other points to several advantages of sales over grant aid, including the fact that sales would force "the local government to consider the entire current and long-range cost of its defense program as an integral part of its economic planning."[8]

All forms of American grant aid—hardware, training, advisory missions—can be purchased, though military sales are usually restricted to equipment and related instruction.

Since sales are more economical for Washington and are sometimes politically more acceptable to the recipient, and since they serve essentially the same objectives as comparable grant aid, no arbitrary ceiling should be placed on them. The $40 million ceiling on combined sales and grants (not including training) to Africa established by the Foreign Military Sales Act of 1968 unnecessarily ties the hands of the executive branch, even though there are only a few states in Africa capable of purchasing sizable amounts of equipment.

Beyond the various kinds of grant aid and sales, the option for emergency U.S. military assistance should also remain open, to be used at the discretion of the President. Such assistance was given to the Congo on at least three occasions when the United States provided transport aircraft to assist the government in dealing with a serious security crisis or to rescue endangered American citizens and others. The 1964 Belgian-American rescue mission to the Congo, for example, not only saved more than 2,000 foreign civilian hostages, but it was a positive factor in determining the outcome of the struggle between the central government and the rebels, though it was not undertaken for this reason.

The major problem in developing a grant or a grant-sales military aid program is to determine the proper balance among equipment, training, and advice. For political-psychological reasons "advice," as such, is not listed in the program budget but, as an essential ingredient in "training" and "technical assistance," its desirability is acknowledged and accepted by both sides. The formalized agency for providing in-country advice is the U.S. military group (which has different names) whose mutually agreed functions include monitoring and advising on all aspects of hardware and training assistance.

Person-to-person advice has had a constructive effect upon a half

7. Quintus C. Atkinson, "The Management of U.S. Military Assistance in Africa South of the Sahara" (Master's thesis, George Washington University, 1966), p. 89.

8. Harry J. Shaw, "The Military Assistance Program: A Study of Interdepartmental Relationships and Influences" (Ph.D. thesis, University of Virginia, 1967), p. 432. See also pp. 430–33.

dozen African armed services, particularly those in Ethiopia and the Congo. The impact of quietly given, in-country military counsel by carefully selected American officers can be substantial, especially if it continues over a long period, operates at several levels of command, and is supported by an appropriate program of equipment assistance. The quality and applicability of the advice is affected by political and professional factors in both states and is ultimately dependent upon the respect for and understanding of the political interests and security needs of the recipient country by U.S. authorities. The advisory role can be eroded if U.S. officers are transferred to new posts as soon as they become proficient. Their duty tours should be adjusted to meet their special qualifications and the needs of the host government.

One of the most enduring forms of advice is that associated with the building of new institutions and facilities in the host state. The U.S. Air Force has assisted at every stage in developing the Ethiopian Air Force. It has trained most of its officers and has supervised, on request, the building of the headquarters base at Debra Zeit, including the Air Training Center with its various schools, and the supporting repair and maintenance workshops. Through this type of continuous and close cooperation, U.S. advisers have been able to transmit not only technical skills, but the habits of discipline, management, and quality control essential to maintaining a modern air force.

In Africa about 85 percent of military aid has been spent for equipment and related costs, the remaining 15 percent for training. In contrast, some 30 percent of the smaller British military aid budget of $14 million for Africa in 1967 went into training. Although the existing U.S. equipment–training ratio probably cannot be drastically altered because of the relatively high cost of hardware and the inability of most African governments to purchase it, Washington should continue to emphasize training over marginally useful equipment. One advantage of training is the significantly greater man-to-man contact and influence compared to an equal dollar investment in hardware. Most equipment is both costly and ephemeral. An expensive jet fighter may crash, and in any event it will wear out or become obsolete. An equivalent investment in officer training or in developing a whole range of military skills cannot be wholly lost, even if high U.S. standards are not fully met or the skills fully utilized. Such training can help the armed forces better perform their security function and at the same time increase the total pool of skilled manpower desperately needed in tropical Africa. Further, the man-to-man contacts provide a valuable channel of communication.

In terms of the larger goals of state-building and political development, longer periods of U.S. training are more valuable than shorter ones. Serious professional training (such as command and general staff) has a greater impact on discipline and efficiency—attributes also in short supply in underdeveloped countries—than instruction in the use of technical equipment, though both kinds are needed. Training in the United States has a greater political and cultural influence on the trainee than training in his home environment, but more intensive exposure to America does not automatically lead to a greater appreciation of American life and institutions or understanding for U.S. foreign policy. Because of the many benefits of military training to both parties, no arbitrary ceiling should be imposed on the number of participants.

When pressures develop in recipient states for the acquisition of "prestige" hardware—new, sophisticated, and perhaps militarily unessential items—Washington usually insists that U.S. guidelines be followed and encourages sales where feasible. In dealing with this problem, which has not been serious in tropical Africa, three factors should be noted. First, the term "sophisticated hardware" cannot be defined in the abstract because of widely differing security, economic, and political circumstances. Second, on occasion it may be in the security interest of the United States to bolster the status of a regime by providing some prestige equipment, such as out-of-date "prestige" planes. Third, if Washington refuses to provide desired hardware, the requesting government may turn to another supplier who has fewer inhibitions, thus depriving the United States of the political and military advantages of ongoing training and spare parts contracts, especially in situations where Washington has been the exclusive or prime supplier of military equipment and training.

The portion of U.S. military aid earmarked for civic action in tropical Africa should remain small, though subject to increase under certain circumstances. The armed forces should focus their major energy on their fundamental security mission and engage in civilian projects only when there is military manpower to spare from this primary task. Security-oriented civic action is more justifiable than development-oriented civic action. The latter might be justified in a country with a scarcity of skilled civilians and equipment essential for building an urgently needed road, bridge, or dam. In such situations an army engineering unit with U.S. training and equipment could properly be enlisted if it were not needed for supporting a military mission. Emergency services can also appropriately be performed by U.S. aided armies, alone or with the help of U.S. military manpower and facilities. In 1968, for example, the U.S. and Ethiopian air forces teamed up to rescue thousands of flood victims in the Ogaden.

The responsiveness and flexibility of MAP aid in Africa has been somewhat limited by an unnecessarily complex and cumbersome administrative structure rooted in "methods used for the rebuilding of European allies after World War II."[9] Military assistance in that area is administered by the commander in chief of the U.S. Strike Command —Middle East, Africa South of the Sahara, and Southern Asia—with headquarters at McDill Air Force Base in Florida; this unified command is operated directly under the joint chiefs of staff. The rather impressive superstructure is probably not essential for the small aid program in tropical Africa. Atkinson recommends that small aid programs "be excluded from the present complex and overly-centralized" Department of Defense system and that the unified commander be eliminated from "the formal review process."[10] He also recommends that the U.S. ambassador in any tropical African state, observing the general guidelines from the State and Defense departments and using "qualified military advisers on his staff, be granted greater authority in the planning, programming, and implementation of the country program."

At several points U.S. military aid and public safety assistance invite a cost-benefit comparison. Though financial costs are quantifiable and benefits are not, a substantial increase in U.S. public safety aid to tropical Africa would be desirable in countries capable of utilizing additional training and equipment in their police services. Even with a substantial cost increase, the public safety program would remain much smaller than military aid which has in dollar terms been ten times larger.

In their task of maintaining law and order the police are the first line of defense against subversion and terrorism; when they meet these problems effectively, the army need not be brought in. The public safety program is designed to help the civil police accomplish this objective.

9. Atkinson, "Management of U.S. Military Assistance," p. 84.
10. Ibid., pp. 88–89.

The less often the army is brought in the less costly will be the internal security task both financially and politically.

The argument that a soldier can do a policeman's job as well as a policeman can be questioned on several counts. A soldier is neither trained nor equipped for police work. His primary vocation is to fight and destroy organized military units, and he is equipped almost exclusively with lethal weapons. A policeman, equipped largely with non-lethal weapons, is trained to apprehend individual civilians, to control crowds, and in general to operate among his fellow countrymen to maintain and restore order, always seeking to perform his tasks with minimum violence. A policeman lives and works in the civilian population, while a soldier lives a more separate existence in a barracks or base. By tradition, doctrine, and training the soldier and the policeman are prepared for different but complementary security roles.

Recognizing the basic distinction between essentially police and essentially military functions, most states provide for military support to the police in certain domestic emergencies. Many governments have established army riot control units, sometimes with American aid, to augment the police during serious challenges to civil order. U.S. advisers have also encouraged Third World states to upgrade their civil capacity to deal with internal disorders, though the debate as to whether the riot-control function should be vested primarily in the army or in the police continues. Political and cultural circumstances differ greatly, but in many if not most cases it would make both security and economic sense to develop this capability first in the police service and later, if necessary, within the army, assuming the resources are not available to do both simultaneously. Normally it is more economical to achieve a given riot-control capability within the police service because the cost of supporting and equipping a policeman is considerably less than that of a soldier.

In some situations a policeman on patrol may cost only one-third as much as a soldier performing the same duty, if the military overhead of heavy weapons and equipment is taken into account. If a larger proportion of security resources is invested in the police service and results in increased police efficiency, the burden on the military can be reduced and more security can be bought for the same investment. The same cost-benefit considerations apply to U.S. security assistance. If public safety aid is increased, resulting in the greater effectiveness of the more efficient security instrument, and military aid is reduced proportionately, Washington will be getting more for its security investment. Since an army will always be needed to deter or deal with serious threats, the problem is one of achieving the optimum balance of resources for both army and police on the part of the donor and recipient states.

In political terms, relatively greater attention to building the police services may have the beneficial effect of reducing the size of the African military forces, some of which are unnecessarily large. The existence of an oversize army may tempt the political or military leaders to engage in an adventure against a neighboring state. Large underemployed armies sometimes become restless, and a clique of dissatisfied officers may decide to overthrow an effective, constitutional regime when there is no political or moral basis for such action.

Administratively, public safety assistance tends to enjoy a greater degree of flexibility and responsiveness than military aid, due mainly to its character, its relatively small scale, and its less complicated bureaucratic channels. Police aid in African states concentrates on technical assistance. It is limited to a few U.S. advisers per country, the training of a small number of selected men, and the provision of small quantities of relatively inexpensive equipment, primarily for demonstration and training purposes. In a crisis, urgently needed equipment and technical advisers can be dispatched in a matter of days.

Over the past two decades the public safety program has been administered by AID and advised and assisted by the departments of State, Defense, Justice, and Treasury, and other U.S. agencies. The small public safety program—which in 1968 amounted to only 2.4 percent of the total AID effort—was supported by AID's global logistical and administrative structure. At the same time, this "orphan of the AID program," as one official put it, sometimes lacked a clear identity and sufficient autonomy to make an effective case before the Congress and to pursue its objectives—quite different from, but compatible with, economic development goals—efficiently. In any new administrative arrangement, therefore, efforts should be made to safeguard the integrity and autonomy of the public safety program whose fundamental purpose, like that of military assistance, is to help the participating countries create an environment conducive to healthy economic and political development.

These policy conclusions and observations are in the first instance applicable to the U.S. security assistance program in Ghana, the Congo, and Ethiopia. But since the fundamental problems of exercising political responsibility and insuring domestic tranquillity are essentially the same throughout the developing world, despite the rich diversity of cultural life, political history, and military tradition, the observations may be considered to have a wider application.

Facts on Ghana, the Congo, and Ethiopia

Unless otherwise specified, the information below on Ghana, the Congo (Kinshasa), and Ethiopia reflects the situation in early 1970. Some of the figures, particularly population and educational statistics, are estimates. All economic statistics are in U.S. dollars.

Categories	Ghana	Congo	Ethiopia
POLITICAL			
Form of government	Republic	Republic	Constitutional and hereditary monarchy
Present regime	K. A. Busia installed prime minister, Oct. 1, 1969	Gen. Joseph Mobutu assumed presidency, Nov. 25, 1965	Haile Selassie became emperor, Nov. 2, 1930
Political franchise	Universal	Largely suspended	Nominal
Independence date and previous status	March 6, 1957, British colony (Gold Coast)	June 30, 1960, Belgian colony	Modern history begins with Emperor Menelik II (1889–1913)
Foreign policy orientation	Neutral, member of British Commonwealth, leans toward West	Neutral, leans toward West	Neutral, leans toward West
Capital	Accra	Kinshasa	Addis Ababa
GEOGRAPHIC			
Area (in square miles)	91,843	904,747	457,000
Location	West Africa, bordered by Gulf of Guinea, Ivory Coast, Upper Volta, Togo	Heart of Africa, bordered by nine countries, Atlantic Ocean	East Africa, bordered by Sudan, Somalia, Kenya, Red Sea
DEMOGRAPHIC			
Population (1968 estimate)	8.4 million	17.5 million	23.5 million
Inhabitants per serviceman	500	470	575
Major tribal groups	Ga, Ashanti, Ewe, Fanti	Kongo, Mongo, Luba, Lunda, Lulua	Amhara, Tigre, Galla

223

Categories	Ghana	Congo	Ethiopia
DEMOGRAPHIC *continued*			
Resident Europeans			
1969	8,500	35,000–50,000	30,000
1960	9,700	115,000	30,000
Resident Americans			
1969	1,500	1,700	6,500
1960	1,000	1,700	5,000
EDUCATIONAL			
Principal languages	English (official), Twi, Ga, Ewe, Akan	French (official), Lingala, Kikongo, Tshiluba, Swahili	Amharic (official), English, Tigriniya Galla
Literacy (percent of population above 14 years)	25	38	5
Primary and secondary pupils	1,461,000	2,766,000	470,000
Percent of population	17	16.5	2
University students	4,800	3,500	3,500
Students studying abroad	1,000	1,200–1,500	1,000
University graduates in country	6,000	300	3,000
ECONOMIC			
Gross national product (1968)	$1.8 billion	$1.5 billion	$1.5 billion
Per capita income	$214	$86	$64
State budget (1969)	$460 million	$370 million	$284 million
MILITARY			
Total armed forces	17,000	37,000	41,200
Army	15,000	36,300	38,000
Air Force	1,000	600 (includes 150 foreigners)	2,200
Navy	1,000	100	1,000
Reserves	2,000	none	7,000
Military budget	$48 million	$37.7 million	$37 million
Percent of total state budget	10	15	14
Percent of GNP	2.3	2.5	2.4
Contribution to UN Congo Force (man-months)	39,203	12,953	119,226
POLICE			
Strength of force	18,600	20,800	31,000
Police budget	$19.9 million	$19.8 million	$22.2 million
Percent of total state budget	4.3	5.4	7.8

Categories	Ghana	Congo	Ethiopia
SECURITY ASSISTANCE **(1960–68)**			
U.S., military	$100,000	$198.5 million ($170.7 million through UN Force)	$147.1 million
Communist bloc, military	$10 million (estimated)	none	none
U.S., public safety	16 officers trained in United States	$2.6 million, including equipment and training of 44 officers	$2.97 million, including equipment and training of 92 officers
Communist bloc, police	undetermined amount (1962–64)	none	none
ECONOMIC ASSISTANCE			
United States (1960–69)	$244.8 million	$405 million	$195.1 million
Communist bloc (1960–67)	$234.9 million	none	$115 million
Western Europe (1960–67)	$70.3 million	$265.2 million	$42 million

U.S. Military Assistance Agreements

Agreement with Ghana

The agreement excerpted below insures the continued application to Ghana of certain treaties, including the mutual defense assistance agreement signed by the United States and the United Kingdom on January 27, 1950. The Ghana agreement can be found in *United States Treaties and Other International Agreements*, Series 4966, pages 240–43. The initial mutual defense agreement with the United Kingdom is found in *Treaties and Other International Acts*, Series 2017.

Agreement effected by exchange of notes concerning the continued application to Ghana of certain treaties concluded between the United States and the United Kingdom signed at Accra September 4 and December 21, 1957, and February 12, 1958; entered into force February 12, 1958:

Embassy of the United States of America
September 4, 1957

EXCELLENCY [*the Ghanaian Prime Minister, Minister of Defense and External Affairs*]:

I have the honor to refer to the informal statement of Minister Gbedemah and the Secretary of the External Affairs Department to the Chargé d'Affaires of the American Embassy on or about February 20, 1957 that the Government of Ghana would regard treaties and agreements between the Governments of the United Kingdom and Northern Ireland and the United States of America affecting Ghana as remaining in effect for three months following March 6, 1957, pending the conclusion of more permanent arrangements. The Minister responsible for External Affairs informed me orally on June 28, 1957, that the Government of Ghana considered this informal undertaking remained in force.

In the view of my Government, it would be desirable to replace the existing informal agreement by a formal undertaking, which might be appropriately registered with the United Nations Organization. Since certain treaties or agreements between the United Kingdom and the United States of America may be either inapplicable or out of date, my Government proposes that consideration be given at this juncture only to continuing in force the following treaties and agreements. I understand that the Chargé of this Embassy transmitted copies of these treaties to the Ministry of External Affairs in April of this year.

.   .   .

Mutual Defense assistance agreement of January 27, 1950 (*Treaties and Other International Acts,* Series 2017).

.   .   .

If the foregoing proposal is agreeable to the Government of Ghana, my Government will consider this note and your replying note concurring therein as concluding an agreement between our respective Governments on this subject.

Accept, Excellency, the renewed assurances of my highest consideration.

WILSON C. FLAKE
American Ambassador

*   *   *

Agreement with the Republic of the Congo

This agreement, effected by an exchange of notes in July 1963, was signed while the United Nations Force was still in the Congo. It can be found in *United States Treaties and Other International Agreements,* Series 5530, pages 142–45. Below is the letter sent from the U.S. ambassador to the Congolese foreign minister setting forth the terms of the agreement.

Agreement effected by exchange of notes concerning the furnishing of defense equipment, materials, and services signed at Leopoldville June 24 and July 19, 1963; entered into force July 19, 1963:

Léopoldville, June 24, 1963

EXCELLENCY [*the Congolese Minister of Foreign Affairs*]:

I have the honor to refer to recent conversations and communications between representatives of our two governments and to advise you that the Government of the United States of America is prepared to furnish to the Government of the Republic of the Congo such military equipment, materials, and services as may be requested by representatives of the Government of the Republic of the Congo and agreed to by representatives of the Government of the United States of America. Such military assistance will be provided to help assure the security and independence of the Republic of the Congo in accordance with such terms and conditions as may be agreed upon by such representatives in accordance with the following understandings:

1. The Government of the Republic of the Congo shall use the military equipment, materials, and services furnished by the Government of the United States of America to maintain its internal security and legitimate self defense. It is understood that the Government of the Republic of the Congo

as a member of the United Nations organization interprets the term "legitimate self defense" within the scope of the United Nations Charter as excluding an act of aggression against any other state.

2. The Government of the Republic of the Congo shall not relinquish or tranfer title to or possession of the military equipment and materials furnished by the Government of the United States of America and shall not use or permit the use of such articles for purposes other than those for which furnished without the prior consent of the Government of the United States of America.

3. The Government of the Republic of the Congo undertakes that it shall take the measures which will be agreed upon with representatives of the United States of America to maintain the security and prevent the disclosure or compromise of classified articles, services, or information received hereunder.

4. In connection with this Agreement, the United States will send, and the Republic of the Congo will receive, a military mission. The Chief of Mission and his Deputy will receive the same treatment accorded diplomatic agents under the Convention on Diplomatic Relations signed at Vienna on April 18, 1961. All other personnel of the mission, including U.S. military personnel temporarily assigned and auxiliary groups of U.S. military personnel who may be serving in, or transiting the Congo, will be accorded the treatment to which technical and administrative personnel of diplomatic missions are entitled under that Convention.

5. The Government of the United States may establish and operate in the Republic of the Congo a United States military Post Office for the transmission of mail between such military post office and other United States post offices, for the benefit of official United States Government agencies and organizations in the Republic of the Congo, the personnel assigned thereto who are United States nationals, and their dependants.

6. The Government of the Republic of the Congo will grant duty-free treatment on importation or exportation of, and exemption from internal taxation upon, products, property, materials, or equipment imported into its territory in connection with this agreement.

7. The Government of the Republic of the Congo will permit representatives of the Government of the United States of America to observe the utilization and progress of assistance furnished pursuant to this agreement.

8. The Government of the Republic of the Congo shall offer to return to the Government of the United States of America military equipment and materials furnished by the Government of the United States of America hereunder which are no longer required for the purpose for which they were originally made available.

If these understandings are acceptable to your Excellency's Government, I propose that this note and your Excellency's note in reply concurring therein shall constitute an agreement between our two governments which shall enter into force on the date of your Excellency's reply.

Accept, Excellency, the renewed assurances of my highest consideration.

EDMUND A. GULLION
American Ambassador

*   *   *

Agreement with Ethiopia

This agreement, which provides for the establishment of a U.S. military assistance advisory group, is more comprehensive than those made with Ghana or the Congo. On the day this agreement was signed and entered into force, May 22, 1953, a second agreement was signed regularizing the existence and operations of the U.S. communications facility (Kagnew Station) at Asmara. The defense assistance agreement can be found in *United States Treaties and Other International Agreements*, Series 2787, pages 421–26.

Mutual Defense Assistance Agreement between the Government of the United States and the Imperial Ethiopian Government:

The Government of the United States of America and the Imperial Ethiopian Government,

Desiring to foster international peace and security within the framework of the Charter of the United Nations through measures which will further the ability of nations dedicated to the purposes and principles of the Charter to participate effectively in arrangements for individual and collective self-defense in support of those purposes and principles;

Reaffirming their determination to give their full cooperation to the efforts to provide the United Nations with armed forces as contemplated by the Charter and to participate in United Nations collective defense arrangements and measures, and to obtain agreement on universal regulation and reduction of armaments under adequate guarantee against violation or evasion;

Taking into consideration the support which the Government of the United States has brought to these principles by enacting the Mutual Defense Assistance Act of 1949, as amended, and the Mutual Security Act of 1951, as amended;

Desiring to set forth the conditions which will govern the furnishing of such assistance;

Have agreed:

ARTICLE I

1. The Government of the United States, pursuant to Section 202 of the Mutual Security Act of 1951, as amended, will make available to the Imperial Ethiopian Government arms and other equipment, materials, services or other assistance in such quantities and in accordance with such terms and condi-

tions as may be agreed. The furnishing and use of such assistance shall be consistent with the Charter of the United Nations. Such assistance as may be made available by the Government of the United States pursuant to this Agreement will be furnished under the provisions and subject to all the terms, conditions and termination provisions of the Mutual Defense Assistance Act of 1949 and the Mutual Security Act of 1951, acts amendatory or supplementary thereto and appropriation acts thereunder. The two Governments will, from time to time, negotiate detailed arrangements necessary to carry out the provisions of this paragraph.

2. The Imperial Ethiopian Government will use this assistance exclusively to maintain its internal security, its legitimate self-defense, or to permit it to participate in the defense of the area, or in United Nations collective security arrangements and measures, and Ethiopia will not undertake any act of aggression against any other nation; and Ethiopia will not, without the prior agreement of the Government of the United States, devote such assistance to purposes other than those for which it was furnished.

3. Arrangements will be entered into under which equipment and materials furnished pursuant to this Agreement and no longer required or used exclusively for the purposes for which originally made available will be offered for return to the Government of the United States.

4. The Imperial Ethiopian Government will not transfer to any person not an officer or agent of that Government, or to any other nation, title to or possession of any equipment, materials, property, information, or services received under this Agreement, without the prior consent of the Government of the United States.

5. The Imperial Ethiopian Government will take such security measures as may be agreed in each case between the two Governments in order to prevent the disclosure or compromise of classified military articles, services or information furnished pursuant to this Agreement.

6. Each Government will take appropriate measures consistent with security to keep the public informed of operations under this Agreement.

7. The two Governments will establish procedures whereby the Imperial Ethiopian Government will so deposit, segregate or assure title to all funds allocated to or derived from any program of assistance undertaken by the Government of the United States so that such funds shall not, except as may otherwise be mutually agreed, be subject to garnishment, attachment, seizure or other legal process by any person, firm, agency, corporation, organization or government.

ARTICLE II

The two Governments will, upon request of either of them, negotiate appropriate arrangements between them providing for the methods and terms of the exchange of patent rights and technical information for defense which will expedite such exchanges and at the same time protect private interests and maintain necessary security safeguards.

ARTICLE III

1. The Imperial Ethiopian Government will make available to the Government of the United States Ethiopian dollars for the use of the latter Government for its administrative and operating expenditures in connection with carrying out the purposes of this Agreement. The two Governments will forthwith initiate discussions with a view to determining the amount of such Ethiopian dollars and to agreeing upon arrangements for the furnishing of such Ethiopian dollars.

2. The Imperial Ethiopian Government will, except as may otherwise be mutually agreed, grant duty-free treatment on importation or exportation and exemption from internal taxation upon products, property, materials or equipment imported into its territory in connection with this Agreement or any similar Agreement between the Government of the United States and the Government of any other country receiving military assistance.

3. Tax relief will be accorded to all expenditures in Ethiopia by, or on behalf of, the Government of the United States for the common defense effort, including expenditures for any foreign aid program of the United States. The Imperial Ethiopian Government will establish procedures satisfactory to both Governments so that such expenditures will be net of taxes.

ARTICLE IV

1. The Imperial Ethiopian Government will receive personnel of the Government of the United States who will discharge in its territory the responsibilities of the Government of the United States under this Agreement and who will be accorded facilities and authority to observe the progress of the assistance furnished pursuant to this Agreement. Such personnel who are United States nationals, including personnel temporarily assigned, will, in their relations with the Imperial Ethiopian Government, operate as a part of the Embassy of the United States of America under the direction and control of the Chief of the Diplomatic Mission, and will have the same status as that of other personnel with corresponding rank of the Embassy of the United States who are United States nationals. Upon appropriate notification by the Government of the United States the Imperial Ethiopian Government will grant full diplomatic status to an agreed number of personnel assigned under this Article.

2. The Imperial Ethiopian Government will grant exemption from import and export duties on personal property imported for the personal use of such personnel or of their families and will take reasonable administrative measures to facilitate and expedite the importation and exportation of the personal property of such personnel and their families.

3. The military assistance advisory group to be provided by the Government of the United States will include an appropriate number of military personnel designated for the training of the Ethiopian Armed Forces and advising in their organization in accordance with such terms and conditions as may be agreed.

ARTICLE V

1. The Imperial Ethiopian Government will:

(a) join in promoting international understanding and good will, and maintaining world peace;

(b) take such action as may be mutually agreed upon to eliminate causes of international tension;

(c) fulfill the military obligations which it has assumed in multilateral or bilateral agreements or treaties to which the United States is a party;

(d) make, consistent with its political and economic stability, the full contribution permitted by its manpower, resources, facilities and general economic condition to the development and maintenance of its own defensive strength and the defensive strength of the free world;

(e) take all reasonable measures which may be needed to develop its defense capacities; and

(f) take appropriate steps to insure the effective utilization of the economic and military assistance provided by the United States.

2. (a) Subject to mutual agreement hereafter, the Imperial Ethiopian Government will, consistent with the Charter of the United Nations, furnish to the Government of the United States, or to such other governments as the Parties hereto may in each case agree upon, equipment, materials, services or other assistance in order to increase their capacity for individual and collective self-defense and to facilitate their effective participation in the United Nations system for collective security.

(b) In conformity with the principle of mutual aid, the Imperial Ethiopian Government will facilitate the production and transfer to the Government of the United States, for such period of time, in such quantities and upon such terms and conditions as may be agreed upon, of raw and semiprocessed materials required by the United States as a result of deficiencies or potential deficiencies in its own resources, and which may be available in Ethiopia. Arrangements for such transfers shall give due regard to reasonable requirements of Ethiopia for domestic use and commercial export.

ARTICLE VI

In the interest of their mutual security the Imperial Ethiopian Government will cooperate with the Government of the United States in taking measures designed to control trade with nations which threaten the maintenance of world peace.

ARTICLE VII

1. This Agreement shall enter into force on the date of signature and will continue in force until one year after the receipt by either party of written notice of the intention of the other party to terminate it, provided that the provisions of Article I, paragraphs 2 and 4, and arrangements entered into under Article I, paragraphs 3, 5 and 7, and under Article II, shall remain in force unless otherwise agreed by the two Governments.

2. The two Governments will, upon the request of either of them consult regarding any matter relating to the application or amendment of this Agreement.

3. This Agreement shall be registered with the Secretariat of the United Nations.

Selected Bibliography

Published information on the role of the armed services in tropical Africa states is limited to general studies; no empirically based case studies are available. Almost nothing has been published on the role of the police. The most reliable source of current information on political and military development until mid-1969 was Africa Report *magazine, Washington, D.C.*

Entries in this bibliography, annotated where titles are not explicit, are arranged under five headings: The Military and Political Development, Tropical Africa, Ghana, Congo (Kinshasa), and Ethiopia.

The Military and Political Development

Almond, Gabriel A. "Political Development: Analytical and Normative Perspectives," *Comparative Political Studies*, Vol. 1 (January 1969).
Summary article on theory of political development and comparative politics, including a basic bibliography.

Almond, Gabriel, and James S. Coleman (eds.). *The Politics of the Developing Areas.* Princeton: Princeton University Press, 1960.
A pioneering effort comparing political systems of Asia, Africa, the Middle East, and Latin America.

Apter, David E. *The Politics of Modernization.* Chicago: University of Chicago Press, 1965.
Examines modernization as a political process requiring political and economic change and adaptation.

Ashford, Douglas E. "How Non-Western are the New Nations?" *World Politics* (January 1962).

Bienen, Henry (ed.). *The Military Intervenes: Case Studies in Political Development.* New York: Russell Sage Foundation, 1968.
Brief case studies of intervention in Africa, Korea, Turkey, and Argentina.

Cramer, James. *The World's Police.* London: Cassell and Co., 1964.

Deutsch, Karl W., and William J. Foltz (eds.). *Nation-Building.* New York: Atherton Press, 1967.
Nine area specialists compare and analyze the long history of nationalism in Europe with its shorter history in the Americas, Asia, and Africa.

Finer, S. E. *The Man on Horseback: The Role of the Military in Politics.* New York: Praeger, 1962.
Examines military intervention as a worldwide phenomenon and systematizes its motives, causes, and consequences.

Goldman, Marshall I. *Soviet Foreign Aid.* New York: Praeger, 1967.
Discusses Soviet and satellite aid programs and trade with Africa, Latin America, the Middle East, India, Egypt, Afghanistan, and Indonesia.

Gutteridge, William. *Armed Forces in New States.* London: Oxford University Press for Institute of Race Relations, 1962.
Deals primarily with the Commonwealth countries in Africa.

————. *Military Institutions and Power in the New States.* New York: Praeger, 1965.
Sees the character of armed forces in a new state as a product of the colonial heritage and the force of nationalism.

Hovey, Harold A. *United States Military Assistance: A Study of Policies and Practices.* New York: Praeger, 1965.
Factual description of U.S. military aid program, with minimum interpretation.

Huntington, Samuel P. *Political Order in Changing Societies.* New Haven and London: Yale University Press, 1968.
Discusses the decline of political order, the undermining of authority, and the legitimacy of government in the Third World. See especially Chapters 1 and 4.

Institute for Strategic Studies. *The Military Balance, 1969–1970.* London: Institute for Strategic Studies, 1969.

Iskenderov, A. "Army, Politics, People," *Izvestya* (Jan. 17, 1967).
Authoritative summary of Soviet view of the role of the army in Africa and Asia.

Janowitz, Morris. *The Military in the Political Development of New Nations: An Essay in Comparative Analysis.* Chicago: University of Chicago Press, 1964.
Deals with the potential and limitations of the military profession for political leadership in the Third World states.

Johnson, John J. (ed.). *The Role of the Military in Underdeveloped Countries.* Princeton: Princeton University Press, 1962.
Series of essays that explore the role of the armed forces in various environments, including Sub-Saharan Africa.

Lieuwen, Edwin. *Arms and Politics in Latin America.* New York: Praeger, 1961.
Analyzes the social and political role of Latin America's armed forces.

Liska, George. *The New Statecraft: Foreign Aid in American Foreign Policy.* Chicago: University of Chicago Press, 1960.
Realistic and imaginative assessment of military and economic assistance as a foreign policy instrument.

Martin, Laurence W. (ed.). *Neutralism and Non-Alignment: The New States in World Affairs.* New York: Praeger, 1962.
Ten scholars discuss the foreign policy of newly independent states.

Nye, J. S. "Corruption and Political Development: A Cost-Benefit Analysis," *American Political Science Review,* Vol. 61, No. 2 (June 1967).

Pye, Lucian W. *Armies in the Process of Political Modernization.* Cambridge: Massachusetts Institute of Technology, 1959.
Pioneering effort relating the military to political development.

———. *Aspects of Political Development: An Analytic Study.* Boston: Little, Brown, 1966.
Chapter 9 deals with the role of the army in political development and modernization.

Rockefeller, Nelson A. *Quality of Life in the Americas: Report of a U.S. Presidential Mission for the Western Hemisphere.* (Reprinted by Agency for International Development, August 1969.)

Rustow, Dankwart A. *A World of Nations.* Washington: Brookings Institution, 1967.
Examines the political evolution of newly independent and modernizing states. Chapter 6 deals with military regimes.

Sutton, John L., and Geoffrey Kemp. *Arms to Developing Countries, 1945–1965.* Adelphi Paper No. 28. London: Institute for Strategic Studies, October 1966.

U.S. Department of Defense, International Security Affairs. *Military Assistance Facts.* Washington: Government Printing Office, March 1970.

U.S. Department of State, Agency for International Development. *U.S. Overseas Loans and Grants and Assistance from International Organizations.* Washington: Government Printing Office, May 29, 1969.

U.S. Department of State, External Research Staff. *Role of the Military in Less Developed Countries: January 1958–February 1964, A Selected Bibliography.* Washington: Government Printing Office, March 1964.

U.S. President's Committee to Study the United States Military Assistance Program. *Composite Report.* Vols. 1 and 2. Washington: Government Printing Office, 1959.
This Draper Committee report contains a thoughtful appraisal of U.S. military assistance.

Westwood, Andrew F. *Foreign Aid in a Foreign Policy Framework.* Brookings Staff Paper. Washington: Brookings Institution, 1966.

Wolf, Charles, Jr. *United States Policy and the Third World: Problems and Analysis.* Boston: Little, Brown, 1967.
Thoughtful, empirically based analysis. Chapters 2 and 6 relate political, economic, and military factors.

Tropical Africa

Andreski, Stanislav. *The African Predicament.* Reading, England: University of Reading, 1969.
Realistic and imaginative analysis of African development and the obstacles that confront a new African state.

Attwood, William. *The Reds and the Blacks: A Personal Adventure.* New York: Harper & Row, 1967.
The former U.S. ambassador to Guinea and Kenya, 1961–66, reflects on his experience.

Bell, M. J. V. *Army and Nation in Sub-Saharan Africa.* Adelphi Paper No. 21. London: Institute for Strategic Studies, 1965.

———. *Military Assistance to Independent African States.* Adelphi Paper No. 15. London: Institute for Strategic Studies, 1964.

———. "The Military in the New States of Africa," in Jacques Van Doorn (ed.), *Armed Forces and Society.* The Hague: Mouton, 1968.

Bienen, Henry. "Foreign Policy, the Military, and Development: Military Assistance and Political Change in Africa," in Richard Butwell (ed.), *Foreign Policy and the Developing Nation*. Lexington: University of Kentucky Press, 1969.

Booth, Richard. *The Armed Forces of African States*. Adelphi Paper No. 67. London: Institute for Strategic Studies, 1970.

Brown, N., and W. F. Gutteridge. *The African Military Balance*. Adelphi Paper No. 12. London: Institute for Strategic Studies, 1964.

Brzezinski, Zbigniew (ed.). *Africa and the Communist World*. Stanford: Stanford University Press, 1963.

Buell, Raymond Leslie. *The Native Problem in Africa*. 2 vols. New York: Macmillan, 1928.

Busia, K. A. *Africa in Search of Democracy*. New York and Washington: Praeger, 1967.
   Published two years before Busia became prime minister of Ghana; examines the requirements of democratic rule in Africa.

Cooley, John K. *East Wind Over Africa: Red China's African Offensive*. New York: Walker and Company, 1965.

Cowan, L. Gray. *The Dilemmas of African Independence*. New York: Walker and Company, 1967.

Emerson, Rupert. *Africa and United States Policy*. Englewood Cliffs, New Jersey: Prentice-Hall, 1967.

Ferkiss, Victor C. *Africa's Search for Identity*. New York: George Braziller, Inc., 1965.
   Examines attempts to reconcile traditional loyalties, colonially derived institutions, and the demands of a modern economic and political system.

Fleming, William G. "American Political Science and African Politics," *The Journal of Modern African Studies*, Vol. 7, No. 3 (October 1969).
   Attempts to show how "the concepts and findings of political science might be applied in the rational planned development of African politics."

Glickman, Harvey. "The Military in African Politics: A Bibliographic Essay," *African Forum*, Vol. 2, No. 1 (Summer 1966).

———. *Some Observations on the Army and Political Unrest in Tanganyika*. Pittsburgh: Duquesne University Press, 1964.

Greene, Fred. "Toward Understanding Military Coups," *Africa Report* (February 1966).

Gregor, A. James. "African Socialism, Socialism, and Fascism: An Appraisal," *The Review of Politics*. Vol. 29 (July 1967).

Gutteridge, William. *The Military in African Politics*. London: Methuen & Co., 1969.
   Examines military intervention in politics of tropical Africa.

Hovet, Thomas, Jr. *Africa in the United Nations*. Evanston: Northwestern University Press, 1963.
   Analyzes the policies and tactics of African states in UN lobbying.

Humphries, Donald H. *The East African Liberation Movement.* Adelphi Paper No. 16. London: Institute for Strategic Studies, 1965.

Hunter, Guy. *The New Societies of Tropical Africa.* London: Oxford University Press for Institute of Race Relations, 1962.
A 1959–61 study on the emergence of new social and political forces in Africa.

Kilson, Martin. "Elite Cleavages in African Politics: The Case of Ghana," *Journal of International Affairs*, Vol. 24, No. 1 (1970).

————. *Political Change in a West African State: A Study of the Modernization Process in Sierra Leone.* Cambridge: Harvard University Press, 1966.

Kitchen, Helen (ed.). *A Handbook of African Affairs.* New York: Praeger, 1965.

Landier, Simone. "The Changing French Military Role in Africa," *Africa Report* (November 1964).

Lee, J. M. *African Armies and Civil Order.* New York: Praeger, 1969.
Analyzes the character and behavior of eighteen tropical African armies against the backdrop of the British and French legacy.

Lefever, Ernest W. "Sub-Sahara Africa: Strategic Issues," in *Research Resources for the Seventies: Proceedings of a Conference on Plans and Needs for International Strategic Studies.* Washington: Center for Strategic and International Studies, Georgetown University (forthcoming).

Legum, Colin. "Peking's Strategic Priorities," *Africa Report* (January 1965).

LeVine, Victor T. "The Trauma of Independence in French-speaking Africa," *Journal of Developing Areas*, Vol. 2 (January 1968).

Lewis, William H. (ed.). *French-Speaking Africa: The Search for Identity.* New York: Walker and Company, 1965.
Several authors examine the political, social, and economic situation of the diverse countries of Francophone Africa.

McKay, Vernon (ed.). *African Diplomacy: Studies in the Determinants of Foreign Policy.* New York: Praeger, 1966.
Drawing on various disciplines, seven writers examine postwar African diplomacy. Chapter 4 deals with military influences.

Moskowitz, Harry, and Jack Roberts. *Africa: Problems and Prospects; A Bibliographic Survey.* Washington: Government Printing Office, 1967.

Nkrumah, Kwame. *Neo-Colonialism; The Last Stage of Imperialism.* New York: International Publishers, 1966.
One of several expositions of Nkrumah's political ideology.

Scalapino, Robert A. "Sino-Soviet Competition in Africa," *Foreign Affairs*, Vol. 42, No. 4 (July 1964).

Spiro, Herbert J. (ed.). *Africa, The Primacy of Politics.* New York: Random House, 1966.

U.S. Department of State, Agency for International Development. *A.I.D. Economic Data Book: Africa.* Washington: Government Printing Office, December 1967.

Wood, David. *The Armed Forces of the African States.* Adelphi Paper No. 27. London: Institute for Strategic Studies, 1966.

Zartman, I. William. *International Relations in the New Africa.* Englewood Cliffs, New Jersey: Prentice-Hall, 1966.

Zolberg, Aristide R. "Military Rule and Political Development in Tropical Africa," in Jacques van Doorn (ed.), *Military Profession and Military Regimes.* The Hague: Mouton, 1970.

Ghana

Afrifa, A. A. *The Ghana Coup: 24th February 1966.* New York: Humanities Press, 1966.
The second chairman of the National Liberation Council in Ghana relates his experiences before, during, and after the 1966 coup.

Alexander, H. T. *African Tightrope: My Two Years as Nkrumah's Chief of Staff.* New York: Praeger, 1966.
The chief of Ghana's Defense Staff from 1959 to 1961 discusses President Nkrumah's policies toward the army and Ghana's role in the Congo.

Austin, Dennis. "The Ghana Coup d'Etat," *Survival* (May 1966).

————. *Politics in Ghana, 1946–1960.* London: Oxford University Press, 1964.
A basic analytical history of political developments.

Bretton, Henry. *The Rise and Fall of Kwame Nkrumah: A Study of Personal Rule in Africa.* New York: Praeger, 1966.
A balanced and critical appraisal of the Nkrumah era.

Feit, Edward. "Military Coups and Political Development: Some Lessons from Ghana and Nigeria," *World Politics,* Vol. 20, No. 2 (January 1968).

Harvey, William Burnett. *Law and Social Change in Ghana.* Princeton: Princeton University Press, 1966.

Hevi, Emmanuel John. *An African Student in China.* London and Dunmow: Pall Mall Press, 1963.
Story of the mass exodus of African students from Peking University written by the former secretary general of the African Students Union of Ghana.

Lefever, Ernest W. "Nehru, Nasser and Nkrumah on Neutralism," in Laurence W. Martin (ed.), *Neutralism and Nonalignment.* New York: Praeger, 1962.

Thompson, W. Scott. *Ghana's Foreign Policy, 1957–1966: Diplomacy, Ideology, and the Nkrumah Period.* Princeton: Princeton University Press, 1969.

————. "Ghana's Foreign Policy Under Military Rule," *Africa Report* (May–June 1969).

Congo (Kinshasa)

Centre de Recherche et d'Information Socio-Politiques. *Congo: 1959 [1960, 1961, 1962, 1963, 1964, 1965, 1966, 1967].* Brussels: Les Dossiers du CRISP, 1959–1967.
Best single source of basic documents on the Congo.

Gerard-Libois, Jules. *Katanga Secession.* Madison: University of Wisconsin Press, 1966.
Thorough and objective study of Katanga's secession based on many unpublished and confidential documents.

Good, Robert C. "The Congo Crisis: A Study of Postcolonial Politics," in Laurence W. Martin (ed.), *Neutralism and Nonalignment.* New York: Praeger, 1962.

Hoare, Mike. *Congo Mercenary.* London: Robert Hale, 1967.
A first-hand factual account by the commander of Commando V, a European mercenary unit that fought Congolese rebels in 1964.

Hoskyns, Catherine. *The Congo Since Independence: January 1960– December 1961.* London: Oxford University Press for Chatham House, 1965.
A detailed record of political developments in the Congo.

Janssens, Emile. *J'étais le général Janssens.* Brussels: Charles Dessart, 1961.
Autobiography of the Force Publique's last commander.

Kitchen, Helen (ed.). *Footnotes to the Congo Story: An "Africa Report" Anthology.* New York: Walker and Company, 1967.
A collection of articles written between 1960 and 1966 by American, British, Congolese, and Belgian scholars, journalists, and officials.

Lefever, Ernest W. *Crisis in the Congo: A U.N. Force in Action.* Washington: Brookings Institution, 1965.
A study of the four-year operation with emphasis on the U.S. role.

———. *Uncertain Mandate: Politics of the U.N. Congo Operation.* Baltimore: Johns Hopkins University Press, 1967.
The UN operation is seen as a drama with the United States, the Soviet Union, Belgium, Britain, and the Congo itself as the principal actors.

Lemarchand, René. *Political Awakening in the Congo.* Berkeley: University of California Press, 1964.
Analyzes the forces underlying the political events of the Congo.

Lumumba, Patrice. *Congo My Country.* London: Pall Mall Press, 1962.
Lumumba's own analysis of the pre-independence situation in the Congo, written in 1956–57.

Merriam, Alan P. *Congo: Background of Conflict.* Evanston: Northwestern University Press, 1961.
Study of Congolese attitudes and reactions to events before and during the first few months of independence.

Monheim, Francis. *Mobutu, l'homme seul.* Brussels: Editions Actuelles, 1962.
Biography of General Mobutu by a personal friend, focusing on the domestic developments in 1960–61.

Reed, David. *111 Days in Stanleyville.* New York: Harper & Row, 1965.
Dramatic and accurate account of the foreign hostages held by Congolese rebels and of the American-Belgian rescue mission.

Young, Crawford. "Domestic Violence in Africa: The Congo," in Charles W. Anderson, Fred R. von der Mehden, and Crawford Young, *Issues of Political Development.* Englewood Cliffs, New Jersey: Prentice-Hall, 1967.

————. *Politics in the Congo: Decolonization and Independence*. Princeton: Princeton University Press, 1965.
Comprehensive study of the impact of colonial policies and four years of independence upon Congolese politics and society.

Ethiopia

Clapham, Christopher. "The December 1960 Ethiopian Coup d'Etat," *Journal of Modern African Affairs*, Vol. 6, No. 4 (December 1968).
Brief and balanced view of the coup.

————. *Haile Selassie's Government*. New York: Praeger, 1969.

Greenfield, Richard. *Ethiopia: A New Political History*. New York: Praeger, 1965.
Examines Ethiopian political developments, including the abortive 1960 coup, against the background of the country's ancient past.

Hess, Robert L., and Gerhard Loewenberg. "The Ethiopian No-Party State: A Note on the Functions of Political Parties in Developing States," *American Political Science Review*, Vol. 58 (December 1964).

Levine, Donald N. "The Military in Ethiopian Politics: Capabilities and Constraints," in Henry Bienen (ed.), *The Military Intervenes: Case Studies in Political Development*. New York: Russell Sage Foundation, 1968.

————. *Wax and Gold: Tradition and Innovation in Ethiopian Culture*. Chicago: University of Chicago Press, 1965.
A thoughtful, psychological-sociological interpretation of Ethiopian character and culture.

Yakobson, Sergius. "The Soviet Union and Ethiopia: A Case of Traditional Behavior," *Review of Politics*, Vol. 25, No. 3 (July 1963).

Index

243

TYPESETTING   *Monotype Composition Company, Inc., Baltimore*

PRINTING & BINDING   *Garamond/Pridemark Press, Inc., Baltimore*